Abba Hillel Silver

Abba Hillel Silver

A Profile
in American Judaism

Marc Lee Raphael

Introduction by Rabbi Alexander M. Schindler

HM *HOLMES & MEIER* *New York* *London*

Published in the United States of America 1989 by
Holmes & Meier Publishers, Inc.
30 Irving Place
New York, N.Y. 10003

BOOK DESIGN BY DALE COTTON

The paper used in this publication meets the requirements of the American National Standard for Permanence of Paper for Printed Library Materials, Z39.48-1984.

Library of Congress Cataloging-in-Publication data

Raphael, Marc Lee
    Abba Hillel Silver : a profile in American Judaism / Marc Lee
Raphael.
      p. cm.
    Bibliography: p.
    Includes index.
    ISBN 0-8419-1059-6
    1. Silver, Abba Hillel, 1893–1963. 2. Rabbis—Ohio—Cleveland—
Biography. 3. Zionists—United States—Biography. 4. Cleveland
(Ohio)—Biography. I. Title.
BM755.S544R37 1989
296'.092—dc20
[B]   89-7581
                                              CIP

MANUFACTURED IN THE UNITED STATES OF AMERICA

For Linda
again, with love

Table of Contents

dency; Reconciliation with Ben-Gurion; Return to
Scholarship; Death; Legacy, 1949–63

Photographs appear between pages 108 and 109.

Abbreviations

The following abbreviations have been used throughout the notes and sometimes in the text:

AECZA American Emergency Committee for Zionist Affairs
AJC American Jewish Conference
AZEC American Zionist Emergency Council
CC Chamber of Commerce
CW Archives Chaim Weizmann Archives (Rehovoth, Israel)
CZA Central Zionist Archives, Jerusalem
CZD Cleveland Zionist District
CZS Cleveland Zionist Society
Corresp. Correspondence (Abba Hillel Silver Papers)
ECZA Emergency Committee for Zionist Affairs
EK Papers Eliezer Kaplan Papers (Central Zionist Archives)
FAZ Federation of American Zionists
HM Files Harold Manson Files (The Temple, Cleveland)
HU Archives Hebrew University Archives
HUC Hebrew Union College
IG Papers Israel Goldstein Papers (Central Zionist Archives)
JAE Jewish Agency Executive
JE Jewish Educational Alliance
NG Papers Nahum Goldmann Papers (Central Zionist Archives)
NJ *New Judaea*
OCUI Ohio Commission on Unemployment Insurance

Abbreviations

PC	Personal Correspondence (Abba Hillel Silver Papers)
PDC	Palestine Development Corporation
PRF	Palestine Restoration Fund
SSW Papers	Stephen S. Wise Papers (American Jewish Historical Society, Waltham, Mass.)
SU	Samuel Ungerleider & Co.
TWA	Temple Women's Association
UAHC	Union of American Hebrew Congregations
UC	University of Cincinnati
UNSCOP	United Nations Special Committee on Palestine
WZO	World Zionist Organization
ZOA	Zionist Organization of America
ZOA Archives	Zionist Organization of America Archives (New York)
n.d.	no date of publication
n.p.	no place of publication

Preface

In biography you have your little handful of facts, little
bits of a puzzle, and you sit and think, and fit 'em together
this way and that, and get up and throw 'em down, and
say damn, and go out for a walk. And it's really soothing;
and when done, gives an idea of finish to the writer that is
very peaceful. Of course . . . it always has and always
must have the incurable illogicalities of life about it. . . .
Still, that's where the fun comes in.

—Robert Louis Stevenson to Edmund Gosse

Despite the fun of biography, there are hardly any scholarly studies
of twentieth-century American rabbis. Solomon Goldman, Jacob
Rothschild, Eliezer Silver, Milton Steinberg, Stephen S. Wise, and
two or three less well-known men have found biographers, but the
total is barely ten books. Even if these men were representative of
the thousands of other rabbis whose careers have not yet been
investigated by scholars, we would still know very little about the
rabbinate in America.

No claim will be made in the pages that follow that Rabbi Abba
Hillel Silver (1893–1963) is "representative" of the American, or
the Reform, rabbinate, because few pulpit rabbis had, as he did, the
manner and bearing of an Old Testament prophet, few have represented world Jewry at the United Nations, headed national Jewish
organizations, or had both streets and a city in Israel named for
them.

Silver had dark, piercing eyes, a lively sense of humor, and an almost legendary grasp of facts and the ability to memorize. An immensely learned man, he was one of the greatest orators of this century; his deep booming voice filled large synagogues and theaters and his books as well as his sermons reflect immense reading, especially in several branches of Hebraic literature. It could not be said of him what James Russell Lowell once wrote about Emerson, "that people do not go to hear what Emerson says so much as to hear Emerson,"[1] for Silver dazzled with his style but also informed with his content. Like many other gifted men, he could turn with equal ease to his peers or to his congregants. He focused his whole attention on whatever subject he was concerned with, but he saw his primary role as a *rav*, a rabbi. Of course, any part of his rabbinate would reveal only a part of the man, just as any one sermon or book will reveal only part of what he wanted to say. That is why I will look carefully at his Zionist ideology and his eating habits, his politics and his humor, his friends as well as his enemies.

Silver was a dominant and magnetic figure, a teacher, preacher, pastor, celebrant, executive administrator, and an active member of the economic and political life of his community. Because many functions of his rabbinate have been performed over and over by countless other rabbis whose names remain unknown beyond the synagogues they served or at most the communities in which they lived, one modest goal of this study is to learn more about the various dimensions of the American rabbinate. Just as Silver rushed home each week from lobbying on Capitol Hill or at the United Nations (arguably making his two most enduring contributions to Jewry) to teach and preach to and marry and bury his congregants, so my narrative will return from Europe, Palestine, New York, and Washington to The Temple in Cleveland.

One recurring danger of biography is that the reader becomes engaged as much with the biographer as with his or her subject. This is frequently the result of what Freud noted in his biography of Leonardo da Vinci: biographers become "fixated on their heroes in a very peculiar manner."[2] Reading Boswell's *Life of Johnson* or Stein's

Autobiography of Alice B. Toklas teaches us as much about Boswell and Stein as about their subjects. I hope that this is rarely the case here. The biographer must to some degree identify with his or her subject; how otherwise to reexperience Silver's feelings, his problems, his struggle? But I never met Abba Hillel Silver, I never heard Rabbi Silver speak, I had no conscious preconceptions about him, and I never imagined writing his biography until I happened to visit the remarkably preserved Abba Hillel Silver Archives at The Temple in Cleveland in 1983. I was overwhelmed by the quantity and quality of the extant sources, excited by the challenges of biography and by the naive optimism that I might come to "know" another person (people are surely unknowable to others and probably to themselves), and I was encouraged by Daniel Jeremy Silver, Abba's son and the senior rabbi of The Temple.

I have constantly kept in mind the advice of Leon Edel, Henry James's biographer, and probed beneath Silver's captivating rhetoric for the essence of his character. I have carried a sense of skepticism and sedulous inquiry into my conversations with one person after another, people who bestowed enormous amounts of adulation on the man, and I tried to remain "sympathetic, yet aloof, involved, yet uninvolved."[3] Silver seemed larger than life to many who knew him only from the distance between pulpit and pew, and I have tried to humanize him as much as possible.

Neither Daniel Jeremy nor his brother Raphael has read a word of this manuscript prior to publication or offered anything but cordial help when asked. John Grabowski and Judah Rubinstein first introduced me to Cleveland; Miriam Leikind shared with me her vast knowledge of Cleveland Jewry and the Silver Papers; librarians and archivists, including Claudia Fechter (Cleveland), Esther Togman (New York), and Michael Heymann (Jerusalem) provided assistance whenever asked; the staff at The Temple was always pleasant and helpful as I conducted my research; G. Micheal Riley, dean of the College of Humanities at The Ohio State University, graciously permitted me a leave of absence for two quarters to facilitate my

Preface

Cleveland research; and various persons in the Department of History and College of Humanities cheerfully typed and retyped this manuscript. The staff at the University of Kent, Canterbury, and at Mishkenot Sha'ananim, Jerusalem, made the bulk of my writing as pleasant as possible. Marc Beckwith, Michael J. Cohen, Evyatar Friesel, Jeffrey S. Gurock, Jonathan D. Sarna, Kenneth J. Weiss, and Steven J. Whitfield each read and commented on at least one chapter of this book; their suggestions have improved the manuscript considerably.

Introduction

There were giants in the earth in those days.

—Genesis 6:4

In the pre-Holocaust, pre–State of Israel Jewish world of less than half a century ago, the American Jewish scene was blessed with the presence of rabbinical giants whose stature was a reflection both of their individual abilities and of the relative powerlessness of their community. Rabbis Stephen S. Wise and Abba Hillel Silver, in particular, were the last of a species of inspired leaders who with tremendously persuasive eloquence and moral intensity tried to influence the American Establishment in ways that the American Jewish community as a whole now strives for with extensive lobbying, philanthropy, and electoral and organizational efforts. The rabbis had their counterparts among giants in the world of business (Warburg, Schiff, Seligman), trade unionism (Gompers, Hillman, Dubinsky), politics and the judiciary (Brandeis, Morgenthau, Frankfurter)—but it was the rabbinical titans alone whose success at organizing the American Jewish community and mobilizing its latent political power made their own role in the Jewish world obsolete. Like the biblical antediluvians, they would become "the heroes of old, the men of renown" of a bygone era.

Perhaps this explains why it has taken until now, over twenty-five years after the death of Abba Hillel Silver, for his first biography to be published. Despite the man's powerful personality, despite his famous oratorical talent, his wide-ranging intellect, and his much-vaunted political skills, Silver's personal career was subordinated to the world-historical cause of redeeming the Jewish people from the genocidal crimes of Nazism by assuring the establishment of the State of Israel. His and his Zionist compatriots' success meant their replacement in the historical spotlight by the leaders of the new Jewish state; it meant, too, their replacement by federations and lay organizations as the main wielders of American Jewish communal influence.

Moreover, the backdrop to Silver's period of greatest leadership was the Holocaust—the annihilation of European Jewry in a shockingly brief period. Against such a backdrop, none but the martyrs of resistance seem to be of adequate stature. At best, the heroism of American Zionist leadership is obscured for us by the kind of raw, rude, contentious politics in which they participated as midwives to the diplomatic birthing of the state of Israel. At worst, American Jewry of the period is viewed as impotent or even as criminally culpable in its inability to halt or even slacken the genocidal onslaught. Indeed, it has become fashionable to charge the American Zionist leadership with ignoring or sacrificing rescue efforts in order to focus on building the *Yishuv* in Palestine and transforming it into a state. (The American Jewish Commission on the Holocaust, formed in September 1981 with Arthur Goldberg as chair and torn by internal dissension within the year, did little to modify this perception.)

The greatness of Abba Hillel Silver and his allies (and rivals) has thus been eclipsed by both their successes and their failures. That these occurred in a dramatically different historical context than our own seems especially hard for young observers to appreciate, so radical has been the improvement of Jewish fortunes since the Holocaust and so qualitative a change in Jewish life has been wrought by the existence of Israel.*

---

*Despite these dramatic changes, the experience of helplessness in the face of slaughter and indifference lingers in Jewish self-perceptions. Notwithstanding the efforts of Jewish religious and secular leaders to help develop a sustaining, positive sense of American Jewish identification—and despite the best-selling assurances of my friend Charles Silberman that

Consider, therefore, the environment in which Abba Hillel Silver labored: In the late 1930s and 1940s, American Jewry, equipped with far less than its present capacity for self-defense, faced an environment peopled by anti-Semitic organizations and individuals: the German-American Bund, the Silver Shirts, the Christian Front, the Black Legion, the Christian Crusaders, the Ku Klux Klan, and over a hundred others; the Rev. Charles Coughlin, General George Van Horn Mosely, Gerald L. K. Smith, the aviator and American hero Charles Lindbergh, and many more. Most of these people and organizations emerged as overnight sensations in response to Hitler's ascension in Germany. None took root (except, perhaps, the obdurate KKK) to do lasting damage to the pluralistic culture of our country. Nonetheless, though in calmer times such stewards of nativism, fascism, and anti-Semitism might have been dismissed, American Jewry could hardly be so glib in the face of the startling rise of the once-ridiculed Adolf Hitler to totalitarian power in Germany.

Prewar Nazism had cast a global penumbra of anti-Semitism. When in the late 1930s the American Jewish Committee and other human relations agencies began conducting public opinion surveys, they uncovered a reservoir of ill will against American Jewry. In fourteen polls conducted between March 1938 and February 1946, one-third to one-half of the respondents considered Jews "too powerful"—with the proportion of those who subscribed to this idea *growing* into a majority during and immediately after the war. Of this hostile sector, 20 percent said in 1938 that they would "drive Jews out of the U.S." to reduce this mythical Jewish power. Over 60 percent of people polled in March 1938 believed that the "persecution of Jews in Europe has been their own fault," entirely or partly. Consistently during the war years, Americans named Jews as a

---

Jews can be "certain" of their place in America (*A Certain People*)—it is the anti-Semitic past with which Rabbi Silver struggled rather than the promising future he helped to create that seems most powerfully to bind the community together.

"menace to America" as often or nearly as often as they named Germans and Japanese.

Many of these opinions fluctuated wildly from poll to poll, revealing more of an American susceptibility to anti-Semitism than a commitment to it. Discrimination against Jews did consistently reveal itself in the fields of housing, employment, and education, and outright physical attacks upon Jews did occur in urban centers during the war years. Anti-Semitism was nevertheless rootless in America, which at best had a tolerant spirit and at worst an ample supply of alternative scapegoats.

When it came to rescue efforts on behalf of the Jewish victims of Hitlerism, however, other ingredients of the American malaise combined with anti-Semitism to create enormous obstacles. David S. Wyman points to these obstacles in his authoritative work, *The Abandonment of the Jews, America and the Holocaust, 1941–1945:* how the Great Depression's 30 percent unemployment rate greatly empowered the anti-immigration arguments of restrictionist legislators (1939 saw no less than sixty bills introduced in Congress to further shrink the xenophobic quota system installed during the 1920s); how the wartime boom failed to alter such sentiments because Americans were fearful that the boom would bust in peace time; how the leading opponents of immigration at the grass-roots level were such groups as the Veterans of Foreign Wars, the American Legion, the Daughters of the American Revolution, and the American Coalition of Patriotic Societies, itself representing 115 organizations with a combined membership of 2.5 million. So extreme was opposition to immigration that in a survey taken in early 1939, 66 percent of the American public opposed a one-time exception to quota limits in oder to allow ten thousand refugee children to enter the United States! "The tendency in Congress," writes Wyman, "was clear, and it frightened the leadership of several refugee-aid and social-service organizations. . . . [T]hey were convinced by Fall, 1943 that a rising tide of public opinion, along with the anti-refugee mood in Congress, endangered the entire quota system." Such activists were able to save the quotas from drastic curtailment or elimination, but they could not "succeed in widening America's virtually closed doors during the war, even to the extent of increasing the tiny percentage of the quotas that was being made available."

Conceivably, a true mass movement in favor of rescue might have moved Franklin Delano Roosevelt to override the Congress, the State Department, the War Department, and all the other forces of obstinate opposition. But the Jewish community on its own had no such ability. We were lonely, without support from the trade union movement (of which Rabbi Silver himself was a champion, resigning in 1921 from the Cleveland Chamber of Commerce to protest its open shop policies and becoming a key player in Ohio's pioneering unemployment insurance movement in the thirties), without a civil rights movement to mobilize, without the many alliances that have been keys to Jewish advancement and to general social progress in the postwar era.

In short, the Jewish leadership was helplessly isolated in its rescue efforts. The genocidal reality of Nazi anti-Semitism had loomed up too suddenly out of the historical continuum of anti-Jewish persecution. It was too much of a moral horror, too much of a crime before God, to be fully grasped. When at last the carefully placed Nazi decoys and concealments were whisked away, some two million Jews had already been slaughtered; the factories of death were speeding up production; America was reeling from the shock of Japanese treachery and military prowess; and the American Jewish leadership was paralyzed. The opportunity truly to make a difference—before the consolidation of Nazi power in Germany, certainly before the conquest of Poland, the nation that became a virtual killing field for Jews—had long since passed. Even the American Jewish boycott of German goods, initiated by Abba Hillel Silver and Samuel Untermeyer in 1933, had been sharply opposed as "provocative" by most mainstream German and American Jewish leaders.

Searching the horizon for even a glimmering of light, Silver and his compatriots found hope and purpose in the possibility of establishing a Jewish national presence in Palestine. The fulfilment of the Zionist vision, said Rabbi Silver, was

> the inescapable logic of events. . . . From the infested, typhus-ridden Ghetto of Warsaw, from the death-block of Nazi-occupied lands where myriads of our people are awaiting execution by the slow or the quick method, from a hundred concentration camps which befoul the map of Europe, from the pitiful ranks of our wandering hosts over the entire face of the earth, comes the cry: "Enough; there must be a final end to all this, a sure and certain end!"[1]

First among the obstacles to that "sure and certain end" was the British government's White Paper of 1939, which limited Jewish immigration to Palestine to seventy-five thousand over the course of five years. It was a policy that squeezed Jews, even those who had managed to become illegal refugees, into Hitler's death trap. Yet at the Twenty-first World Zionist Congress in Geneva in August 1939, Chaim Weizman advocated a policy of cautious compromise with Great Britain in order to preserve unity against the Nazis, and Abba Hillel Silver in one of his first appearances on the world Zionist scene spoke in support of Weizmann's approach.

This would mark the last time that Silver would advocate Zionist dependency upon the powers-that-be. ("The tragic problems of the Jewish people in the world today cannot be solved by chiefs of government or prominent officials sending us Rosh Hashanah greetings!") Courted by Weizmann and others to commit himself to Zionist politicking, Silver became a dynamo of militant Zionism. Within three years he had electrified the Biltmore Conference in New York with an historic speech urging—and winning, under the leadership of David Ben-Gurion—an unequivocal demand for the establishment of a Jewish commonwealth in Palestine. By 1943 Silver had control of the Emergency Committee for Zionist Affairs and had turned it into a remarkable powerhouse of lobbying and agitation.

Throughout this period, Silver's strategy was to mobilize the Jewish rank and file and to build widespread popular support for the establishment of a Jewish state. "The most effective representation in a democracy is through organized public opinion," he argued. "We have nothing to lose now but our illusions. We have a new life to build for our people!" Distrustful of the Roosevelt administration, he insisted upon political independence for himself and for Zionism. (Silver was a registered Republican, but he supported candidates of both major parties for high public office; he opposed Roosevelt's third term as president as a violation of "a tradition which reflects the political wisdom of the American people, a custom which is even more powerful than a law . . . indicat[ing] that free government is not dependent on any one man, however good and able he may be.") This strategy brought Silver into a head-on collision with Nahum Goldmann and especially with Stephen S. Wise, who advocated using channels of influence that Wise himself had established over a forty-year span of public service and Zionist activism.

Their furious factional fights and the general inability of American Jewry to join ranks quickly to strive for rescue and postwar statehood have also been the object of retrospecive criticism. Hitlerism, after all, did not distinguish among Jews. Zionist or anti-Zionist, communist or capitalist, Orthodox or Reform, German or Eastern European—none of these differences were visible among those who stood before open graves or gas chambers. How, then, could the Jewish leadership in America (or in Palestine, or in the Warsaw Ghetto itself!) allow ideological or even stylistic differences to slow their resistance to the Nazi holocaust and obstruct their efforts to reclaim a Jewish national presence in Palestine?

Here, too, we must leaven our judgments about the key actors by recalling their historical context, most especially the statelessness of the Jewish people. Israel has since supplied a focus for unified pride and unified concern in the Jewish world (as well as a new forum for fierce Jewish infighting); few but the most ideological Jews would today call themselves "anti-Zionist." During the first half of our century, however, it was the Zionists who were considered "ideological" by mainstream Jews of every persuasion. Zionism was a small, minority movement. Silver's own Central Conference of American Rabbis (Reform) was on the record as anti-Zionist until 1937—and both rabbinic and lay battles over Jewish nationalism wracked the Reform movement right through the war years. Likewise the Conservative and Orthodox branches of Judaism (including most Chassidic sects) were opposed to what they regarded as a pseudomessianic, dangerously secular pipe dream—while the influential American Jewish Committee and the not-to-be-discounted Jewish Left, both socialist and communist, were decidedly against Jewish nationalism, preferring other political destinies for the Jewish people.

History overruled them all, and the Zionist cause was pushed to the fore, morally and politically, in the name of Jewish survival. "What is really driving us toward Palestine," Silver would ask in the spring of 1943 as chair of the United Palestine Appeal, "and why is our movement irresistible? Our sages say that two Arks led the Children of Israel through the wilderness and on to the Promised Land: the Ark wherein lay the body of Joseph, and the Ark of the Covenant. Two Arks! An Ark of death and an Ark of faith!" It was too late, he argued with his fellow Jews, "to wage anew those interesting ideological battles of a generation ago, the generation which preceded the Balfour Declaration." The "vast ghostly company" of murdered Jews "all the way back to the universal holocaust in the days of Chmielnicki . . . give us no rest . . . admonish us against all vain illusions and false hopes. It is their innocent blood which will not be covered up, until out of their martyrdom a new life is born—the free and redeemed life of their people."

In their lifelong and visionary Zionism, Stephen S. Wise and

Abba Hillel Silver were both exceptional and united. Perhaps it would be more accurate to view their rivalry as a functional partnership. Together they hitched their dream of Israel to the great draught horse America. Silver the militant swept Great Britain and other obstacles out of its path; Wise the diplomat fed, groomed, and encouraged the beast (and helped other, non-Zionist Jews to hop onto the wagon). Eventually the mighty horse did its labor. Then other Jewish leaders took over the reins.

Rabbi Silver's Zionist commitments were unwavering from boyhood and predated his involvement with Reform Judaism by nearly a decade. When in 1911 eighteen-year-old Abba Hillel Silver opted for rabbinical training (and general college studies) in Cincinnati at Hebrew Union College, the stronghold of Reform Judaism, his fellows in the Dr. Herzl Zion Club, of which Silver had been president since becoming *bar mitzvah*, must have been appalled. The radical eight-plank Pittsburgh Platform of 1885 was still very much binding upon Reform Judaism, and its fifth plank was pronouncedly anti-Zionist: "We consider ourselves no longer a nation but a religious community and therefore expect neither a return to Palestine nor a sacrificial worship under the administration of the sons of Aaron nor the restoration of any of the laws concerning the Jewish state." The historical forces that would eventually move Reform Judaism to redefine itself ("to recognize and reassert the spiritual and ethnic community of Israel and take sympathetic cognizance of the Palestine that is being built," in the words of Rabbi Abraham Feldman of Hartford) were not yet fully in place. Instead, the movement was the captive of its past, of its revolutionary period of anti-Orthodox rationalism and rejectionism. Reform's sense of itself as a missionary, "universal" faith was so incompatible with national aspirations that Rabbi David Einhorn (1809–79), the radical Reformer of Baltimore's Har Sinai who was eventually driven from his pulpit for his antislavery views, could seriously urge the observance of Tish Ab'av, traditionally a day of mourning for the destruction of the Jerusalem temples and the initiation of the Jewish exile, as a day of celebration!

Silver not only remained impervious to the anti-Zionism within the Reform movement, he indelibly impressed his Zionist faith upon the movement as a whole. The process took three decades and many people played a role in it, not least the almost three million Eastern European Jews who immigrated to the United States between 1881 and 1920, reducing German Jewry, who were most strongly attached to classical Reform, to a small minority. (At the time of the Pittsburgh Platform, only three hundred thousand Jews lived in America, many from Germany.) These immigrants' Americanization, including their movement away from the strictures and visible trappings of Orthodoxy, and Reform's process of redefinition, including a moving away from its rather cold intellectualism and reserved style of worship (and its eventual institutional transplantation from Cincinnati to New York, the teeming center of American Jewish life), constituted a mutually reinforcing evolution. Eastern European Jewish self-consciousness as a "national minority," a people within peoples, also paved the road to Reform's acceptance of Zionist objectives.

Abba Hillel Silver argued this point in a momentous 1935 debate before the Central Conference of American Rabbis (CCAR) in Chicago, in which he urged the abandonment of Plank Five of the Pittsburgh Platform. "It is idle," he said,

> to talk of our people as no longer a nation but a religious community, in the face of the fact that millions of Jews are today recognized by the law of nations as national minorities in Poland, Lithuania, Czechoslovakia, millions more as a distinct nationality in Soviet Russia . . . and hundreds of thousands in Palestine where a Jewish homeland is being created under the terms of a mandate of the League of Nations which recognizes not only the national existence of the Jewish people but its historic claim to a national home. It is not only idle today to repeat the "religious community" shibboleth of the early Reformers but also quite

fantastic. . . . Should we not rather regard it as providential that in these days when formal religion is losing its hold upon great numbers of our people and when this loss threatens to undermine our existence as a people, that the national and racial sentiment has been rekindled among many of them so that they wish to remain Jews and to link up their destiny with the destiny of Israel in some if not in all of the spheres of its creative life?

Silver's opponent in this debate was Rabbi Samuel Schulman of New York, a powerful and venerated speaker at the age of seventy-one. A classical Reformer, Schulman nonetheless complained to the CCAR of the lack of "mystic passion" and the excess of "self-satisfied rationalistic pride" in Reform Judaism and called for greater Jewish distinctiveness and ritual observance in the movement "as a discipline and a hallowing and purifying influence in our lives." He conceded that "perhaps we are beginning a new chapter in Jewish history and are ready for a new synthesis; that while we need above all clarity of thought, moral courage, freedom and fearlessness in uncompromisingly upholding our own idea, yet history may determine that the best of what we have given to the world as the modern anti-nationalist party in Israel and the good that may be indirectly contributed by the nationalist revival in Israel, may come to be harmonized. For both Herbert Spencer and Hegel tell us that that is the law of history." Dialectics aside, however, Schulman maintained that "the particular character of Israel as a community is to reject ordinary nationality and to be what it is, a religious community. . . . The home of a group whose essence is loyalty to the universal God is and ought to be all over the world."

Rabbi Silver in turn was not upholding the strictly secular nationalism that dominated in Palestine; rather, he spoke for what his ally Rabbi Barnett Brickner termed (in the discussion that followed the debate), "spiritual Zionism . . . a synthesis by which all that is spiritually creative in the Jewish people shall be released." Silver did not reject the messianic universalism or missionary purpose of

Reform Judaism, he only refused to see either as a substitute for Jewish nationalism. He urged "the sense of classic harmony in Jewish life . . . the *total* program of Jewish life and destiny—the religious and moral values, the universal concepts, the mandate of mission, as well as the *Jewish people itself*, and all its national aspirations." This was indeed the Zionism of the Eastern European immigrants, the "folk" from whom the Lithuanian-born Rabbi Silver drew his personal and political strength. Most of these people would never bestir themselves to make *aliyah* to the Jewish state, but they would come to see Israel as their spiritual homeland, the main repository of Jewish values and the main preserver of their Jewish identities.

In their breadth of understanding about the meaning of Judaism and Jewish peoplehood in the modern world, Rabbis Schulman and Silver did not stand as polar opposites. Still, they incarnated by virtue of their age, descent, and demeanor, opposing tendencies within Reform Judaism: the one a noble conservatism that feared Zionism's potential to diminish permanently the prophetic, universal character of Judaism, the other a militant realism that viewed the flesh-and-blood fact of Jewish suffering as alterable only through a national restoration in Palestine. That Rabbi Silver had the impetus of history on his side was revealed in his rhetorical strategy: he spoke concisely and rather impersonally, with ample biblical references that were of greater historical than theological importance. By contrast, Schulman's presentation was considerably lengthier, more pious, and at times almost bitterly personal. The discussion among the rabbis in attendance, moreover, centered exclusively on Rabbi Silver's paper. Clearly the day and the future were his.

Two years later, new Guiding Principles of Reform Judaism were adopted by the CCAR in Columbus, Ohio. Principle Five (which aroused such passions that the entire document was nearly tabled) declared Judaism to be "the soul of which Israel is the body" and went on to affirm "the rehabilitation of Palestine, the land hallowed by memories and hopes," as holding "the promise of renewed life for many of our brethren. We affirm the obligation of all Jewry to aid in its upbuilding as a Jewish homeland by endeavoring to make it not only a haven of refuge for the oppressed but also a center of Jewish culture and spiritual life." The declaration was hardly Zionistic—it carefully declared Palestine to be *a* center, not *the* center of Jewish life—but it ended the isolation of Reform Judaism from the mainstream of American Jewry who were becoming increasingly devoted to Jewish efforts in Palestine. "If the younger men of the Central Conference want [the Guiding Principles]," declared Rabbi David Philipson, who fifty years before had attended the convocation that adopted the Pittsburgh Platform, "I will move its adoption." In truth, that task had been performed two years earlier by Abba Hillel Silver.

Just as he spoke within the Reform movement as a Zionist, so Rabbi Silver spoke within the Zionist movement (and beyond) as a rabbi: as a teacher and preacher deeply committed to his own prestigious synagogue where he served for nearly half-a-century and to the synagogue in general as the central institution of Jewish life. His convictions derived from the core of Judaism as he understood the tradition—and his understanding was deep, for he literally steeped himself in the *Tanach,* so much so that scriptural passages became an integral part of his internal vocabulary and patterns of communication. Rabbi Silver didn't merely cite verses in his oratory; the Torah spoke through him. Rabbi Silver wasn't merely rabbinical in his political style; his politics proceeded from his identity as a rabbi.

In 1925 and 1926 Henry Hurwitz's *Menorah Journal,* the most influential Jewish publication of its day, ran a series of articles highly critical of organized Judaism. Elliot E. Cohen launched a savage attack against the synagogue and the rabbinate ("The Age of Brass"), while Horace Kallen, the secular prophet of "cultural pluralism" and himself a Zionist, urged better Jewish education but without religious renewal—a "Hebraism" that would go beyond a religion-centered Judaism. Kallen called Judaism "a small part of the total fullness of the life of the Jewish people."

Silver launched an angry counterattack, "Why Do the Heathen Rage?" which editor Hurwitz first requested and then suppressed. (The piece was consigned to publication in four issues of the *Jewish Tribune*). In it, Rabbi Silver defended the modern rabbinate and synagogue against the intellectuals who sought to supplant religious institutions with secular alternatives. The reformer of Reform presented a vigorous defense of the mission idea of Reform Judaism as an inspirational ideal that prompted Jews to global action and preserved an essential value of Judaism. Twenty years later, well after the *Menorah Journal's* demise, he would repeat his defense before the Fortieth Biennial of the Union of American Hebrew Congregations in Boston (14–17 November 1948):

> To the thoughtful Jews it is becoming increasingly clear that there are no substitutes in Jewish life for religion. Neither philanthropy nor culture nor nationalism is adequate for the stress and challenge of our lives. All these interests can and must find their rightful place within the general pattern of Judaism. But the pattern must be of Judaism, the Judaism of the priest, the prophet, the saint, the mystic and the rabbi; the Judaism which speaks of God, and the worship of God, and the commandments of God and the quest for God.
>
> There have been many false prophets of *ersatz* Judaism in our midst who have frequently misled our people. There were professional social workers, for example, who announced that a full complement of scientifically administered hospitals and orphanages and other social agencies were a sufficient "vade mecum" for the Jewish people, and that the synagogue and religious schools were quite unnecessary. . . . There were certain educators who resented the intrusion of religion in their ultra-scientific curricula. Judaism, they said, was not a religion, but a way of life—that is to say, *their* way of life . . . non-religious or anti-religious. Jewish education should, according to them, not be religious at all, only nationalistic or linguistic. . . .

There were those Jewish spokesmen who offered Jewish nationalism as a substitute for Judaism, forgetting that nationalism as such, unredeemed by a moral vision and responsibility, had sadly fragmentized our world, provincialized its peoples and is driving nations madly from one disaster to another.

This holistic sense of Judaism and Jewish life has become the hallmark of Reform Judaism in the postwar years as we take on the dual challenge of being both broad and deep, flexible and rooted, as a modern religious movement. For Abba Hillel Silver, such an approach was the hallmark of his career. As Harold P. Manson wrote in 1949:

No real understanding of Dr. Silver—the man and the leader—is possible without an appreciation of the fact that he is first and foremost *Rabbi* Silver, a person of deep spiritual convictions and a profound scholar. . . . He regards his pulpit in Cleveland, Ohio, with the reverence and devotion of one for whom there can be no greater calling in life. If we bear this fact in mind, many things which at first glance appear mystifying become crystal clear: why he underwent the physical discomfort of spending many days of each week on trains and planes, commuting between New York and Cleveland or Washington and Cleveland*—this over a period of six years—in order to be back in his pulpit on the Sabbath; why, even in the midst of the most severe crises in his political life, he could be found at The Temple happily engaged in teaching a class of children. . . .

When we view Dr. Silver in the light of his dedication to the spiritual essence of Judaism, we are better able to understand his unshakable faith that the Zionist cause would triumph, no matter what the obstacles, as well as the quality akin to mysticism which is present even in his most "political" utterances—a quality which some regarded as a contradiction of his basic character, but which those close to him understood to be the true expression of that character.

---

*A good deal of this commuting time may have been devoted to homiletic preparation: Rabbi Silver once told me that his average sermon, which was usually more than an hour

Yet even Harold Manson who authored "Abba Hillel Silver—An Appreciation" in the 1963 *Festschrift* produced to honor Rabbi Silver's seventieth birthday would say in a 1971 interview that for Rabbi Silver "[t]here was really no gray area, nothing in between, in political or personal decisions. It was really *entweder oder kinderlach*, you want me, I'm here. You don't want me, I'm not here." In the schismatic Jewish world in which Abba Hillel Silver wielded his tremendous influence, he was often regarded as ruthless and militant, an avid polemicist, a general who thrived on the battlefield and defined his compatriots in reductionist terms as either allies or foes. Perhaps this was a reaction to his patrician manner, his egotism, his impermeable privacy; but perhaps, too, there is among his detractors an element of "murmuring against Moses," the biblical figure to whom Rabbi Silver bore significant resemblance and about whom he wrote his last book, *Moses and the Original Torah*.

Like Moses, Abba Hillel Silver had had to be called to leadership, to the responsibility of nation-building. Although a lifelong Zionist, he eschewed the infighting that was the day-to-day reality of Zionism until he was summoned by other Jewish leaders, including those whom he eclipsed or demolished in later years.

Like Moses, he was revered more than loved—a leader aloof from the people yet embodying their most precious hopes.

Like Moses, he undertood a multiplicity of roles that demanded incredible endurance and spiritual discipline.

Like Moses, he helped make tangible the dream of land for the people of Israel and then surrendered the mantle of leadership to practical men, administrators, and warriors.

---

in length and drew some two thousand listeners to The Temple each Sunday, required two days of thinking and writing and one day of memorization and practicing delivery. His famed eloquence, reflected in the title of this biography, was the result of inspiration and charisma, no doubt—his height and stature, his bushy hair reaching up toward the heavens, and his penetrating bass voice all contributed to the effect—but the true undergirdings of his power as an orator were arduous effort, concentration, scholarship, and rehearsal.

And like the great liberator and teacher of the Torah, Abba Hillel Silver possessed a panoramic, inclusive vision of Judaism and the Jewish people that was unique among his more nearsighted contemporaries. While the theories and plans of others were being swept away by the storm winds of history that so radically altered the Jewish landscape in our time, Silver stood upon the rock of thirty-five centuries of Jewish reality and saw through the tempest to the future.

"(T)here is clearly visible in Judaism," he wrote in his most enduring book, *Where Judaism Differed*, "a steady and dominant coherence, a self-consistency, which links together all its stages of change and development and gives it structure and unity of tone and character. It possesses the unity not of a system but of a symphony. In their total and continuous integration, the key ideas—unity, freedom, and compassion—came to be sufficiently distinctive and impressive as to be unmistakable."

Let his words, as ever, speak for themselves: Abba Hillel Silver's own life could not be better described.

Rabbi Alexander M. Schindler
President, Union of American
Hebrew Congregations

Abba Hillel Silver

Chapter
One

Abe was wholly self-possessed and self-confident; he ruled
the [Dr. Herzl Zion] Club [1906] with an iron hand.

—Emanuel Neumann, 7 January 1975

The halls of old Ohio University are still echoing your
inimitable oratory and the audience is still wildly
applauding.

—William Blumenthal to Abe Hillel Silver,
23 April [1912]

In 1902 Dinah Silver left the Lithuanian village of Neustadt-
Schirwindt with her children Pearl (13), Maxwell (11), Abraham
(9), and Rose (4) to join her husband, Rabbi Moses Silver, who had
emigrated to New York City in 1898, and her daughter Bessie, who
had emigrated in 1899 after graduating from a Russian school.
Taking a train to Bremen, the family sailed on 24 May and arrived
in New York City on 5 June.[1]

Rabbi Moses Silver and Dinah (Seaman) both left strong im-
prints on Abe, who would become by the late 1940s the most
recognizable rabbi in America. Dinah (1860–1948), who had attended a government-sponsored Russian high school, could con-
verse in Russian, Yiddish, German, and Polish, and she supervised
the young boy's studies during the years that her husband was across
the sea. Rabbi Moses (1861–1949), the son and grandson of distinguished rabbis, had already spent a decade at Talmudic acade-
mies before he received ordination and married Dinah in 1886. He

ran his father-in-law's toilet soap business in Neustadt for more than a decade, in part because all of Dinah's siblings had departed for America and in addition because there was little need for another rabbi in Neustadt. Rabbi Moses also joined the nascent Zionist movement in these years, immersed himself in Hebrew literature, and acquired fluency in Hebrew speech as well. He provided his son even before the age of five with a command of spoken Hebrew and a sensitivity to Zionist affairs.[2]

During the years that Rabbi Moses lived apart from his family and saved the steamship fare for his wife and children, he worked primarily as a poorly paid teacher in a Lower East Side Hebrew school on East Broadway (Talmud Torah Mahazikei Ha-Dat) and later in the Talmud Torah of Boro Park. The years in New York were lonely and sad ones: he saw Bessie, who lived with a wealthy but childless aunt and uncle on the Upper East Side, only on Sundays; he was informed, by mail, that his youngest son had died of penumonia shortly after he left; and he was forced to spend a much longer time alone than he had anticipated. His young charges as well as the nascent Zionist activities seemed to provide most of his satisfaction. He explained this movingly in an address he delivered to a Zionist youth club on its fifth anniversary in 1909, later published in the Hebrew monthly *Ha-B'surah*:

> I am a friend and pal to the boys. . . . I am interested in everything in which they are interested. . . . I can penetrate into their inmost souls, easily unlock their closed hearts, and kindle the holy flame that will grow and be fanned gradually into a mighty Jewish fire.[3]

When Abe met his father at Ellis Island, the boy was dressed in a sailor suit (pants and blouse) and sported long, curly earlocks. On the way home to the apartment Rabbi Moses had rented for the family, he left the women in a restaurant and took Abe to a barber who removed his earlocks. Rabbi Moses Silver was already providing concrete evidence of how he envisioned Abe accommodating himself to the new land. The family ate in a kosher restaurant and conversed in part in Hebrew; on the other hand, Abe was supposed to look and dress like an American boy.[4]

In the fall of 1902 Abe began formal studies in America. He attended P.S. 25 and later P.S. 62 in the mornings, while pursuing his Judaica and Hebrew studies in the afternoons at Yeshiva Etz Chaim (later, the Rabbi Isaac Elhanan Theological Seminary), named after the famous Yeshiva of Volozhin. There was time, nevertheless, for both work and fellowship. Abe had a good singing voice and a strong liturgical background and he found jobs in local synagogues as a High Holy Day "choirboy," as a Hebrew and *bar mitzvah* tutor/teacher as well as an English tutor of older immigrants, and as a delivery boy for the silk neckties that his sisters made at home.[5]

Two years after Abraham Silver's arrival in America in July of 1904, Theodore Herzl, the founder of the modern Zionist movement, wornout before his forty-fifth birthday by his Herculean efforts on behalf of the Jewish people, died. The death of Herzl grieved Rabbi Moses enormously, as his son recalled many years later:

> When Dr. Herzl died, my father, who loved Zion with a passionate love, said to us with tears in his eyes, "A prince and a leader has this day fallen in Israel." A few days later he took us to a great memorial service which was held in one of the large synagogues on the Lower East Side of New York, where men and women wept bitterly as if for a lost son.[6]

Rabbi Moses suggested to his two sons that a fitting tribute to the departed Zionist leader would be the organization of a Zionist boys' club on the Lower East Side dedicated to spreading the Zionist program and cultivating the Hebrew language. Thirteen-year-old Maxwell, eleven-year-old Abe, and their friend Israel Chipkin, aged eleven, all students at the same yeshiva, recruited other boys from the yeshiva and on 28 August 1904 at the Silver home (at 360 Madison Street), they officially organized the Dr. Herzl Zion Club, with Maxwell Silver as president. Boys aged eleven to sixteen with some knowledge of Hebrew were eligible to join and to contribute five cents a week in dues—a penny of which went to the Jewish National Fund to purchase land on behalf of the Jewish people in Zion. The club soon outgrew the Silver residence, and they secured the Hebrew Immigrant Aid Society on Canal Street and later the United Hebrew Charities on East Broadway.[7]

The Dr. Herzl Zion Club conducted its Saturday evening meetings mostly in Hebrew, and it sponsored programs that discussed Zionism, Jewish history, and Jewish literature. The boys debated topical themes of Jewish interest, brought well-known Jewish lecturers—such as Rabbi Adolph Moses Radin and Zevi Hirsch Masliansky—to the club, raised funds at synagogues and on the streets for Zionist causes, and ate robustly at a cheap deli after members had solicited at synagogues and lodges. One member, Jess Schwartz, recalled that the boys raised money "from Christie Street to Lewis Street and from Monroe Street to Houston Street," and that "not a synagogue or lodge hall remained unvisited." They also, Schwartz remembered, "went from synagogue to synagogue, from house to house, selling [Jewish] National Fund stamps."[8]

The club gained sufficient prominence within a year that Abraham Goldfaden, the "father of the Yiddish theatre," offered to write a Hebrew-language play for the "actors" of the club. He not only wrote the script but the music as well, and in March of 1906 at Clinton Hall Goldfaden directed the boys in *David Ba-Milchomo* (David At War). It was, perhaps, the first Hebrew play produced in America, and it received positive reviews.

Its success (it was performed again at Clinton Hall in March of 1907 and April of 1908) enabled the club to install a modest Hebrew library, while its popular appeal boosted club membership. By 1909 in fact there were five branches of the club: a senior and junior branch, a girls' branch, and branches in Harlem and Jersey City.[9]

The active membership of the club included a gallery of future American Jewish leaders: Samuel J. Adams, Abraham J. Feldman, Benjamin Friedman, Joseph Baron,. Maxwell Silver and Barnett Brickner became rabbis; Abraham H. Friedland, the future Hebrew poet, short story writer, and educator whom the youngest Silver boy would later bring to Cleveland as the head of the Cleveland Bureau of Jewish Education, Louis Hurwich, and Israel Chipkin distinguished themselves in Jewish education; Jesse Schwartz and Emanuel Neumann became prominent Canadian and American national Zionist leaders; George Sokolsky gained fame as a Far Eastern correspondent and author; and Sol Cohen became a noted New York Jewish communal and Zionist leader.[10]

Abraham Silver played a prominent role in Dr. Herzl Zion Club affairs. By 1906, following the celebration of his *bar mitzvah,* he was made the president, and according to one member he was "its natural leader for years thereafter." He was, noted this same member with words Zionist colleagues would echo four decades later, "wholly self-possessed and self-confident," and "ruled the club with an iron hand." Nevertheless, "the crowd seemed to like his strong rule," and echoing future congregants' reactions, they "acepted his judgment without protest." In 1906 thirteen-year-old Abe made his first public appearance as a delegate from a Zionist youth group, and an extant photo from this convention in Tannersville, New York, shows him—in short pants—to be the only youngster at the convention. One year later, three years after the club had been chartered by the national Federation of American Zionists, Abe represented the Dr. Herzl Zion Club at the Tenth Annual Convention of the FAZ and, although he was only fourteen, addressed the convention.[11]

Abe also acted in nearly every play the club performed and frequently with considerable success. Two thousand people—an audience that "filled the old People's Theatre to the roof, howled with laughter," and "joshed Pharaoh in Yiddish"—attended the club's 1909 Hebrew language performance of *Moses* and saw the "handsome young Prince Moses" played by Silver. This four-act play (originally titled *The Exodus From Egypt*), written by Jacob Meir Salkind, the author of numerous Hebrew plays for kids with music by Perlmutter and Wohl was "appropriately costumed in biblical robes and well-acted by amateurs," according to one New York theater critic. The critic singled out the performance of Abraham Silver, noting that it "would have done credit to a professional actor."[12]

Not everyone in the New York Jewish community applauded the young Zionists, for militant anti-Zionists existed on the Lower East Side and especially uptown. On one occasion, several members recall (in slightly differing versions) when the nonsectarian Jewish Educational Alliance served as the club's meeting place, two members of the alliance's board of directors appeared at a meeting. The Zionist activities, Hebrew conversation, and even the group's name disturbed these uptowners, whose commitment to the Jewish Educational Alliance's "Americanization" programs led them to brand such activities as "un-American," and they demanded that either the "Herzl" or the "Zion" be removed from the club's name or the alliance would no longer welcome them.

Sol Cohen recalled that the two guests were the JEA director, Dr. Henry Fleishman, and the distinguished educator, Julia Richman, and that Dr. Fleishman demanded that the club members cease speaking in Hebrew if they wished to continue to meet in the JEA. All the witnesses agree that Abraham Silver (aged fifteen, if this event occured in 1908 as Benjamin Friedman claims) rose, rejected all the demands, and noted that any language in which King David wrote his psalms and Isaiah preached his vision of universal love and brotherhood was good enough for the Dr. Herzl Zion Club. And, so it is said by some, the directors retracted their demands in the face of Silver's powerful response; others said that although they were impressed by Silver's oratory, they evicted the club members. Whatever were the results, Silver entered his first ideological battle in an area that would engage most of his active career.[13]

While the Dr. Herzl Zion Club occupied every Saturday evening of young Silver's New York City youth, he spent his Friday evenings with hundreds of other Jewish children and adults in the audience (with, however, a favored place) rather than on the stage. The Educational Alliance attracted immigrant adults and children to a wide range of activities, including sports, clubs, drama lectures, a reading room and library, steam bath, and much more. George Sokolsky, a Dr. Herzl Zion Club member and later an international correspondent and author, recalled that "there [Educational Alliance] I would spend all my time outside of school, sometimes until midnight or one o'clock. [Zevi Hirsch Masliansky] would lecture at the Alliance every Friday night. Nobody stayed home."[14]

The alliance was also the arena for fights, Sokolsky and others recall; fights over socialism, anarchism, and Marxism. "You were brought up in an atmosphere of that sort," he reminisced, and "we were all politicians; we all belonged to parties—kids, I mean—and we used to have fights about the thing—fist-fights."[15]

Silver did not remember the battles, but he recalled Masliansky without hyperbole.

> Among my unforgettable memories of those years were the lectures of the Rev. Zevi Hirsch Masliansky which I attended regularly every Friday evening at the Education Alliance. Masliansky was the most popular preacher-lecturer on the East Side in those days. Thousands flocked to hear him. . . . I sat every Friday evening in the wings of the stage of the Educational Alliance—Rev. Masliansky was fond of me and had invited me to sit there—and I listened to the captivating flow of his eloquence. After these many years I can still taste the sweet honey of his words.[16]

Possessed of tremendous skill as a Yiddish orator as well as intelligence and learning, Masliansky had such renown that the Yiddish press heralded his arrival in America (1895) and thousands of Jews thronged to the synagogue where he delivered his first sermon. For over a quarter-century he preached at the educational alliance on Friday evenings, and his delivery became the stuff of legends.[17]

Isidore Singer, the managing editor of the *Jewish Encyclopaedia,* called him the "professor extraordinary of Jewish eloquence at the Russo-Judaean People's University of New York." Louis Lipsky, the noted Zionist leader, remembered late in his life a Masliansky lecture in Rochester fifty years earlier:

> I have never forgotten that experience. He was so thoroughly alive as a speaker. He raked his audience fore and aft with invective, sarcasm, lamentation, sentiment, and with appeals to faith and loyalty. . . . He alternated from comedy to tragedy, varying his tone, the tempo of his sentences, and in interludes, rested in a soothing chant. [He was] a great and moving speaker . . . [who] gave [one] the feeling of establishing contact through him with an endless Jewish tradition.

For Charles Angoff, the celebrated novelist and chronicler of Boston Jewry, Masliansky was "Moses and Aaron and Samson and Joshua and all the Maccabbees" and possessed "a voice that was now thunder, now a violin."[18]

It is not at all surprising that Masliansky inspired Silver and that we will hear many of Silver's enthusiastic followers describing his oratory in much the same manner. Though as integral to the Lower East Side as a peddler, Masliansky dressed fashionably, looking the part of a dignified American gentleman. More importantly, he was a spellbinding orator with a full tenor voice, startling and dramatic movements, and the ability to thunder, whisper, and thoroughly captivate an audience for two hours. He "poured forth," Silver once noted, "a brilliant cascade of sparkling phrases . . . wisdom and inspiration." And he was by no means merely a traditional preacher who drew lessons from Scripture and Talmud, but a new-style preacher who spoke over and over on Jewish nationalism ("He was not merely a speaker on Zionism," Lipsky recalled; "he was the chanter of its song"), Jewish pride, and Jewish hope while drawing heavily on current thought and daily experiences to express his positions with absolute conviction. Silver tasted the "sweet honey" for a lifetime; almost every portrait of Masliansky, *Ha-Matif Ha-Leumi*, The National Preacher, could be just as easily applied to Silver. Perhaps from Masliansky on Friday evenings week after week Silver learned the eloquence and firm conviction that dazzled and convinced a generation or two of American Jews. [19]

In 1908, six years after his arrival in America, Abe Silver entered Townsend Harris Hall [High School]. It served as a "prep school" for the College of the City of New York and actually functioned as a department of the college. A boys' school that boys completed in three years and whose graduates in large numbers went on to City College, its alumni association reads like a Who's Who of New York City. Abraham H. Silver's transcripts from semesters 1 and 2 of 1908–09 and from semesters 1 and 2 of 1909–10, when he lived at 1488 5th Avenue have been preserved, and they reveal him to have carried a heavy load of secular courses to complement his yeshiva studies and busy club life. He had four semesters of Latin, Greek, English, math, and history, as well as two semesters of German during these two years. [20]

At the same time, he served as the editor of *The Hebrew Herald* (published in English by the Dr. Herzl Zion Club on its fifth anniversary) and its Hebrew counterpart, *Ha-B'Surah*, contributing an elegant Hebrew and English editorial (hoping to "nationalize our generation of youth") and several poems. He seems to have been a good history and language student, an excellent literature and composition student, and an average math student, although it is not entirely clear what the transcript numbers (rather than grades) represent. It is quite clear, however, that his studies in the nine years he attended New York public and private schools enabled him to enter and excel in a university and rabbinical seminary program at the same time—completing both within a period of four years (1911–15).[21]

Despite a rigorous Orthodox upbringing and an active passion for Zionism, Abraham Silver, along with half-a-dozen or so fellow club members, left New York and enrolled in the anti-Zionist, nontraditional Hebrew Union College. A rabbinic student, Jacob Tarshish, noted that "in the second year [1911–12] . . . the size of our class increased by one—a tall and gaunt youth from New York, Abba Hillel Silver." Was Silver misled into thinking that this reform rabbinical seminary, located across the street from the University of Cincinnati, where he would concomitantly pursue his B.A., was supportive of his personal values and commitments?[22]

Not at all. He knew the HUC to be a bastion of anti-Zionism and had heard of the sharp controversy over Zionism that had led to the resignation in 1906–07 of three faculty members. Nevertheless, his intellectual commitment to Orthodoxy was slight; his father, grandfather, great-grandfather, and great-great-grandfather had been rabbis and, Silver once noted, "predetermined me for it [the rabbinate]"; his "greatest ambition," ever since childhood, a neighbor later recalled, "was to preach to the world the love of men toward themselves and God"; he knew of several prominent reform rabbis in New York who also championed Zionism; and he probably knew little about the "denominational" divisions between Orthodoxy and Reform. Five years after his ordination, a reporter asked him about his boyhood ambitions and Silver replied: street car conductor; policeman; teacher; minister. Some of his friends as well as his brother Maxwell recall that when Abe was asked why he was enrolling at a bastion of anti-Zionism, he replied, probably apocryphally, "to conquer it."[23]

But that he did, in several ways. First, and perhaps most importantly to him, his Zionist ardor and involvement never diminished. Benjamin Friedman (HUC, 1917) recalls that Silver organized and constantly led student discussions and debates on Zionism; that

Zionism and his life were bound up inextricably; and that he arranged for prominent Zionists, such as Nahum Sokolow, to address the student body and be hosted by the college. Chosen by the students to respond to Sokolow, he delivered his words in fluent, modern Hebrew.[24]

Abe Silver, together with the newly appointed Professor David Neumark, founded *Ivreeyah*, a Hebrew-speaking club during the 1911–12 year—an organization that outlived Silver's tenure at the college. Together they organized Zionist programs in Cincinnati's immigrant community that featured Hebrew and English lectures by faculty and Silver. These were usually held at the Jewish Settlement, and several extant broadsides indicate that Mr. Abraham H. Silver, still under twenty years of age, would be the featured speaker. One such evening in 1912, celebrating the fifteenth anniversary of the Hebrew monthly *Hashiloach*, received a lengthy summary in New York City's Yiddish-language *Jewish Daily Forward*, while Silver's Hebrew oratory was frequently lauded in the Yiddish and Hebrew press. By his senior year, Silver was the featured speaker for the Cincinnati Zionist Society.[25]

Abe's oratorical skills received abundant opportunity for growth during his student years, though they seem to have been richly developed upon his arrival to the HUC. One classmate noted that "We had never before heard such eloquence; . . . quietly, with steady march, and in his magnificent clarion voice, [he] expressed his ideas with firm tread, giving weight to every sentence."[26] In addition to preaching in the College Chapel to student and faculty acclaim, Silver made a deep oratorical impression outside the HUC. In 1912 as a University of Cincinnati sophomore at the UC Law School, he won the Cincinnati Arbitration and Peace $15 "Peace Prize" for the best address on international peace. His victory (the second-, third-, and fourth-place winners were all HUC students) gave him one of the ten places at the interstate Intercollegiate Peace Association's contest in Athens, Ohio, and although he only took the $50 second prize with his address against fortifying the Panama

Canal, he left an indelible impression in Athens. The *University Weekly News* called him "an orator of natural eloquence" who "combines a powerful magnetism with an Arabic abandon that fairly sweeps one off one's feet"; the *Athens Daily Courier* claimed the decision to give Silver second place was outrageous, for "most of the audience fully expected that Mr. Silver would be given the first prize." One of the judges even wrote Silver a personal letter: "The halls of old Ohio University are still echoing your inimitable oratory and the audience is still wildly applauding. The School of Oratory yesterday by vote decided that you deserved first prize. The only adverse comment was 'Too good.' Your oration was faultlessly faultless."[27]

Silver's extracurricular activities did not end with Zionist programs and public speaking, for he continued to improve his public presentation of self by renewing his love of the theater. This time, however, it was in Greek rather than biblical drama, as Abba Hillel Silver (a name he began to use only at the age of twenty) played Aeschylus in the first American presentation of Aristophanes' *Frogs.* Translated and directed by Dean Joseph E. Harry for the UC Drama Club, the play and Silver were a great success. The city press lauded him, while the campus newspaper review stated that he was "a poet just acting natural, and therefore forceful, oratorical and artistic."[28]

Besides drama, Silver swam on the swim team, served as vice president of the Debating Council (1911–12), as president of the Speakers' Club (1912–13), and as an active member of ZBT fraternity and the Social Science Club. In addition, he founded, edited, and dominated until his graduation *The Scribe,* a monthly literary magazine published by the university beginning in January 1914. He served as editor-in-chief of volume 1, which included five issues (January–May 1914), and his many editorials reveal a broad grasp of academic, political, and economic affairs as well as a deep social consciousness. A few months after starting up *The Scribe* he founded and edited the *HUC Monthly*. He wrote all the editorials and some of the articles for both journals until his graduation from UC (June 1915) and his ordination from the HUC on 12 June 1915.

Although Abba Hillel began to write poetry at a very young age, his most creative period as a poet came during his years in Cincinnati and he was stimulated greatly by the opportunity to publish his poems in the journals he edited. He saved numerous poems from these years—unpublished longhand verse in notebooks and clippings of published poems in scrapbooks—and many reveal the care with which he chose, revised, and then again revised his words.

The dominant theme of his poetry during this period of enormous outward success is somewhat surprising: darkness. Although "A Wine Song" (1910) is an ode to libation, the brew is necessary because of the depths of human sorrow. "On the Silence of the Night" (n.d.), set in Toledo, Spain, during the Inquisition, is a poem about despair; "God's Greater Gift" (1912), in which the "wild winds moan," addresses the "deeper woe" and "ruins of life-long dreams"; while "Lonely Lights," published first in the *Young Judaean* in 1913 and reprinted in the *American Zionist* in 1964, is set in "my cheerless attic room," and is filled with the "gloom" of the "doomed soul of the dreamer." Abba Hillel Silver's despair is so intense that he wonders, "Shall I, buried in the darkness,/Ever see the rising sun?"

No event seems to have occasioned the strains of gloom and despair that run through the poetry of the young man who drank deeply of the variegated vines of life and who was generally described by his friends of late adolescence as filled with a zest for life. Rather, Silver seems to have anticipated the malaise, or at least the self-examination, more characteristic of a man at least twice his age. The ever-present "brooding, despair, darkness and death" that "sink like mists into my soul/And choke its feeble light" ("A Twilight Prayer," 1911) seem to appear most often in the context of the young poet's search for the meaning of life in general and his career plans in particular. This outwardly self-assured and enormously self-confident young man, already with the seasoned maturity of middle age, knew that "Human life is full of futile quests and heart-breaking pursuits." He seemed desperately to seek "one bright ray of supple warmth . . . one ray of light," so that the "shades shall melt/And shadows shall depart."[30]

Silver certainly did not permit either his secular or religious studies to suffer while he pursued his extracurricular writing and activities. His report cards indicate that he took a demanding schedule at both schools, accelerated through the HUC and UC, and only once earned a grade under ninety in any course. He was a student instructor in the department of (medieval) biblical exegesis (1913–14, 1914–15), the valedictorian of his HUC graduating class (he spoke on "Dreams and Visions")—which included the distinguished student and later halachist Solomon B. Freehof—and in 1914 the faculty awarded him a set of the *Jewish Encyclopaedia* for his prize-winning essay "The *Am Ha-Aretz* in the Period of the Soferim and Tannaim." His senior thesis, a five-chapter work on "Divination in Ancient Israel," demonstrated a fluency not only in biblical Hebrew but in German and Greek too.[31]

During the HUC years, Silver gained important rabbinic and pulpit experience teaching Sunday school at the Reading Road Temple and as a student rabbi. His gifts of oratory as a visiting preacher were noted everywhere he went to serve. His pulpits included congregations in Williamsport, Pennsylvania (High Holy Days, 1912), Chelsea, Mass. (High Holy Days, 1913), at Lake Michigan summer resorts, while studying one summer at the University of Chicago (1914), and Huntington, West Virginia's Ohev Sholom (1914–15), which he served on a biweekly basis throughout his senior year after rejecting an offer from Chelsea.[32]

A *Chelsea Evening Record* reporter noted the power of his voice and the grandeur of his vocabulary and was especially moved by a phrase in Silver's Yom Kippur sermon: "to draw him out of the valley of phlegmatic submission to convention and expediency and urge him on to climb the hostile heights of truth." In Huntington, after Rosh Hashanah services, he was described by one reporter as a "brilliant orator," and after Yom Kippur another reporter noted that he "moved his congregation to tears by a stirring sermon on the Atonement" and then offered a prayer for peace that "was one of the most beautiful ever offered in Huntington."[33]

Besides his deep-rooted Jewishness, excellent training in Judaica and Hebraica, and the sense of direction and mission his Zionist activism had provided him as a youth, Silver's academic successes reflected his maturity. Freehof saw this immediately, recalling that "it was evident at the very beginning that Abba Hillel Silver was different in temperament from most of us . . . more mature, or at least more adult than most of us." His maturity included "a premature reserve and the capacity, characteristic of mature leadership, for listening patiently and in silence." More pointedly, and to be noted by many thereafter, "there seem[ed] to have been no triviality about him from the very first time we met him[;] we were rather boyish and he was already in temperament a man."[34]

The years in Cincinnati changed Abba in one dramatic area: his physical appearance. He returned to a Dr. Herzl Zion Club reunion only twenty-two or twenty-three years of age, tall and lanky, but "elegant in dress, polished in manner, faultless in speech," and having "shed the habits, manners and the accents of his earlier environment." One club member in fact felt that "he seemed *goyish*."[35]

The external changes hid a person far more worldly, sophisticated, and learned than before, but they "had not touched the core of the man—his inner spirit." He left the HUC passionate for Zion, gifted as a performer and speaker, deeply commited to the Hebrew language, and, perhaps the most important contribution of the college, filled with an enormous thirst to implement the Reform Jewish emphasis on prophetic justice and social ethics. These various fires, "kindled" (in the words of the same boyhood friend who thought him, initially, changed) "at the parental hearth and in the company of his youthful comrades," were not at all smothered. They were only "banked against the time when they were to burst into ardent flame."[36]

Chapter
Two

[Silver] uncrossed his legs, placed his hands on the two
arms of the chair, and pushed himself up with elaborate
slowness—a Lincolnesque giant bestirring himself from
repose. Then the voice began, like a soft syllable prying
loose an avalanche, its music, packed with enormous
power and gaining force with each word, until the air
quivered with pathos, rumbled with wrath, and glowed
with sheer grace of phrase and thought. When he closed
his eyes, mine were opened on a realm of harmony and
rapture. When he stepped back and lifted his mighty
arms, an intellectualized thunder rolled up and out from
him, and shook the clustered lights and swept from pew to
pew into the choir loft and out through the windows into
the night.

—Abraham L. Feingold, 1916

Abba Hillel Silver began his rabbinate in 1915 at Wheeling, West
Virginia's Congregation Leshem Shomayim (the "Eoff Street Temple"), at a $2,500 a year salary.[1] Encompassing nearly all of Wheel-
ing Jewry, the congregation had been established in 1849 and had
already been served by full-time ordained rabbis. Leshem
Shomayim was small, and Silver later noted that as a result "I came
close to people whom I saw, perhaps for the first time, as individual
human beings in the setting of their everyday lives," and "I found
great warmth and helpfulness among these people." More than forty
years after leaving those congregants, he said that "to this day I
cherish pleasant memories of them." They too cherished good

memories of him, as attested by numerous letters of affection that he received for years after he left and by gala celebrations whenever he would return.[2] No less important was his introduction to Virginia Horkheimer—the daughter of one of the congregation's most active members—for Silver would return to Wheeling a few years later to wed Ginny, on 2 January 1923.[3]

In addition to the personal contacts of a rabbinate in a small town, Silver immediately took to heart the lessons of social justice and prophetic involvement he had been taught at home, had had reinforced at rabbinical school, and had been developing in his student editorials. He jumped actively into the larger Wheeling society, helping to organize the West Virginia Conference of Charities and Corrections and serving as its first vice-president, actively participating on the board of directors of the Wheeling Associated Charities, and serving on the advisory board of the West Virginia Woman Suffrage League.

Silver's involvement in the suffragist movement was far from perfunctory. He spent most of his weekends while a student rabbi in Huntington, West Virginia (1914–15), at the home of J. and Irene Broh; Irene was a leading suffragist and reformer. When he went to Wheeling as an ordained rabbi—to no small extent as the result of J. Broh's contacts and letters—he was immediately recruited by Irene into the "flying squadron." Ten West Virginia men and women (attorneys, judges, politicians, and clergy) spoke at their own expense to groups in thirty or more different locations, and Irene Broh, more than fifty years later, still recalled one of Silver's impassioned addresses. The Huntington Equal Suffrage Association relied on him at least twice for the 1916 campaign; at his first appearance he gave an "eloquent address," and on another occasion, according to an eye-witness, he provided "renewed inspiration" for campaigners who had "grown weary on the 'last lap' of the race." The head of the Huntington Equal Suffrage Association wrote Silver that "the memory of your address will remain for many years to come," and he was praised for his "generous donation of time and service."[4]

The Wheeling press was filled with admiration for his speeches. Immediately upon his arrival he spoke at the Wheeling YMHA, and an editorial in the *Wheeling Daily News* called his address "one of the most impressive and beautiful sermons ever delivered in this city." Near the end of his rabbinate in Wheeling (where he was known, at least to the teenagers, as "The Voice"), the president of the organization called his speech to the Elks' Club (of which Silver was a member) "the most eloquent and inspiring address ever given in Wheeling."[5]

Silver's rabbinate in Wheeling also gave him a generous introduction to the impact a rabbi could have on the non-Jewish community. He campaigned vigorously for local charities, participated in and spoke at the statewide meeting of the Conference of Charities and Corrections ("a masterly bit of literary art, an artistic gem" one reporter wrote of his speech), and he stumped tirelessly (but unsuccessfully) for the Woman's Suffrage Amendment to the state constitution. Communal service was early on an essential ingredient of his rabbinate.[6]

One event that attracted national attention provides us with much insight into the youthful Silver's values and courage. Sen. Robert M. LaFollette had been contracted by the Eoff Street Temple Lecture Committee to present a public lecture on 8 March 1917. On Monday night, 5 March, more than a hundred angry but "representative, patriotic American citizens of Wheeling" met in a hastily assembled gathering and demanded that Rabbi Silver cancel LaFollette's contract. They objected to his leading a filibuster in the Senate against the Armed Neutrality Act—granting President Wilson the authority to arm United States ships—and they called him an "enemy of our country." They were not alone, of course, in their feelings about LaFollette. Teddy Roosevelt, immediately after the Senate filibuster, wrote that LaFollette "has shown himself to be an unhung traitor, and if the war should come, he ought to be hung."

Silver was informed of the meeting and he rushed to the hall and spoke at some length to the hostile crowd. He explained that whether or not any individual agreed with the Senator's position, LaFollette had every right to vote as his conscience dictated and every right to lecture anywhere. The crowd's leaders interrupted Silver, told him that if LaFollette came to Wheeling they would arrange to "rotten egg" him, and demanded that Silver poll the lecture series subscribers. Silver agreed to do so, arguing that a democratic vote seemed reasonable, but not before a "parting shot of inimitable oratory" at the crowd: "Men of your like are the real menace to democracy; you fan your shallow patriotism into a flame of furious intolerance which consumes all the sanctities of a nation."

The subscribers voted to cancel LaFollette by a four-to-one margin, and Silver was very displeased. After the cancellation of the lecture, on Friday night 9 March Rabbi Silver preached on "Patriotism, White and Red." He argued that LaFollette and his allies had every right to oppose Wilson if their consciences told them to do so, that excessive patriotism is fanaticism and bigotry, and that certain rights must be beyond even a democratic vote. This commitment to a minority view, even in the face of a hostile audience, would guide Silver throughout his career. [7]

The young rabbi, fresh out of the seminary, did not fail to make an overwhelming impression on teen-age boys contemplating the Reform rabbinate. One of them, Abraham L. Feinberg, lived a streetcar ride away from *Leshem Shomayim* in Bellaire, Ohio, and he heard from his father in the spring of 1916 that "The Divine Voice" had "electrified the vast audience" at a rally for Jewish war refugees in Wheeling; that he "knew Talmud like the yeshiva prodigies in the old country, and was a Litvak [Lithuanian]!" Abe went to Wheeling to hear the "Lincolnesque giant . . . whose bushy brows barely saved his black torchlike eyes from a hairy jungle of the same colour that reached down over the forehead," and, in the "back row of a long narrow sanctuary" was transformed. Abe took it all in and came back repeatedly on the streetcar to hear more of the "intellectualized thunder." That same spring Silver took sixteen-year-old Abe Feinberg on walks through the West Virginia hills and encouraged his decision to become a rabbi.[8]

It is hardly surprising that a young man of Silver's talents would seek a forum larger than Wheeling or that a larger congregation would seek him. Temple Beth El in Providence tried hard during 1915–16 to convince Silver to break his contract and come to Rhode Island. He repeatedly said no, although he did agree to a visit. When Dr. Kaufmann Kohler, president of The Hebrew Union College, heard of Silver's rejection of the much larger congregation, he was pleased that the young rabbi had put principle before temptation. Kohler assured Silver that "in a few years larger opportunities will come to you commensurate with your growing power and the fine qualities of mind, heart and tongue with which a good Lord had endowed and blessed you."[9]

When colleagues urged him to pursue larger pulpits aggressively, Silver explained that he would never "go after" any position, for he "detested the wholesale marathons that disclosed the nakedness of our colleagues scrambling for positions before the gaze of a disillusioned public." True to his word, Silver declined several invitations—from colleagues and from Cleveland congregants—to pursue the attractive position held by Rabbi Moses Gries, who was retiring from The Temple in Cleveland to manage the Gries family assets. Rabbi Samuel Mayerberg wrote Silver to "go after it—for no man in the country could fill that pulpit as you can," but Silver politely said no to him and to Alfred A. Benesch, a prominent Cleveland attorney and member of Gries's congregation. But the leaders of Cleveland's Tifereth Israel (The Temple) doggedly pursued Silver and convinced him to give a guest sermon that, according to Rabbi Louis Wolsey of Cleveland's Euclid Avenue Temple, was the "*finest Jewish sermon* ever heard." Solomon B. Freehof, a professor at the

HUC and dear friend of Silver's, wrote to him after the trial sermon that "it is supposed to be a 'goyish' congregation," while Rabbi Lee Levinger informed Silver that "only a fool would try for Cleveland." Why these admonitions on the part of Silver's friends?[10]

Cleveland's Tifereth Israel had been founded about the same time as the Wheeling congregation (1850) but, located in a major urban center, it had grown to become one of the most prominent Reform congregations in America, with more than seven hundred families, nearly nine hundred pupils in the Sabbath School, and a $25,000 annual budget in 1916. The congregation's third rabbi, Moses J. Gries (1868–1918), had served The Temple for a quarter-century when he announced his retirement effective at the end of May 1917—during the High Holy Days of 1916.[11]

Immediately after Gries's resignation announcement, Max Raisin, one of Silver's colleagues, lamented the loss of this distinguished rabbi. Raisin noted that Gries had developed The Temple "from a very small body to one of the largest Jewish congregations in the world," and that its seven hundred plus families constituted "the finest elements of wealthy and cultured Cleveland Jewry." Raisin also noted Gries's "large salary" and "social position in that important community," which was "truly enviable." It is not hard to understand why some of Silver's friends told him to "go after it."[12]

The bad news was that Gries was one of a small number of radical Reform rabbis who had stripped most ritual, custom, ceremony, Hebrew, and even services from the celebration of the Sabbath, choosing instead to worship—in English with richly Protestant hymns—on Sunday mornings. Gries had introduced Sunday morning worship (10:30–11:45 A.M.) one year after his installation, eliminated Sabbath worship one-half-year later, and he refused to read the weekly Bible portion from the Torah scrolls, insisting the verses be read from an English Bible. There is evidence that his reforms, radical though they were, were widely accepted; we do know that the minutes record no serious challenge to them during more than two decades.[13]

Despite the wide acceptance of Gries's idiosyncratic Judaism, the leadership probably did not imagine, when selecting Gries's successor, that Abba Hillel Silver—fluent in Yiddish and Hebrew, outspoken in his Zionist convictions, and passionately committed to Hebrew—would leave these customs unchallenged. But Silver's oratorical skills and commanding presence won over the committee, though it took plenty of time to make its decision, perhaps as a result of Silver's outspoken commitment to Hebrew and to Zion. The choice of Silver, made at a congregational meeting on 29 April 1917, suggests that some part of The Temple's leadership felt that radical reform had gone far enough and that the pendulum must swing back. Silver disappointed very few of them when he began his Cleveland rabbinate on 1 August 1917, because simultaneously he brought great prestige to The Temple with his oratory and began to restore much, if not quite all, of what almost everywhere constituted the program of Reform Judaism. According to Silver, his reforms "did not encounter any marked resistance."[14]

Silver's initial years at The Temple coincided, of course, with the Great War, and though the years from 1917 to 1919 would be occupied primarily with Zionist activities, the new rabbi devoted abundant time and energy to the cause of the Allies. He presented his first public talk ("a patriotic address") in Cleveland on 17 August 1917 at Euclid Beach, where a sizeable number of "Jewish boys" were gathered for festivities before leaving for overseas duty. Before a reported fifteen thousand listeners, Silver expressed optimism that the war would "end all wars," that it would "do away with the reasons for war," and that it would bring "happiness and freedom to all mankind." Furthermore, he argued, "in fighting the battles of America," Jewish young men "fight for Judaism and for humanity."[15]

The following summer for a period of two months Silver went to

France as an agent of the Committee on Public Information (CPI) and as a representative of the French High Commission. The Secretaries of War, Navy, and State had proposed the formation of an official information agency to President Wilson in April 1917, and Wilson established the CPI and chose the prominent and brilliant muckraker George Creel to head it. Before the war ended this enormous propaganda apparatus had distributed seventy-five million copies of more than thirty pamphlets about America's relation to the war, issued six thousand press releases, and sent numerous speakers—many with first-hand impressions—on the stump. There, at Verdun and elsewhere, Silver's hopes for meaning and value from the war began to fade and a sense of sadness emerges in his diary of the trip. By the latter part of August, as he was preparing to leave France, he recorded his inner turmoil and clear sense of the war's meaninglessness:

> My mind is confused from the inrushing of hosts of impressions of the day! Varied emotions were stirred within me as I passed from place to place! I felt the horror of it all, the glory of it all and the wonder of it all. But above all an unconquerable spirit of depression has been with me all day. I could not help hearing the woman's sob and the child's plaintive cry—"Mon Petit Mari; Mon Petit Papa cheri."[16]

These, however, were private feelings, and when Silver returned to Cleveland to speak about his trip and when he toured the country for the CPI, he enthusiastically embraced the war effort, supporting the United War Work and Fourth Liberty Loan drives and even enrolling together with other "prominent Clevelanders" for the draft. In September 1918 he told four hundred Cleveland City Club members ("Some Impressions from the Front") that "Our American boys in the trenches and battle lines are learning a new and wonderful lesson; they are learning the lesson of fraternity and human troubles [and] of unbounded generosity." Furthermore, as "souls now face souls, men are forgetting their prejudices."[17]

Two months later Silver was on the road, speaking on behalf of the CPI in Oklahoma ("Several times the audience was so enthused that it stood and cheered the speaker"), Texas, New Mexico, and Arizona ("With the eloquence and the fervor of a learned man with a burning message"), as well as, later on, Ohio ("The rabbi spoke for nearly an hour; the crowd sat as if held under a magician's sway"). In each city through the fall of 1918 and the early months of 1919 Silver used different words to deliver the same message—the Great War is serving as a crucible of brotherhood and equality. Not until the end of the war and the disillusionment produced by the Peace Treaty of Versailles did Silver like so many other one-time enthusiasts admit publicly to despair. "What a God damned world!" exclaimed ex–Bull Mooser William Allen White in 1920, as the old order settled back into place and crushed many of the aspirations the war had lifted. By 1920 Silver would speak of the "confirmed feeling of the almost absolute futility of war" and even of his opposition to the proposed League of Nations—"a sinister plot of European nations to disguise their imperialism and preparations for war."[18]

From the initial days of his rabbinate in Cleveland—when he shared the dais at Cleveland's Hippodrome with Rabbi Stephen S. Wise for a memorial tribute to the orthodox Rabbi Samuel Margolies—and vigorously throughout his entire career, Silver used his extraordinary oratorical gifts on behalf of the Zionist cause. By the early months of 1919 Palestine had begun to dominate his lecture topics on the road and, increasingly, that judgment entered his sermons and lectures at home.[19]

In Youngstown in January 1919 Silver launched the three-million-dollar Palestine Restoration Fund campaign (Youngstown was assigned a ten-thousand-dollar quota by the Zionist Organization of America). He argued that American Jews, now that European Jewry stood in disarray, must take the primary role in rebuilding Palestine for all Jews who wished to live there, and that it was no more disloyal for an American Jew to support Palestine than for an Irish or Polish man or woman to send money back home. In February he spoke on Palestine to the largely non-Jewish Rochester Ad Club, and the editor of the club's weekly predicted that "Someday, Rabbi Silver will be known all over the world for his ability as a public speaker." In March his "golden voice" raised one million dollars at a Chicago Zionist rally; and in Toledo in April Silver's lecture opened the Palestine Restoration Fund (PRF) campaign and raised twenty-five hundred dollars.[20]

The year 1920 began in the same manner, except that now Silver spoke from first-hand experience after a visit to Palestine the previous summer with his rabbinical school pal Jack Skirball (1896–1985). In January he traveled to the Dallas–Fort Worth area for a Zionist fundraiser, where "his appeal, time after time, brought the diners cheering to their feet"; in April he went to New Orleans to launch the eighty-thousand-dollar PRF campaign and spoke "with an eloquence that set his audience aflame with enthusiasm."[21]

In the summer of this same year, the twenty-seven-year-old Silver departed for the International Zionist Conference in London's Memorial Hall, the first post–World War I meeting of world Zionist leaders, as one of the thirty-nine members of the American delegation. Despite the attention the press gave to the open conflict between American and European Zionist leaders, especially Louis Brandeis and Chaim Weizmann, over the nature and tasks of the World Zionist Organization, reports from the latter days of the conference took note of Silver's powerful oratory and passionate commitment to Zionism.[22]

The American delegation chose Silver to deliver the final address of the conference—part of a "demonstration" to celebrate Great Britain's acceptance of the mandate for Palestine—and he did not disappoint his elders. Emphasizing "joy, hope, and trust," despite the divisiveness of the Brandeis-Weizmann quarrels, he pledged that American Zionists would "completely fulfill their duty." The *London Jewish Guardian* reporter who covered the conference took note of the presence of Lord Arthur James Balfour, Major Ormsby-

Gore, Weizmann, Brandeis, Lord Robert Cecil, and, in the chair, Lord Rothschild, as well as

> a tall young man who stepped forward. His voice was musical; his words were like honey; golden-tongued oratory quickly enthralled the audience and held it spellbound. Those who heard his message will long remember it for its passion, its oratory, its skillful intonation, its climax.

The correspondent for the *American Hebrew*, David Dainow, called it

> the most eloquent speech of the evening. Rabbi Silver . . . has a powerful, rich voice of vibrant quality. His rhetoric was of an inspired nature, which aroused the audience at moments almost to a frenzy of enthusiasm.[23]

A few days later (12 July) Silver addressed an enormous Zionist demonstration at the Royal Albert Hall; the auditorium was "packed to its extreme capacity" and "thousands who sought admission" were turned away. A British reporter described Silver's "remarkable oration" enthusiastically:

> It was a magnificent effort, magnificently accomplished, the work of a master of oratory, a man who has the ability of controlling vast audiences by the power of his tongue, by his dramatic capacity deftly employed so that his art seemed but natural. Soon after he brought his audience spell-bound the meeting closed.[24]

Silver's gift of speech and passion for Zion were now known to almost every major Zionist leader.

Several facts about Silver's Zionist addresses of 1919–20 as well as to a lesser extent those of 1915–17 and 1917–19 are clear. First, he drew enormous crowds everywhere and nearly every newspaper noted the number of people turned away from his lectures. Second, the crowds were wildly enthusiastic about him and editors lauded him. A Fort Worth–Dallas editorial noted that "many who heard him last night—themselves veterans of the pulpit—pronounced him as one of the greatest orators the Jews possess," while the Fort Wayne [Indiana] *News* claimed that Rabbi Stephen S. Wise called Abba Hillel Silver "the finest orator I have ever heard." Third, Silver never suggested that his listeners themselves go to Palestine and participate in the drama of creating a Jewish homeland, but he suggested that they contribute money to those who wished to do so. Fourth, and most important, Silver presented a consistent Zionist ideology from the very beginning of his rabbinate. He was a fervent disciple of Ahad Ha'am, a cultural Zionist, and he "came to the movement through his love of Hebrew Culture and Literature." He never qualified his love of Zion, Hebrew, or the Jewish people, and he withheld none of his enthusiasm in his sermons, lectures, or even his interviews and communications with Cleveland leaders of The Temple when he sought the pulpit. He had two long con-versations about Zionism, for example, with Temple leaders in Cincinnati and one in the Gries's home in Cleveland, and he discussed Zionism with the "search" committee first in Wheeling and later in Cleveland. He explained to Gries and to the laymen his commitment to a "spiritual and cultural centre in Palestine," and the manner in which Hebraic culture might radiate from this center and "galvanize Jewish life the world over." He did not stress the political side of Zionism in these years (he would usually state that the "political thrust of Zionism is for me secondary"), but he always emphasized that should the nations of the world establish a Jewish state in Palestine, "I cannot see where that would be detrimental to the status of the Jews in America." In his correspondence with the Clevelanders, he went on to make clear his readiness to withdraw his name from consideration if anything in his Zionist ideology "would militate against a mutual sympathy of pulpit and pew." Thus, as he wrote Rabbi Stephen S. Wise in 1917, "I go to Cleveland a free and independent man."[25]

Within a twelve-month period during 1920–1921, three Zionist gatherings—in London, Buffalo and Cleveland—dominated the Anglo-American scene. All the earlier differences between the Europeans and the Americans, between Chaim Weizmann and his followers and Louis D. Brandeis and his aides, had been mere skirmishes compared to the "opening salvo of the real battle between East and West" that erupted in London. The London conference had revealed tensions that were leading to a collision course (one historian called it "a major convulsion that shook the world Zionist movement") from which it would be impossible to retreat.[26]

Brandeis returned home from London under attack from some American Zionist leaders for his behavior overseas. At the National Executive Committee sessions on 29 and 30 September 1920, American Zionist leaders especially criticized Brandeis for his seemingly hostile attitude to Weizmann and the International Organization and for his lack of consultation with his own delegation. The National Executive Committee, still dazzled by his London oratory, asked Silver to convey these criticisms to Brandeis in a private meeting, and Silver carried out this unpopular task in Washington on 12 October. He then prepared for the executives a four-page transcript summary of his conversation, corrected and approved by Brandeis, a report that largely argued that "ignorance of the facts" and "misunderstandings" had led to the attack on Brandeis. This meeting with Brandeis bound Silver intimately to the Supreme Court justice and led him to dramatically blast Brandeis's foes a few months later in Cleveland.[27]

At National Executive Committee meetings in August, September, and October 1920 as well as in less formal gatherings of Zionists, American Zionist opposition to Brandeis and his aides rallied around Louis Lipsky and Emanuel Neumann, and this conflict dominated the 1920 ZOA convention in Buffalo later that fall, with the Brandeisians carrying the convention. The 1921 convention, held in Cleveland (5–8 June) only seven months after Buffalo—with Chaim Weizmann present—served as a forum for "both sides to reiterate their stands with great passion," and all spring each side jockeyed for position in the forthcoming confrontation.[28]

Stephen S. Wise, Julian Mack (zoa president), Jacob de Haas, and Silver, in the absence of Brandeis, bore the brunt of the battle for the Brandeisians, while Weizmann, Ussishkin, and Louis Lipsky fought for the Europeans and the American opposition. The latter, heavily supported by loyal followers, triumphed decisively over the Brandeis supporters, and the repercussions of this were felt throughout the decade of the 1920s, even though some conciliation moves began as early as 1922.

The two hundred and fifty delegates to the Cleveland conference heard all the old contentions repeated with a passion that suggested the delegates were denouncing each other's positions for the first time. There were several areas of contention: first, Brandeis supporters opposed the one hundred million dollar wzo–*Keren Hayesod* agreement hammered out by the Europeans because of their fear that investment and charitable funds would be mixed up and that the apparatus would be poorly managed; the Brandeisians believed that they could raise large sums for well-managed attractive investments in Palestine but not to succor poor Jews; and the *Keren Hayesod* (Palestine Foundation Fund) was directed largely to conditions of the masses of Jews in the diaspora rather than those in Palestine. Second, the Europeans felt that the Brandeis followers would entrust the interest of the Zionist movement to the care of a non-Zionist executive more capable of business skills in managing funds than of fervor for Zionism, whereas the Brandeisians felt that a small autocratic clique of European directors paid scant attention to American Zionists. Third, the followers of Brandeis sought to minimize (or eliminate) the policy-making role of those factions (such as East European Jewry) making little or no financial contribution and to prevent funds from reaching non-Palestinian (that is, East European) Jews. Weizmann viewed Zionist fundraising as supportive of Jewish culture everywhere (called *Gegenwartsarbeit* ["work

in the present"] in Zionist parlance), while the Brandeisians wanted
to restrict fundraising to rebuilding Palestine.[29]

Despite the interruptions, jeers, and frequent outbursts of antag-
onism, several speakers on both sides presented carefully organized
and forceful arguments. Neumann, Lipsky, and Weizmann triumphed over Felix Frankfurter, Mack, Wise, and Silver, and the
American Zionist leadership, repudiated at the convention by a
better than 2–1 vote, had no voice but to resign. Nevertheless, the
thirty-seven Zionist leaders who resigned—including de Haas,
Frankfurter, Mack, Silver, and Wise—vigorously attempted to implement their own economic program for Palestine.[30]

In his presentation to the conference on the evening of 6 June,
Silver claimed that he was not interested in attacking or defending
anyone and that he "never questioned the sincerity" of either side
in a conflict, which, according to Silver, turned "brother against
brother." Immediately, however, he launched into an impassioned
defense of Brandeis and Mack. In response to "all of the cruel things
that have been said [about them]," Silver urged the delegates "to lay
a wreath of tribute at the shrine of their names." Delegates (including Lipsky) heckled, jeered ("Throw him out"!), and interrupted
him continually, but he yielded not an inch to any one of them. "I
will have my words, friend, whether you like it or not . . . You can
all stand on your chairs and howl [me] down . . . No one can read
me out of the movement."[31]

Silver dealt with the dispute over the *Keren Hayesod,* whether
non-Zionists should participate in the controlling agency in Palestine, the extent to which Zionist fundraising should support
diaspora Jewish culture, the Buffalo convention, and some other
minor matters, and he concluded by placing himself firmly on the
Brandeis side ("I must stand and fall with our administration").
Lipsky immediately followed with a ringing attack on Silver, which
the latter vigorously denounced ("Absolutely false; I want the record to carry that; absolutely false.") An exasperated chairman,

after listening to the attacks and counterattacks by Silver and Lipsky, could only say: "One man says he said it. The other says he did not. What in thunder has it got to do with the issues before this Convention?"[32]

At the Buffalo convention during late November 1920, the delegates proposed and created the Palestine Development Corporation [PDC] to hasten industrial and agricultural development in Palestine. Businessmen in consultation with scientists and engineers would suggest projects and the PDC would circulate information about and sell stock in projects or prospective projects in Palestine.[33]

Silver, as soon as the convention ended and the PDC apparatus was set in motion, had an additional cause for which to stump. Within a year he headed the Central Committee of the Palestine Development League and chaired the PDC, and in 1922 he increased his speaking commitments on behalf of Palestine's economic development. In one whirlwind campaign from late August to early September 1922, Silver spoke in St. Paul–Minneapolis, Seattle, Portland, San Francisco, Oakland, Los Angeles, and San Diego with hopes of raising four and a half million dollars (nationally) for the Rosenberg hydroelectric project through the sale of stock at fifty dollars per share.[34]

Silver's appeal rarely disappointed either his listeners or the campaign organizers and together with Rabbi Stephen S. Wise he was the most eagerly sought-after Zionist speaker in the land in the early 1920s (and for years thereafter). In Philadelphia during May 1921, he "kicked off" a campaign for Palestine and was called "an orator of the ages who spoke with the divine thrill of the universal soul"; in Detroit several months later he was introduced as the "silver-tongued orator of the pulpit," and the audience "cheered his fundraiser for several minutes at the conclusion"; in Scranton in April 1922 "he won his listeners' attention, and they would have stayed the night through"; and in Reading, Pennsylvania, early in

1923, "the entire crowd [rose] to their feet as he entered the hall." In all four cities Silver's keynote talks led to dramatic returns.[35]

When Silver in 1924 finally threw his support to the *Keren Hayesod*—the new financial fund created at the London conference but opposed by Brandeis and not established in the United States until Weizmann's visit to America in the spring of 1921—he became one of its leading boosters. With his captivating oratorical skills and without any remuneration except for travel expenses, Silver laboriously crisscrossed the states east of the Mississippi on behalf of the fund. In May, to initiate the thirty-five-million-dollar *Keren Hayesod* campaign, he addressed large gatherings in Boston, Buffalo, Chicago and New York City (at Carnegie Hall); a reporter for the *Boston Globe* who attended the Boston lecture wrote that "Rabbi Silver used inflections, cries, gestures and shouts that very few orators would have cared to try, yet [there was] not the hint of a false note in the address."[36]

Despite a schedule of travel and speeches that made Silver, in the words of a reporter from Erie, Pennsylvania, the "most sought for man in the ministry," Silver's primary activity centered on his congregation and the community of Cleveland. He preached and lectured at The Temple virtually every Sunday morning from the early autumn to the late spring and took a deep intellectual and practical interest in the society outside The Temple walls. He not only addressed social injustices and civil liberties frequently in his lectures before his congregation, but he involved himself in the political and economic issues within his community.[37]

His deep commitment to justice probably emerged when he was an immigrant boy in New York City, open to the influences of his parents and teachers. It was refined and given an ideological base at the Hebrew Union College, because the movement's leaders repeatedly spoke of the "social ideals of prophetic Judaism" as well as the "immortal prophetic cry for justice." In editorials in college magazines and in sermons in Wheeling, Silver invoked the prophets to explain his activities on behalf of free speech, woman's suffrage, and even the moral and ethical issues involved in the Panama Canal. Looking back in 1954 upon his own commitment to social justice, he invoked the prophets, the "fearless spokesmen of God's moral law to men," to explain his affirmation of Reform Judaism's demand for "unremitting action" and "unwearied moral effort" to "build the good society." At the "heart of the message of Hebraic prophecy," he argued, "is a summons to men not to rest content with the evils of society . . . but to set to work to correct them." This helps explain why, for Silver, the prophets were such a potent symbol of social involvement and were never divorced from society: "they were interested primarily in the moral tone of their nation and of society generally," and especially in "social righteousness and human brotherhood."[38]

Silver delivered sermons and lectures on a variety of social issues, most of which did not sustain his attention. These included support for five municipal taxes on the ballot (in 1920), a bitter attack on police incompetence and what he termed a "meaningless" vice crusade (in 1921), an exposé of a local university's racist question ("Are you of the Jewish race?") on its admissions application (in 1922), a strong statement embodied in a minority report for the municipal committee of the Chamber of Commerce in opposition to federal censorship of the movies (in 1922), several sermons and lectures, including one in the City Club's Public Square Forum, in defense of "absolute free speech" (in 1923), and an unsuccessful appeal to the Akron, Ohio, Board of Education to oppose scriptural reading in the public schools (in 1924).[39]

Most of these issues, even though they were passionately felt at the moment, occupied Silver's time and energies only briefly. With the turmoil in industrial labor of those same years, however, it was different; he catapulted himself into this arena with enormous energy, intellect, and courage. In the first lecture that he delivered on the subject of labor on 17 February 1918, during World War I and Labor Loyalty Week, he castigated the strike of shipbuilders.

He argued that even if their wage demands were just, they were "unpatriotic and dangerously criminal" to have struck "at a time as critical as this, when the whole world is prayerfully watching every bolt and every rivet which is put into a ship that is to carry a new hope to a struggling world." He called the strike "reprehensible" and urged "every patriotic American citizen and every devoted lover to the cause of labor" to condemn the action.[40]

With the world war at an end and the demands of patriotism no longer central, Silver began to study and analyze industrial tension far more thoroughly than he had before. Cleveland offered a cauldron of industrial conflict—237 strikes occurred in 1919 in Ohio—and from 1919 to 1924 Silver preached frequently from his pulpit, lectured widely in the community, and wrote occasionally for the general press on the subject of labor and management.[41]

As the industry that lined the shores of Lake Erie grew, steel dominated Cleveland's industrial sector. The successful Russian Revolution and its promises led five thousand marchers to carry red banners and placards reading "Workers of the World, Unite," through Cleveland's streets on May Day 1919. They were met by seven hundred policemen and countless thousands of hostile spectators who started a bloody riot. Postwar frustrations led to the giant nationwide strike of more than three hundred thousand steelworkers beginning in late September 1919. In Cleveland, the mills shut down almost completely for several weeks and Mayor Davis, until stayed by court action, prevented strike-breakers from entering the city.[42]

Silver in a lecture on 19 October 1919 that was reprinted virtually verbatim in Cleveland's daily newspapers as well as in the city's Yiddish weekly, analyzed the industrial tension in the steel industry "after thoughtful and careful and prayerful study and reflection and meditation." He attributed the massive strike to "postbellum psychology," arguing, as have subsequent labor historians, that the vigorous opposition of steelowners to workers' demands immediately after World War I frustrated the heightened expectations of the newly organized steelworkers. He correctly pointed to intensive organizing efforts made the previous year in the steel mills, and he noted perceptively how the organizers of "industrial democracy" had used the concomitant Fourth Liberty Loan and the final battles of the war to link unionization and patriotism.

Silver quickly dismissed communism and socialism as having any serious impact on American workers and strongly supported trade unionism, collective bargaining and, "in the last resort," strikes, as the only weapons available to "the pigmy [pitted] against the giant" of "selfish and nearsighted" capital. Most centrally, he denounced the "open shop," an idea that came to life in a national movement by 1920. He argued that the open shop—in principle a place of employment where the employer was not allowed to discriminate against a worker because that person was or was not a union member—was a thin disguise for an antiunion drive. He illustrated this argument with the case of the steel industry, which on the one side declared that it stood for the open shop and on the other side rejected collective bargaining, employed labor spies and strike-breakers, "systematically suppressed free speech and the right of public assemblage," discharged men for union activities, and frequently controlled the press and local public officials.

This 19 October 1919 lecture was by no means exclusively in praise of labor, for Silver accused it of acting, "in recent years," in a "manner so arbitrary, so despotic, so disregardful of public interests and public welfare as to trouble and confound its truest and best friends." He noted that workers had engaged in more than two hundred strikes in September 1919 alone, and he believed that they "plunged the country into strikes at the slightest provocation." Nevertheless, he delineated the methods that were being used to destroy unionism. He noted that the demands of the steel strikers—including collective bargaining, an eight-hour day, one day rest in seven, the end of the twenty-four-hour shift, and overtime for Sundays and holidays, when "analyzed dispassionately," were reasonable. He urged employers to recognize organized labor and the right of collective bargaining. And he expressed the strong fear that should the steel strike collapse, other industries would "use this failure as a fulcrum to remove unions within their shops."[43]

Such statements took more than a little courage, for not only did Silver anticipate that his lecture "will prove unpopular," but he knew full well that the congregation's president (from 1915 to 1927) and a key man in Silver's hiring, Benjamin Lowenstein (1859–1945), strongly opposed the closed shop. Lowenstein, the president of the Landesman, Hirschheimer Co., Manufacturers of Ladies', Misses' & Children's Coats & Suits, faced a strike himself in the summer of 1919 and wrote Silver in France, as the lines were being drawn more tightly in the garment industry, that he "will not have anything to do with this so-called union." Silver responded to Lowenstein as he did to most critics of his strong positions on social issues, that "no religious leader dare shirk these problems if justice and truth and democracy are part of his doctrine and part of his theology," and as he did to most militant antiunionists, "that any man who . . . sets about fighting trade-unionism without first finding an equally effective and beneficent substitute to protect the interest of the workingman, and to insure his further progress and development—that man is an enemy of society, and I care not who he is."[44]

Silver lectured again on workers and employers in "Labor Relations in Cleveland" on 28 March 1920, and he began by asserting that "the industrial relation is the most vital in human affairs and human life, and the one that stands in most need of religious interpretations." He indicted religious institutions for losing their "prophetic vision and their prophetic courage" and failing to "challenge the social conditions about them," for being "the agencies of power that is," and for forgetting that "the prophets of Israel never hesitated in applying their religious convictions to the industrial [sic] problems of their day." Silver also discussed a report of the Cleveland Chamber of Commerce that not only denied recognition to the closed shop but also did not recommend collective bargaining nor concede to employees the right to be represented by men of their own choosing. His lecture—to a congregation whose members belonged disproportionately to the Chamber of Commerce and took pride in his standing-room-only addresses to that organization—insisted that neither socialism nor capitalism was "sacred or divine," that business desperately needed to "find a soul," and that labor must "magnify man." Such lectures regularly led one or two non-Jewish businessmen to write Silver and applaud his courage. George L. Fairbanks heard this particular talk ("a corker"), called his courage "commendable and praiseworthy," and asked how Silver, "head of a rich temple, dared" to do what "Christian pussy-footers wouldn't" do.[45]

Later that same year on 19 December 1920, as the push for the open shop by the National Association of Manufacturers united the propaganda efforts of numerous local business and industrial agencies, Silver spoke on "The Coming Industrial Struggle—The Open vs. the Closed Shop." In his strongest language to date he argued that the open shop crusade was nothing more than "a determined effort to destroy trade unionism," and that calling it the American Plan was "unmitigated balderdash and bunk," for it suggested that "any other arrangement is un-American and unpatriotic." Once again he defended in some detail his familiar propositions that the right of labor to organize and bargain collectively is beyond question, and that labor and management must talk together to resolve their differences.[46]

By the summer of 1921 Silver had spoken on "economic subjects" to numerous civic and religious audiences and was widely perceived, according to the press, as having "tried to avoid catering to anybody." When twenty-five thousand men in the building trades struck in May 1921, tying up forty million dollars worth of building in Cleveland for more than a month, Silver was a logical choice of the *Cleveland Plain Dealer* and the Joint Conciliation Board (seven employees and seven employers) to serve as one of the seven "public" representatives to form a twenty-one-member committee whose wage scale recommendations would be binding. He joined the other members in proposing an offer that both contractors and unions finally accepted early in June, despite the opposition of the Chamber of Commerce, and in asking for a permanent, impartial board with public representatives. He also served as the sole arbitrator in the plumbers' dispute. Both sides in binding arbitration submitted briefs (on 2 June) and argued their cases (from 4 to 10 June) before him; he announced a settlement that gave the plumbers $1.10/hour.[47]

A year later on 21 May 1922 Silver lectured on "Coal: An Interpretation of the Coal Strike" and repeated much of his argument in the City Club's summer open forum before several hundred listeners in Public Square. As nearly six hundred thousand bituminous coal miners struck for the second time in three years, Silver delineated the "moral delinquency" of the coal mine operators for their repeated refusals to meet with John L. Lewis and the United Mine Workers, even after strong urging by the secretary of labor, the House Committee on Labor, and the attorney general (on behalf of President Harding). Silver argued that the miners' charges go "to the very heart of industrial morality and ethics." Silver had a tremendous ability to describe the pathos of the Central Competitive Field miners (Western Pennsylvania, Ohio, Indiana, and Illinois) and the "industrial feudalism and economic autocracy and exploitation" of a typical town controlled by the mine owners. According to listeners, he thundered the message that nearly every "elemental right of American citizens" was being denied to striking miners in coal towns, and, most of all, he decried the fact that the "vast American public" is "almost totally indifferent to the situation."[48]

Silver's passion for the "open shop" finally erupted into more than just lectures. On 11 December 1922 he submitted a letter of resignation to the Chamber of Commerce and the following April the Cleveland press made this correspondence public. In his letter Silver charged that the men who controlled the Chamber of Commerce "systematically engaged in smashing the closed shop, destroying organized labor and eliminating collective bargaining," and pointed out that the chamber was a civic organization, not an "association of employers." The chamber's Committee on Labor Relations publicly reaffirmed its opposition to the closed shop, while several men, most notably Newton D. Baker, former president of the Chamber of Commerce and former U.S. secretary of war, tried privately in a "downright way" to persuade Silver to reconsider. But he rejected all entreaties and released much of the correspondence to the press (with Baker's approval). Silver's dramatic move resulted in numerous scathing anti-Jewish attacks in letters to him and the subsequent resignation of some non-Jewish members who opposed a civic organization campaigning for the open shop. In addition, the chamber's directors published a blistering assault on Silver in the Chamber of Commerce's publication and reaffirmed their opposition to unions and union activity.[49]

Silver's vigorous defense of some of labor's interests represented only a part of his involvement in political matters. Early in 1919 a new national organization, the Committee of Forty-Eight (a loose group of Progressives sculpted out of the Bull Moose movement that year), issued a call for a conference of those radical intellectual forces in America that stood outside the ranks of either the labor or farmer movements (these two groups coalesced into the Farmer-Labor Party in 1920). Drawn largely from men who opposed what they called "rule for profit" rather than social betterment and who felt that sound and constructive radicalism had been coopted by President Wilson's befuddling liberalism, the committee's call for a conference appealed to Abba Hillel Silver and he lent his name to the committee's efforts and publicity. After Harding soundly defeated Cox in the 1920 presidential election (and the Farmer-Labor Party received only 290,000 votes nationally), the committee believed the time was unusually ripe for enticing liberal Republicans and liberal Democrats into a third party. Silver continued to pay his membership dues and to permit the committee to use his name, but little came of the organization's efforts. Early in the autumn of 1924 Silver gave his support to the LaFollette-Wheeler ticket for president, and he viewed the LaFollette campaign (Progressive Party) of unionists, farmers, and socialists as the sequel to the Committee of Forty-Eight. In October in the *New York Times* Silver wrote that the ticket promised to be the nucleus of a new Progressive or Liberal Party—fusing together liberal Democrats and liberal Republicans—but his hopes for this new party (though it polled five million votes) were aborted once again.[50]

While Silver played a prominent role in the campaigns for Liberty Loans, Palestine development, and worker's rights, he also continued to minister to a gigantic congregation. Silver's rabbinical duties at The Temple, which he handled alone for ten years, were extensive. He taught the Confirmation class on Thursday and Friday afternoons at 4:30 P.M., conducted worship services in the religious school on Sundays, and preached nearly every Sunday morning between Rosh Hashanah (September) and Shavuot (June). He officiated at a sizeable number of weddings and funerals, counseled extensively, and coordinated virtually every synagogue activity. Scores of letters attest to his impact on the betrothed, the sick, and the bereaved. A mourner in 1925 wrote that "words cannot express our appreciation of your sympathy and condolence during our recent sorrow"; a physician in 1926 noted that "your visits to my mother at Mt. Sinai Hospital have brought wonderful results in her mental condition"; and another mourner told Silver "how much we appreciate your kind and peaceful service at mother's funeral and the sweet simplicity of it was so overwhelmingly sensitive."[51]

Silver also coordinated the efforts that culminated in the erection of a new and magnificent temple. By June 1924, when the last service was held in the thirty-year-old building at East 55th and Central, the congregation had grown to more than twelve hundred families (more than five hundred families had joined since Silver arrived) and the congregation was greatly in need of larger facilities.

For example, beginning in 1919, High Holy Day services were conducted simultaneously in The Temple and, initially, in East End Baptist Church because of lack of adequate space, and on many Sunday mornings during the year Silver's preaching drew standing-room-only crowds with significant numbers turned away. The old Temple seated only twelve hundred people (it had about six thousand members and twelve hundred children in the Sunday School in 1925), and by the end of the world war, most Temple members had begun to move away from the neighborhood.[52]

In March 1920 the congregation authorized the purchase of land at the junction of East 105th and Ansel Road; in June Silver wrote a long letter urging that a new building seating at least eighteen hundred and having more than twenty-five classrooms be erected; in December 1922 excavation began after the trustees chose Charles R. Greco of Boston as the architect; in May 1923, the cornerstone was laid; and by late September 1924 the almost $1,500,000 Byzantine structure, whose sanctuary would seat nineteen hundred and whose golden dome still towers over a part of the University Circle skyline, was ready for use.[53]

The structure of the new building reflected the three types of activities in the congregation—religious, educational, and social/recreational—which explains the three main parts of the building: the temple itself; the offices and school; and the gymnasium. The three-story-high school had twenty-seven classrooms, while a swimming pool (never built) was to have connected directly to the school above and the gymnasium below. A special feature, surely for Abba Hillel Silver's benefit, was the sanctuary's sound system; it "eliminated all echo from the standpoint of the speaker, without at the same time smothering the resonance and tone of the organ, which are equally necessary to the best effect."[54]

Silver nurtured the entire project, from the search for a new site, which began in 1919, to planning the details of the ark and the gymnasium. When the trustees raised his salary to fifteen thousand dollars on 1 March 1923, they cited his attention to the work involved in planning the new temple, and when they raised it again two years later to twenty thousand dollars they did the same.[55] After the completion of the spectacular eighty-five-foot-high blue-vaulted domed structure—which one architect called "as nearly perfect a structure of its kind as exists in the world today"—Silver even took an active interest in the "selling of pews" (seats, as each "pew" contained two "seats"). Annual dues of fifty dollars gave an individual or family all membership privileges except a reserved seat, and the trustees, with much support from the rabbi, raised $380,000 by auctioning seats on 14 September 1924. The pews ranged in cost from one hundred to twenty-five hundred dollars each (there were 240 of the former and twenty-one of the latter). Silver's appeal at a special meeting of the Budget Committee, New Temple Finance Committee, New Temple Building Committee, New Temple Pew Committee, and the Executive Board one month before the auction led sixteen of the twenty-nine leaders present to pledge themselves to purchase $22,750 worth of seats.[56]

Only once during Silver's rabbinate in Cleveland did he even briefly consider another pulpit. Chicago Sinai, a Reform congregation much like The Temple, conducted a rabbinical search during 1922–23. The leadership of Sinai invited Silver to preach in the fall of 1922 and he overwhelmed them with his oratorical gifts and charisma. The president of the Hebrew Union College, Julian Morgenstern, apparently initially urged Sinai to pursue Silver, but once Silver visited Chicago he won the job on his own. Friends as far away as New York City heard rumors that Silver had accepted the new position, but he explained to the Chicagoans and to Dr. Morgenstern that he could not leave Cleveland in the midst of his "vast project" (building campaign), for the congregational leadership "launched this project" in order to "assist me in my work."[57]

Although there is no record of Silver's own contribution to the building campaign, he shared his financial resources generously with friends, family, and even strangers. He made personal loans to poor rabbinic students from Cleveland; he generously loaned money—sometimes repeatedly—to siblings and in-laws who needed it desperately; sent $150 to his parents every month after their move to Palestine in 1924; supported *schnorrers* and other wandering, needy Jews nearly every week; donated generous amounts to an extensive list of Jewish philanthropies and several nonsectarian charities; and headed a private campaign to raise money in support of a new gymnasium for the Jewish community of his birthplace (Neustadt-Schirwindt). [58]

Before concluding this summary of the first decade of Abba Hillel Silver's rabbinical career, I should try to explain his extraordinary impact as a public speaker while he was still a young man in his twenties. Enough descriptions of his lecturing style exist for us to make some efforts at understanding his appeal. First, people would frequently remark on the excitement he generated by his presence alone, even before he began to speak. A writer in the *Steubenville Herald-Star* who described Silver as "the big, virile, intellectual king" noted that "even before he speaks one feels the tremendous power inherent in him." Of course, his reputation usually preceded him, so that, as in Reading, Pennsylvania, "the entire crowd [rose] to their feet as he entered the hall." His "powerful physique suggesting strength of character in every feature," his long bushy hair and his dramatically placed *pince-nez* (which he removed and cleaned dramatically before he began) all contributed to a commanding presence. [59]

His lectures were always written out in full and usually covered about fifteen to twenty typescript pages. Hence, he spoke for thirty to forty minutes, only rarely, as in Columbus, Ohio in 1919, for an hour, where despite the length the "crowd sat as if held under a magician's sway." He thought through his subjects clearly and organized them unusually well—he "knows," a reporter in Wheeling noted, "what he wants to say and knows exactly how to say it." [60]

The thesis of every message Silver delivered was immediately clear, and the evidence for that thesis unfolded in a coherent fashion. Listerners often remarked on his seriousness (he rarely told jokes or even used stories) and, while he occasionally resorted to broad and even inaccurate generalizations ("whenever a Jewish community failed to kindle the lamp of learning and relied solely on worship, observance, and philanthropy, it ultimately disappeared"), he usually dissected a topic with the logician's precision.[61]

His delivery, however, was spirited and energetic. Everywhere listeners commented upon his gifts of speech, voice, and drama. When necessary, he could use an "even, well-modulated and musical voice" to "allay and soothe any resentment his words may arouse." More often, however, as in Allentown, Pennsylvania, he was "a Caruso singing in rhythmic prose" with a "depth of poetic thought and a mystical something of omnipotence [which] held his hearers in the deep silent stillness that bespoke a tribute to the golden voice and the glorious poesy that tripped from the tongue like odor from a rose and the wondrous beauty of the dawn gliding into the daylight."[62]

Silver spoke with an abundance of animation, and he "used inflections, cries, gestures and shouts that very few orators would have dared to try—yet with not the hint of a false note in the address." He could alternate, therefore, "an appeal to judgment and an appeal to emotions," as a Pittsburgh observer noted, and he had a "keen appreciation of dramatic values, with the aid of his deep, clear, musical voice and wealth of expressive words."[63]

Perhaps most crucial, he did it all by memory without the help of a text. Silver almost never spoke extemporaneously—"I feared that the inspiration of the moment may be late in coming," he recalled later—but he also hardly ever (and not until much later in his life) resorted to a manuscript. He wrote every lecture out carefully, revised and revised it, and then memorized all of it. The effect upon the audience was rarely surpassed in American oratory of Silver's generation.[64]

And what of his youth, for Silver achieved this fame well before the age of thirty? Dr. Nettie Erskine, the Steubenville writer, noted this and explained the effect of his age. "Rabbi Silver is only twenty-eight," she wrote, "and yet the happiness and the sadness, the glory and the seriousness of life are already traced on his face, and he appeals to one as being possessed of all the dignity and all the spirituality and all the power which must have thrilled the great prophets who have been the leaders of his people."[65]

Did Silver ever question his preaching and its role in the syn-agogue? Repeatedly through the 1920s and 1930s he did so, es-pecially as he began to lecture more and more on secular subjects (to preach, for Silver, meant to talk on religious motifs; to lecture meant to address secular concerns). He frequently "called down" from the pulpit those who arrived after the services just to hear him speak, arguing that the "primary and essential purpose "of the synagogue was prayer. In numerous letters he pointed out how Reform Judaism had imitated Protestantism in subordinating wor-ship first to the sermon and later the lecture, and how this had reached "preposterous extremes" by the interwar years. He fre-quently urged laypeople to demand more "preaching," and did all he could, short of inserting prayer in the midst of his lectures, to make the worship service more than "an introduction to the ser-mon."[66]

The first decade of Silver's rabbinate did not pass without crit-icism—however mild—preserved in his papers. It is in the form of letters from his boyhood friends from the Lower East Side and from his brother Maxwell. The latter, unable to hold any rabbinic post for very long, continually berated Abba for not trying hard enough to place him (Maxwell) in this or that position. Boyhood friends complained that "Abba Hillel" never had time for personal corre-spondence and, in response to their long and newsy letters (fre-quently seeking advice) they received only a formal line or two. They were right. Though Silver did manage to find the time to attend the wedding in New York City of Solomon Cohen, his old friend from the Dr. Herzl Zion Club, those childhood pals whose professional lives no longer touched his he soon forgot, despite their sad letters that sought a piece of his fame. Already by 1924, though only thirty-one, he had an abundance of fame in Cleveland's Jewish and non-Jewish community as well as elsewhere in America. Generously paid, spaciously housed at 1485 East 106th Street in Bratenahl, comfortably seated in the latest model Cadillac, widely acclaimed, leading one of the world's largest synagogues, in demand as a speaker day after day, and with most of his career before him, he dedicated The Temple on 19–21 September 1924 with optimism for the future and confidence in his career choice and its location.[67]

Chapter
Three

I am an extremely over-worked and hard-driven man.

—Abba Hillel Silver to Louis J. Kopald,
16 January 1928

The second decade of Silver's rabbinate began as auspiciously as the first decade ended. At The Temple a packed sanctuary of about two thousand people assembled for his opening lecture of 1926–27. They saw a tall and commanding figure with a large head of black hair and heard the musical bass voice that carried strongly to every corner of the immense sanctuary with an effortless delivery, conversational in tone yet filled with power. In response to his message, the congregation "spontaneously exploded with constant ovations." At the Free Synagogue in New York in January 1926 as the guest of Rabbi Stephen S. Wise, Silver was "greeted," according to the New York *Times*, "by one of the largest congregations in the history of the Free Synagogue." In Wisconsin, speaking on "Jew and Christians: Will They Ever Meet?" Silver "held his large audience spellbound by the force of his silver-tongued eloquence and clear logic," while in Chicago "his address hypnotized the crowded temple to such an extent that he himself appeared to them as a young prophet. His voice protested, thundered and appealed." Silver continued to be in great demand to speak to churches, synagogues, schools, colleges, fundraising events, and conventions all over the land.[1]

It was inevitable that Silver would need rabbinical assistance at The Temple, and at his tenth anniversary celebration (in 1927) the

President, Benjamin Lowenstein, announced that Rabbi Leon
Feuer (1903–84), a recent graduate of The Hebrew Union College,
a recipient of a scholarship from The Temple while a rabbinic
student, and a summer replacement for Silver for several years while
attending HUC, would become "assistant minister." Feuer as a teen
in Cleveland had been in awe of Silver and, he once recalled, "he
decided to become a rabbi" after "hear[ing] Abba Hillel Silver
preach." Upon Feuer's acceptance of the position, Silver wrote to
him that "eagerly I am awaiting you as colleague and co-worker."[2]

Feuer's hiring was rather typical of rabbinic placement in the
1920s. Here is how Feuer recalled it:

> I came home during my senior year for Passover and, as usual, I made
> my usual call on Rabbi Silver. I always went to see him when I came
> home, and he always bought lunch, and he said, "Are you doing
> anything special for lunch?" I said no. He said, "Well, let's have lunch
> together." Instead of going to our usual luncheon place which was a
> delicatessen near the corner of 105th and Euclid, he said "Let's go
> downtown." We went downtown and we went to the Hollenden Hotel
> in Cleveland which was a very fine hotel, a very fine dining room. We
> didn't go into the public dining room. We went into the private dining
> room and there, to my surprise, were four or five members of the Board.
> We sat and talked. I was asked a few casual questions. Nothing was
> mentioned about a position. No offer was made. Luncheon broke up.
> The men wished me goodbye. I remember one of them saying to me, if I
> recall correctly, we'll see you soon. I thought nothing of it and they left
> and Rabbi Silver and I walked out. We went out to get his car and on
> the way to his car he leaned over and said, "Congratulations"! I said
> about what. He said, "You've just been elected my assistant." He had
> never asked me whether I wanted to be his assistant. But he knew I
> did.[3]

Rabbi Feuer, at age thirty-one, left The Temple in late 1934 after
seven years of service to become the head of the Collingwood
Avenue temple in Toledo, where he remained until his retirement.

As soon as Feuer's resignation became public, Silver (and the president of the HUC, Julian Morgenstern) were flooded with letters of inquiry about replacing Feuer. Almost all the queries came from rabbis who well understood that the opportunities to preach were virtually nonexistent but who felt that the chance to assist Silver was too valuable to pass up.[4]

Silver for his part knew exactly what he sought, if not precisely whom. In fact, he sought two assistants. The men would split such responsibilities as preaching at Sabbath morning religious school services and Sunday morning high school assemblies; conducting and addressing Sunday morning religious school assemblies; teaching part of the confirmation class, high school classes, alumni study groups, the preconfirmation class, and midweek Hebrew classes; editing The Temple Bulletin; assisting with the High Holy Day services; and conducting the life-cycle ceremonies (weddings and funerals) of nonmembers. This would leave Silver in charge of Sunday morning and the main High Holy Day services, pastoral work, several classes (especially the confirmation class) and the general "planning, supervision [and] policy" of The Temple. Silver, according to Feuer, "left nothing to chance." In words that recall his teenage friend's description of his Herzl Club presidency, Feuer continued, "No member of The Temple became a member of the Board unless he approved of him. Nobody became president of the sisterhood or brotherhood unless he thought they were fit for the office and truly represented what he felt [were] the right values."[5]

To administer the religious school was a serious matter at The Temple. A summer school program existed all through Feuer's ministry for those children who had failed the spring final exams. And promotion the next fall depended upon the successful completion of the academic examinations—in the spring or at the end of the summer. One summer, while Silver was in Palestine visiting his parents, Feuer wrote that more than forty students had failed their final exams and that thirty of the forty were enrolled in summer school while the others engaged private tutors.[6]

Silver hired Rabbi David Sherman (1909–) to begin in January 1935 on a temporary basis and Rabbi Melbourne Harris (1903–) as a more permanent assistant and head of the religious school beginning in September 1935. Harris, thirty-two, had directed a religious school in San Francisco (for two years) and then he had served as rabbi in Peoria before coming to Cleveland. Silver's notes on Harris reveal that he was the "ideal junior [?]" that he would "work well with young people," and that he "has presence" and is "good-looking." Silver chose him over several well-qualified and subsequently quite prominent applicants, and the formal relationship endured for nine years, while their friendship continued throughout Silver's lifetime.[7]

During the 1920s The Temple, as so many other Reform and Conservative synagogues, had steadily added cultural, social, and recreational programs to its worship and educational activities. The synagogue-center, first established by Rabbi Mordecai M. Kaplan in New York City in 1916 and brought to fulfillment by Rabbi Israel Levinthal in Brooklyn in the 1920s, was replicated in numerous cities during the 1920s. Some congregations showed movies, housed orchestras, and fielded athletic teams, while others made space available for scout troops, dramatic clubs, and book groups. Some congregations had rabbis directing their social and recreational activities; others had full-time recreational leaders guiding the swimming, basketball, and gymnastics. All these activities shared one thing in common: they brought hundreds of Jews into the facilities.[8]

The Temple not only intended to build a gymnasium in the new edifice (a locker room with showers was installed), but recreational and social programs for various ages filled the congregational calendar in the late 1920s. In 1929, however, Silver and the trustees made a bold decision—to eliminate the social and recreational ("community center") activities of The Temple. The reasons were many.

First, the secular activities appealed largely to neighborhood people—nonmembers of the congregation—and not to Temple members, who increasingly lived further than walking distance from The Temple. Second, Temple members belonged to social and recreational clubs—especially country clubs—of their own, and they found little need for The Temple's facilities. Third and perhaps most important, there was little evidence that dances, plays, basketball, and parties drew young people to worship services. Because the bait of amusement drew few into worship and study, these activities had little relationship to The Temple's purposes. As Silver put it at the seventy-ninth annual congregational meeting that approved the new policy: "Activities of a purely secular and recreational nature aimed at entertaining people . . . contribute little or nothing to spiritual life." Finally, the more affluent members of The Temple stayed away from the secular activities of The Temple because The Temple "no longer represent[ed] homogeneous social groups," that is, wealthy members exclusively, but it "reflect[ed] all the social strata in a community." Because upper-middle-class members in the suburbs did not frequent social and recreational events with lower-middle-class members still in the city, the former found little rationale for continuing the "time, money and energy expended" on the synagogue-center concept. By the end of the year, The Temple minutes note, "the Old Gymnasium had been converted into an Assembly Hall."⁹

During Silver's tenth anniversary his congregation honored him with a trip to Palestine—his first since 1919—to see his parents, and the National Society of Scabbard and Blade, a ROTC honorary society, gave him the dubious distinction of blacklisting him, along with fifty-five other "dangerous un-American personages" who revealed "communistic tendencies." Actually, Silver appeared on numerous blacklists in the late 1920s: one group, the ROTC (whom Silver called "American fascists"), challenged his patriotism because he pleaded for the World Court (1923); another challenged it because he joined the American Civil Liberties Union; and yet another because he corresponded with Scott Nearing, the notorious pacifist and Socialist. One member of the Daughters of the American Revolution—described by Silver as the "ladies auxiliary of American fascists"—wrote that "he should have remained in Lithuania where he was born."

The DAR accused Silver—as well as a number of other prominent but foreign-born Americans—of being agents operating on orders from Moscow, that is, "Red internationalists," and thus urged local chapters to include his name on their list of banned speakers. The lists, usually of potential speakers of prominence, attempted to include those men and women with alleged communist or socialist leanings, as evidenced by membership in the ACLU or pacifist groups. Silver, active in the ACLU throughout the 1920s (he was elected to the National Committee in 1927) and increasingly an opponent of an unnecessarily large peacetime military establishment, was an especially visible target for the somewhat paranoid daughters. [10]

Upon Silver's return from Palestine he not only lectured several times each week in Cleveland and elsewhere on Palestine Jewry but he jumped head first into Cleveland politics. Cleveland was a somewhat atypical city; with an amazingly diversified industrial base and a heavy percentage of immigrants among its million or so inhabitants, it had voted for La Follette for President in 1924 and during the war gave Charles Ruthenberg, an outspoken and jail-worn Communist, an enormous vote for mayor. In 1929 Cleveland scrapped its time-honored and conventional municipal government, adopted a new and advanced charter written by a college professor, and soon afterward installed the first city manager of a truly metropolitan city. Opposing the powerful Cleveland Federation of Labor, Silver defended the city manager (an able administrator and forceful executive "*sans peur et sans reproche,*" he pleaded) and the city-manager system of government against the attacks of those who sought to overturn this progressive governmental reform. Silver's defense of this reform represented the first time since his rabbinate began in Cleveland that he spoke from a political platform, and his vigorous (and successful) defense of the city manager/charter commission plan was front-page headline news in the autumn of 1927. His second appearance on political platforms came the following spring when he again had to defend (successfully) the manager/charter plan against those who wanted to return to the mayoral system with all its (according to Silver) "old rottenness."[11]

The unsuccessful referendum for the abolition of the managerial office in 1927 and 1928 was not the end of the fight. Silver would have to defend the city-manager plan again and again (in 1929, in 1931) against an all-out onslaught (the "3-D" [Davis, Danaceau, Downer] amendment) by various political bosses and their supporters who sought a complete return to the old order. Silver, one of the organizers of the Progressive Government Committee, wrote columns in all three Cleveland newspapers (Democratic, Republican, Scripps-Howard—all three supported the city-manager system), organized a vigorous house-to-house campaign, and helped provide the scant three thousand vote majority (of ninety-seven thousand total votes) in the 1929 referendum.[12]

In the midst of Silver's political activism, the Macmillan Company published his first book, *Messianic Speculation in Israel: From the First Through the Seventeenth Centuries* (1927). It was to be the first in a series of publications stretching over three decades, and the remarks of John Haynes Holmes (1879–1964), clergyman, pacifist, and civil libertarian, were typical of numerous professional colleagues: "How did you do it? . . . I envy you, admire you, acclaim you!" The nucleus of the book consisted of his doctoral thesis at The Hebrew Union College (submitted in 1925), the result of several years of research and critical analysis of medieval Hebrew sources and modern, mostly German, critical scholarship. Silver methodically investigated the theme of the arithmetical calculation of the coming of the Messiah, as this millenarian chronology had occupied numerous distinguished Jewish medievalists, such as Rashi, Nachmanides, and Abarbanel. He wrote from a strong nationalistic (perhaps even Zionist) perspective, with exile from the land, the longing to return to the land, and the relationship between messianic speculation and national redemption central to his analysis. Silver wrote the book exclusively in Cleveland and relied heavily on gracious librarians, especially at the Jewish Theological Seminary and the HUC, continually to send him the abundant sources utilized and documented in the volume.[13]

The book received many favorable reviews. Moses Gaster (1856–1939), chief rabbi of the Sephardic communities of the British Empire, lauded it in England in *The Jewish Guardian*, and similar reviews appeared in American newspapers and magazines. The complex messianic calculations undertaken by Jews century after century enthralled some of the reviewers; Silver's "vast command of sources" and his ability to summariz[e] an enormous literature with great succinctness" impressed others; and his impressive grasp of world history and Christian thought caught the attention of two reviewers. None disagreed with the assessment of an English scholar that "we have before us a scholar and a profound thinker."[14]

One year later in 1928 the Block Publishing Company published Silver's *The Democratic Impulse in Jewish History*, a forty-three-page, ten-thousand-word essay linking the "democratic" thrust in Reform Judaism to earlier developments in the Jewish past from biblical times through the Middle Ages. In part one of the booklet, Silver sails through Jewish history, gathering various manifestations of courage and humanity and fusing them into the "democratic impulse." There is little careful and scholarly investigation; "democracy" is sometimes used to denote a system of government, sometimes to denote the implications of the "mission" theory, and sometimes something else; here at least, eloquence and good historical analysis were not synonymous.

Part two, in contrast, was a significant statement on Reform Judaism and Zionism. Silver vigorously rejected one hundred years of Reform Jewish antinationalism and argues persuasively—at a time when he was almost alone in doing so—that "universalism and nationalism . . . are never antithetical," (p. 43) and hence the basic tenets of Reform demand an embracing of Palestine.

In 1931 his first collection of sermons and essays, *Religion in a Changing World* (New York: Richard R. Smith) became a Religious Book Club of the Month selection for January. His publications served to spread his reputation even further; by the late 1920s Silver was receiving scores of lecture invitations each year from all over the country. Early in February 1929 he finally agreed to a lengthy speaking tour and combined the lectures with the UAHC Biennial Convention in San Francisco. His stops with all expenses paid by the invitees included Houston's Temple Beth Israel, El Paso's Temple Mt. Sinai, Portland's Jewish Union Council and Temple Beth Israel, San Francisco's Temple Emanu-El and Shearith Israel, Los Angeles' Temple Emanu-El, and Omaha's Jewish Community Center. At each stop he delivered a different lecture (all of which he had already presented at The Temple), almost always spoke to enormous crowds, and had the entire trip arranged and promoted (including generous newspaper ads) by the Ellison-White Lecture Bureau of Los Angeles.[15]

Silver's fee arrangement for lectures remained consistent for decades, and he would explain it frequently to those who inquired. He gave his services absolutely free to all charitable organizations in or out of Cleveland, as well as to national movements such as Hillel, United Palestine Appeal, Community Chest, and the Jewish National Fund. In addition, he usually paid his own travel expenses for fundraising keynote addresses. For lectures before clubs, societies, brotherhoods, and similar organizations with regular lecture programs, Silver requested an honorarium.[16]

Silver could certainly use the honorariums, because he made very generous contributions to general and Jewish philanthropy year after year and loaned money to nearly everyone who asked for it. He sent a generous check to his parents in Palestine every month, sent large chunks to cousins and uncles in the east who could not hold jobs or who had invested unwisely, and he sent smaller (but still generous) amounts to needy (and sometimes not so needy) Jews who wrote to him or asked in person. Armond Cohen, a conservative rabbi in Cleveland for half a century, recalled that Silver would "empty his pockets out to any beggar who came to see him," while Joseph S. Shubow, another rabbi, wrote to Israel Goldstein about Silver's "remarkable generosity, especially to students, writers, scholars and homeless." Sometimes he remembered the loans a year or two later—and wrote a letter urging a small repayment—and occasionally he received a check with the reply. But his losses in the late 1920s alone were in the thousands of dollars.[17]

It seems fair to note that Virginia and Abba were not without the means to donate generously and loan money freely. In addition to Abba's handsome salary (his 1932–33 salary of $16,200 was four times greater than that of Rabbi Feuer) and frequent lecture honorariums, Virginia had received a generous dowry from her parents. These funds permitted the Silvers to invest considerable sums in the stock market throughout the late 1920s. In 1928 Virginia sold one hundred shares of General Motors for $12,524 and six weeks later bought $14,000 in municipal bonds. In late 1928 the Silvers bought $4,242 of Atlantic Refining, $5,359 of General Motors, and $1,352 of Simmons; in early 1929 $2,100 of U.S. Electric Light and Power; in the summer of that same year $12,230 of Richman Brothers; and on 4 November 1929, the eve of the crash, one hundred shares of Sears Roebuck for $20,395. All of these purchases came in the wake of the rental of an elegant home late in 1927 on Lake Shore Blvd., in fashionable and expensive Bratenahl on the edge of Lake Erie. Interestingly, it was the home of the late Rabbi Moses Gries and was owned by his son Robert of The May Co.[18]

Silver not only gave generously but he also solicited vigorously for a variety of causes. He wrote numerous personal letters trying to raise money for Talmud Torahs and Hebrew high schools, including for his hometown of Neustadt-Schirwindt; he continually tried to interest his congregants in the Cleveland High School and Institute (Talmud Torah); and he even wrote ten to fifteen personal letters to affluent congregants when needy yeshivot in Brooklyn and New York City approached him. In 1929 he wrote twenty letters to friends in an attempt to raise five hundred dollars for a Herzl Memorial Issue of the *New Palestine,* and shortly thereafter he told a rabbinic colleague in New York that "I have been in twelve money raising enterprises within the last nine months and I have exhausted myself and I am afraid, my community."[19]

In addition to generous philanthropic gifts and vigorous fundraising, Silver gave his time and passion to two causes of enormous importance to him. His strong interest in the impact of industrialization on American society began in the 1920s, and throughout the decade he spoke frequently and worked energetically for unemployment insurance. Ohio was one of the earliest states to have unemployment insurance legislation proposed in the legislature (1916) and was one of two states to seriously consider such legislation throughout the 1920s. His sermon of 25 March 1928, "Our National Debt to the Unemployed," summed up years of thinking and urged that "above all, a law should be passed establishing compulsory unemployment insurance for all working men." His sermon of 2 March 1930, "The Working Man," described unemployment as the most serious single problem in the United States; and following a campus lecture, Silver pleaded for unemployment insurance in an interview that same year with Clarence Barbour, president of Brown University.[20]

By late 1930 Silver headed the Cleveland Committee for Unemployment Insurance, personally opening (21 October) and vigorously publicizing the Ohio campaign for passage of an unemployment insurance law. No state in the entire country had unemployment insurance, but the Cleveland committee had readied a bill (the "Ohio Plan") and would submit it to both houses of the Ohio General Assembly in January 1931 as the [Senator James A.] Reynolds (D-Cleveland) and [Representative Horace] Kiefer (R-Springfield) bill. The genesis of the "Ohio Plan" was a small meeting called by members of the Consumer's League of Ohio on 17

April 1928 and addressed by Silver; subsequently, his "personal intervention" brought some small liberal manufacturers to meetings of supporters of unemployment insurance. Senate Bill No. 25/ House Bill No. 71, or the "Ohio Plan," was written by three or four people, over several months, in Silver's study at The Temple. At the joint hearing of the Senate Labor and House Insurance Committees on the evening of 17 February 1931, "benches around the edges of the Senate chamber were filled" (three hundred spectators attended) as Silver made an "eloquent impassioned plea for the proposed measure." The combined lobbying of the Ohio Farm Bureau, the Ohio Chamber of Commerce, the Ohio Manufacturers' Association, and other industrial associations led the Senate Labor Committee to postpone indefinitely action on the bill; Silver responded with a blistering open letter to the four Senators who had voted for postponement.[21]

That same year President Herbert Hoover appointed Silver to a national advisory committee on unemployment relief, and in March Governor George White named Silver and ten other Ohioans (most of whom favored unemployment insurance) to a commission to study unemployment insurance proposals and report to the governor by the end of 1932 so that a proposal could be readied, if necessary, for the 1933 General Assembly. The Ohio Council of Retail Merchants immediately denounced the commission, calling its members "unimpressive theorists" who have advocated "scattered-brained public policies and legislative panaceas."[22]

The commission met and deliberated during 1932 and eventually it released a four-hundred-page report strongly advocating unemployment insurance. Silver became convinced that unemployment insurance was so critical an issue that it required federal involvement and that state action would likely follow quite easily. In a sermon on 3 April, "Why Cleveland Is Not Taking Care of Its Own," Silver argued forcefully and comprehensively for federal job insurance. New York Senator Robert Wagner, of course, had been advocating this for a decade or more, but even as late as 1934 the

Wagner-Lewis Federal Unemployment Insurance Bill died in committee, despite Silver's "electrifying testimony" in Washington. While Silver's appeals had no discernible effect on Congress immediately, he did distribute the sermon together with a personal letter to the Ohio delegation. Not that he had much confidence in either political party. We noticed in chapter 2 his interest in and support for alternative political configurations in the 1920s; on the eve of the 1932 election he denounced both the Democrats and Republicans and argued, in his lecture "A Rabbi Reviews Politics," that only the Socialists addressed the critical economic issues of the day.[23]

Silver's speeches and writing did call forth a strong reaction from one member of the governor's commission, James F. Lincoln, the vice-president, who strongly opposed unemployment insurance and strongly disliked Jews, whom he (correctly) accused of spearheading the welfare state that had brought an end to the covered-wagon "individualism" whose passing he lamented. Unemployment insurance, Lincoln argued, was the

> most menacing and revolutionary piece of legislation ever proposed in the history of Ohio [and] a threat to Christian charity, family love, neighborly kindliness and human brotherhood.

Not only was his opposition to any unemployment insurance plan a patriotic and moral crusade, Lincoln (correctly but inappropriately) identified the Ohio Plan with the three Jewish commission members. He continually noted their birth in "Old Russia," used I. M. Rubinow's full name (Isaac Max, the commission member with the expertise in statistics), spoke of the communist origins of the Ohio Plan, and used every opportunity to launch ad hominem attacks:

> Is it reasonable to suppose that men cradled in Old Russia can have absorbed our American traditions and ideals sufficiently to make them trustworthy guides for the descendants of the men and women who

61

came over the mountains in covered wagons in social and political problems of major importance and revolutionary character?[24]

When the governor's commission reported that it strongly favored an unemployment insurance bill shaped to a great extent by Silver, Lincoln told seven hundred members of the Associated Industries of Cleveland that Silver was unqualified to write such a bill because he was "Russian-born," had no understanding of the "American spirit of initiative, individual responsibility and self-reliance," and hence could not "be trusted with the handling of the major social and political problems of this country." Despite this attack, the commission's proposal was introduced as the Ohio Plan in the state legislature (1933) and after fierce lobbying by its proponents and opponents, it passed the House (eighty to forty-five) but was again tabled in the Senate (eighteen to ten). Nevertheless, it was frequently cited by Sen. Wagner and other proponents of federal unemployment insurance. The plan, which provided for combined employee and employer contributions and state administration, also became a widely accepted national model for the state unemployment insurance bills introduced more and more frequently in 1934–35 and the following years, and it was jointly reintroduced in both chambers of the Ohio legislature in 1935. The momentum of the Social Security Act (signed into law in August 1935), the threat that states without laws would receive no rebate from the 5 percent tax to be levied in all states, and the vigorous lobbying of the ocui all helped the Boyd Bill pass the House again in 1936. Tough opposition remained in the Senate, but the realization that if no bill passed by the end of 1936 Ohio would lose millions of dollars in rebates finally pushed the Senate—in a special holiday session—to pass a bill quickly. When it was signed into law on 17 December, the Cleveland *Plain Dealer* spoke of Silver as the "father of the unemployment insurance movement in Ohio."[25]

While Silver's deep concern for the unemployed revolved largely around Ohio, his vigorous participation in the boycott-of-German-goods movement took him into the national arena. As a result of the sabbatical his congregation gave him after fifteen years of service, Silver was present in Germany when the Nazis took power following the 5 March 1933 elections. He immediately began to write a series of editorials in various newspapers urging American Jews to protest the treatment of German Jews. As early as the spring of 1933 he suggested that the only hope for German Jewry lay in emigration to Palestine. Late in the spring, in an interview in the Philadephia *Inquirer,* for the first time he urged a boycott of German goods and became an active member of Samuel Untermyer's American League for the Defense of Jewish Rights, when in 1933 it began to spearhead the boycott movement. He traveled far and wide to join or be the keynote speaker at rallies to denounce Hitler and to urge intensification of the boycott of German materials, goods, and products; he actively recruited Jews and non-Jews for the national Non-Sectarian Anti-Nazi League to Champion Human Rights (when Untermyer resigned in 1938, Silver became the president), an organization created by the American League for the Defense of Jewish Rights; he convinced governors, mayors, labor leaders, and other prominent persons to join him on the rally platform; and he wrote editorials, columns, and letters to numerous newspapers demanding that readers refuse to purchase German goods. [26]

In chapter 2 we discussed Silver's commitment to Zionism and how he immersed himself in Zionist activities in the midst of a busy rabbinate. While this zeal did not take the form of a national office, it did mean feverish activity within Cleveland and numerous trips to lecture on behalf of Palestinian causes. This pattern, to a large extent, continued throughout the late 1920s and 1930s, but in addition Silver was drawn—or steadily entered—more and more into the orbit of national politics.

In Cleveland itself he remained unusually active. In 1925 Silver organized a dedication of the newly established Hebrew University of Jerusalem, and six thousand celebrants packed the gymnasium at Western Reserve University. In 1927 he established at The Temple an *Avukah* chapter of college students interested in Zionism and launched its monthly programs by verbally dueling with a Zionist debate team from England. In 1930 Silver organized an anti-British rally at the Jewish Center to protest England's stopping immigration to Palestine and, according to a reporter in attendance, "moved the great crowd [twenty-five hundred] to tears."[27]

In that same year Silver helped organize a mass protest rally through downtown Cleveland against British policy in Palestine. Sometime in the late 1920s he convinced The Temple's Women's Association [TWA] to give an annual scholarship to the Hebrew University; by 1931, during the TWA's thirty-fifth anniversary celebration, the scholarship (in honor of Abba Hillel Silver) amount reached five hundred dollars and the first recipient, Gedaliah Allon, an honors student in the Hebrew University's first graduating class, later distinguished himself as a historian of Judaism in the early Christian centuries. Within The Temple, long a bastion of classical Reform Judaism, which generally deemphasized "peoplehood," especially the use of Hebrew language, Silver had step by step introduced the study of Hebrew into the religious school curriculum. No later than 1927–28 and probably several years earlier, every student in the school was required to learn Hebrew, while a midweek afternoon program enrolled a modest number of more advanced students.[28]

One temple member wrote Rabbi Silver a letter in which he discussed the impact of the Hebrew program on his son during 1934–35.

> My son, Herbert, a fifth grade pupil at The Temple, has shown a keen interest in his study of Hebrew—so much so that he has been advanced in his class, takes special Hebrew on Thursdays, and has had private instruction by his teacher at home. He has also in recent months expressed a deep interest in and regard for any news relating to Palestine. As a matter of fact, he has exacted a hopeful promise from me to send him to Palestine for a visit as a Confirmation gift.[29]

Not all the congregants, however, were delighted with the Hebrew program; scattered letters in Silver's files attest to the fear some held that studying Hebrew was only the first foot in the door that would then open to a full-blown Orthodoxy. One member scored Silver in 1928 for teaching Hebrew in the religious school and thus taking time from "religion." Such thinking characterized those for whom Reform Judaism was a creed or faith—and only a faith—and who viewed studying Hebrew as they would wearing phylacteries, wrapping oneself in a *tallis*, or observing *kashrut* laws. Reform Judaism was a creed of belief, they argued, and the language of this denomination must be English.[30]

All Zionist activists, of course, supported the study of Hebrew, and few cities boasted more committed Zionists than did Cleveland. Cleveland Zionists throughout the 1920s and early 1930s formed one of the most active chapters of the Zionist Organization of America [ZOA]. Silver certainly did not dominate the Cleveland Zionist District [CZD]; in fact, in 1933 and again in 1934 he declined invitations to serve on the executive committee and told the ZOA president that "I cannot be forced or inveigled into working with them." The specific leaders Silver detested were A[braham]. H[yman]. Friedland (1892–1939) and Ezra Shapiro (1903–1977). He once called them "miserable leaders" and "the Talmud Torah Zionist clique," and he "resolved to keep away rather than to engage in unpleasant controversy."[31]

While the precise reason(s) for Silver's refusal remain vague, by early 1935 a fierce battle of words and actions had split the Cleveland Zionists apart. Silver discussed these tensions in an interview with a Cleveland *Plain Dealer* reporter during January of 1935; he called the CZD a "Zionist racket" and its leaders "cheap racketeers" who were "out to get [me]." The issues involved seem rather petty, notwithstanding the passage of half-a-century. An example: it is certain that the author, translator, and literary critic, Maurice Samuel, when addressing the Noon Forum of the City Club in Cleveland, denigrated Silver in response to Silver's plea, when Samuel had been a ZOA employee, to reduce the mounting deficit of the ZOA by reducing the number of employees! Silver felt confident that certain leaders of the CZD had urged Samuel to attack him and publicly vowed revenge. They, however, moved more quickly than he did.[32]

Another issue that caused tension was a series of editorials Silver published in the *Jewish Daily Bulletin* in 1934. A. H. Friedland, director of the Cleveland Bureau of Jewish Education, took these editorials as an attack on the Hebrew schools and sent strong letters of denunciation to the heads of bureaus of Jewish education all over the country. Yet another brouhaha developed over a cultural event ("Romance of a People") that Friedland and Shapiro promoted and Silver refused to support because he claimed all the money would go to the production and none to the cause of Zionism.[33]

When the CZD leadership learned that the ZOA had invited Silver to deliver the keynote address to the National Conference for Palestine in Washington, all the officers signed a letter to the ZOA president stating that "Silver's public appearance at the Conference . . . would completely demoralize Zionist life and leadership in Cleveland," for his views are "an insult to Zionist ethics." Morris Rothenberg, the ZOA president, communicated the complaints to Silver; Silver wrote angrily to Rothenberg, and after suggesting that "you and the ZOA keep out of it," noted that "I go only to such places where people are very eager to have me and as you know they frequently pay very handsomely to have me come." He then announced his decision ("entirely of my own making") not to keynote the conference.[34]

"The fight is on," one columnist, Phineas J. Biron, noted correctly. Quickly Silver responded to the local attack by announcing his resignation from the Cleveland Zionist District and immediately afterward his intention to organize another Zionist society. An overflow crowd of twelve hundred filled The Temple's Mahler Hall on 12 February and approved Cleveland Zionist District No. 2. The speakers produced a litany of grievances against the CZD, highlighted by Silver's impassioned speech reviewing his own grievances and naming the men who tried to "get me." The most prominent opponents were A. H. Friedland and Ezra Z. Shapiro. Friedland, a fine Hebrew poet and a boyhood friend of Abba's whom Silver brought to Cleveland to head the Bureau of Jewish Education and subsequently became president of both the CZD and the Ohio Zionist Region, grew to dislike Silver intensely. Stories abound in Cleveland about his jealousy of and antipathy for Silver, and one participant in the skirmishes of the 1930s relates that Friedland, even when racked with cancer, became obsessed with the need to find fault with Silver.[35]

Cleveland Zionist District No. 2 became the Cleveland Zionist Society with Abba Hillel Silver as president at its formal inauguration meeting late in February. The CZD immediately sought to use the ZOA to fight the CZS; one of the district's officers traveled to the Hotel Astor in New York City to speak at the administration committee of the ZOA on 3 March 1935. He denounced Silver's "free-lance" attitude, that is, his indifference to the CZD (he called it "boycott" and "sabotage"); praised the ZOA for convincing Silver, "who had done nothing [!] to promote Zionist activities in Cleveland for many years," to withdraw as the conference speaker; told the ZOA leaders that Silver had called the CZD a "racket" in the presence of newspaper reporters; and at the organizing meeting of the CZS had called one of the CZD leaders (Isaac Carmel) a "venomous rattlesnake," another (Aaron Garber) "a broken-down real estate man," and yet another (Ezra Shapiro) "a cog in the wheel of a political machine"; and, finally, that in announcing CZS in the *Jewish Daily Bulletin,* Silver had claimed that the new organization would bring "honest Zionism" to Cleveland.[36]

Even more fascinating was the ZOA leadership's discussion following the complaint. Apparently, some of the ZOA leaders resented Silver's "free-lance" position and his refusal to cooperate with the CZD. One man blamed him for "the downfall of Zionism in Cleveland," saying that "he refuses to submit to discipline," and also noted something that several of Silver's friends and associates have stated in various ways—"if he is not in control of something he is opposed to it." Louis Lipsky, who strongly disliked Silver, castigated him more vigorously than any other leader; he moved to send a resolution to the CZD praising their "integrity, loyalty and devotion" and condemning Silver for his "wanton attack upon the reputations of the Cleveland Zionists." Lipsky resisted the argument of Rabbi Louis I. Newman to conduct an inquiry first and then, if necessary, condemn, and his resolution carried. Only Newman, together with Silver's boyhood friend Sol Cohen, voted against the resolution.[37]

The ZOA not only condemned Silver but subsequently denounced the formation of the CZS and then rejected its application for admission. Several Zionist publications and individual leaders pleaded for an end to the name-calling and abuse, and it did end rather quickly. The momentum of the new society could not be slowed and it signed up scores of new members during March and April. The ZOA quickly understood the implications of additional Zionist members for its treasury, and agreed late in March to recognize the new Cleveland Zionist Society.[38]

The original CZD was quickly dwarfed by the membership, programs, and vitality of the CZS, and Friedland and Shapiro initiated a series of three reconciliation meetings. A "Memorandum of Peace" emerged, highlighted by Friedland and Shapiro apologizing for their letter to keep Silver off the program, Silver apologizing for his criticisms of Friedland and Shapiro, and the ZOA embracing both groups. By early 1936 the CZS was nearly five hundred strong, and Howard Kohrman, the son of the CZD's president, could dare to enter the society's oratorical contest with his father's permission if not his blessing, though competition between the two groups and even obstruction and subterfuge continued for some time. CZD leaders even attacked Silver (who was in Europe at the time) at the ZOA's 1936 convention upon his election as vice-president of the national organization; they waited, however, for the ten minutes of applause to subside.[39]

In addition to organizing the new society, Silver continued to devote considerable time and effort to Zionist affairs in Cleveland. He lectured frequently at The Temple on Palestine and Zionism, introduced Hebrew study into every grade of the religious school, presented visiting speakers from Palestine and Europe (Nahum Sokolow, president of the World Zionist Organization in 1932), brought films from Palestine—including the first all-talking film (in Yiddish) produced there—and especially he devoted himself to the Hebrew University. He established, in addition to a scholarship, the Cleveland Committee for the Hebrew University, honored the rector and other Hebrew University officials at banquets and dinners, and ceaselessly *"schnorred"* for the academy.[40]

While the drive for a Jewish state in Palestine would become the overwhelming focus of Silver's rabbinate during the 1940s, together with numerous other Zionist activities it certainly occupied a large part of his rabbinate in the 1920s and 1930s as well. Many of his congregants may have been uncomfortable with the suggestion that The Temple was a "Zionist congregation," but Silver did not seem to have been deterred in the least by the probable non-Zionist attitude of most of the members. He could not, obviously, impose his views on his congregants, but he made sure The Temple sanctuary, meeting rooms, and classrooms buzzed with programs, speakers, appeals, and his lectures on Zion and Zionism. Large numbers of Reform rabbis of these two decades not only served non-Zionist congregations but were themselves non-Zionists, so Silver might properly be seen as a kind of "renegade" Reformer. His congregants ignored such "aberrant" behavior for at least three decades, though on the eve of Jewish statehood a small number of anti-Zionists would announce their resignation from the congregation and form a new synagogue (see chapter 8).

Turning from Zionism to higher education, a university close to home also captured some of Silver's attention during the 1920s. Nationally prominent Western Reserve University stood a short walk from The Temple, and Silver lectured on the campus on several occasions during the decade. On at least one occasion, he helped President Vinson and Dean Cutter secure critical funds for the School of Applied Social Sciences from Cleveland's Richman brothers. By 1928 Silver's reputation and support had earned him an honorary Doctor of Letters degree—the first Jew, President Vinson informed him, to be so honored by the university. His initial contact with the university's administration, however, was potentially combative; he wrote the university president in 1918 about rumors of anti-Semitism in the Dental School. Seemingly unaware of the manifest contradiction between nondiscrimination and a *numerus clausus*, the school's superintendent assured Silver that not only did the admission committee fill its entire "quota" of "Jewish boys" (noting that fourteen of fifty-six freshmen, thirteen of thirty-eight sophomores, and twenty-five of seventy-four seniors were Jews), but that reports of discrimination against Jewish students in patient assignments were unfounded. In October 1918, for example, the superintendent noted that twenty-five Jewish seniors had sixty-five patients (2.6 each) while the forty-six "Gentile" seniors saw only 101 patients (2.01 each). Silver, not about to challenge the entire notion of Jewish quotas in higher education (perhaps because the quota was so generous!), was satisfied with the response.[41]

Robert E. Vinson, who took over as Western Reserve's president in 1924, not only presented Silver with the honorary degree, he preached one Sunday morning at The Temple and he invited Silver to join him from time to time at dinners honoring university guests. But Vinson was the focal point of a controversy that, more than half-a-century later, still excites passions in Cleveland but whose details remain unclear. The central actors in the drama were Silver and Solomon Goldman (1893–1953), the rabbi of Cleveland's B'nai Jeshurun (1918–1922) and then Anshe Emeth (later the Jewish

Center and then the Park Synagogue) from 1922 until he left Cleveland quite suddenly in 1929. Goldman, himself a gifted orator who would draw enormous crowds to the cavernous Anshe Emeth auditorium for his Sunday morning lectures at the end of the 1920s, had a long and, according to his widow Alice, a warm relationship with Silver. Exactly the same age, they had attended the same yeshiva (Yitzhak Elchanan) on New York's Lower East Side, shared *latkes* (potato pancakes—arguably Silver's single favorite food) with their wives at Goldman's Cleveland home throughout the 1920s, and the two couples dined together at Silver's home as well. But by 1927 their relationship had soured, at least privately; Goldman inexplicably lost his fondness for Silver, whom he called a "prima donna," and Silver reacted negatively to the mention of Goldman's name for years to come.[42]

Nevertheless, he and Silver coexisted in prominent congregations on the same street until their break in 1929. According to the most common version of the story, a group of Cleveland Jews (M. Berick, M. Guren, R. Herz, and L. Levi) busied themselves raising money for a Jewish Studies chair at Western Reserve University, with Goldman as the intended occupant; when Silver, envious and hurt, got wind of the effort he demanded that the Board of Trustees and the university president, in return for his support of their institution, scuttle the campaign. Goldman's biographer, Jacob Weinstein, supports this account of events, though without giving any evidence, when he notes "the strange hostility shown by Rabbi Abbba Hillel Silver when Goldman was being considered for a lectureship at Western Reserve University." And Alice Goldman recalls that it was during Pesach 1929, when they traveled to Palestine on the U.S.S. Providence (and even visited Abba's parents!), that a cable arrived informing her husband that Silver had aborted the so-called "Goldman Chair."[43]

No written sources exist in the Goldman or Silver Papers to confirm this scenario and the only extant document on the matter categorically denies Silver's role. Vinson, in a letter to Silver after a phone call from the latter, noted that he didn't know "when I have been more surprised than at the story that you have communicated to me this morning of the rumors" about the Goldman-Silver affair. He confirmed in letters to both Silver and Goldman that Silver had never met with the Board of Trustees, that the Board of Trustees had never had the slightest discussion of any individual occupying the hypothetical chair, and that they had never considered offering such a chair to anyone. Armond Cohen, a native Clevelander and friend of both Silver and Goldman during his long rabbinate (over half a century) at Park Synagogue, confirms the truth of Vinson's claim that Silver did not involve himself either in the chair or its potential occupant. He explains that the fundraisers simply never succeeded in their goal of raising enough money to fund a Jewish Studies chair. Nevertheless, otherwise objective Clevelanders take Goldman's side and insist that Silver, or at least leaders from The Temple, aborted the chair and did so only because Goldman might be its occupant. While the details of the matter will remain shrouded in mystery, Silver did write a friend in Chicago about "a great deal of talk" concerning a "Department of Semitic Languages and Literature at Western Reserve, largely due to a certain am- bitious Rabbi who thought that he would fit into the picture if such a department could be created," and Goldman did leave Cleveland for Chicago immediately after the correspondence from Vinson. He and Silver, as nationally prominent Zionist leaders in the 1930s and 1940s, crossed paths and podiums frequently. There is no evidence of the slightest amicability in their subsequent correspondence or in reports from those who worked with both of them, but whether Silver squashed Goldman's hopes we cannot know. Their antipathy was surely a loss for the fragile American Jewish community, which was so dependent on internal strength as it battled on behalf of European brethren threatened by hostile forces.[44]

Silver traveled outside of Cleveland more and more frequently through the late 1920s and 1930s on behalf of Zionism and Pal- estine. He keynoted dozens of fundraising dinners, banquets, and meetings on behalf of Palestine Jewry; and he participated actively in ZOA national conventions—often as a mediator or healer of factional disputes. At the 1926 convention in Buffalo he mediated between Jabotinsky Revisionists and their attackers, while at the 1928 convention in Pittsburgh he "was hailed as the man who could end the bitter factional fighting that marked the early sessions of the organization." This was no exaggeration; several leaders described him as the "power-broker" in the conflict between the Louis Lipsky and the Stephen S. Wise factions of American Zionism.[45]

In 1929 Silver went to Zurich for the sixteenth Zionist Congress as an American delegate and was chosen a vice-president of the WZO. His reactions to the congress, when interviewed upon his return and as he expressed it in lectures, were rather negative. He found "too many leaders" to be "brilliant people who all wished to be spokesmen," who were "argumentative in the extreme," and "amazingly longwinded." Nevertheless, he took to the stump vigorously in the wake of the congress and the expansion of the Jewish Agency to include non-Zionists, addressing thousands of listeners at regional and national meetings, fundraisers, and banquets on behalf of Zionist organizations. By the 1930s, Silver's reactions to agenda items at World Zionist Congresses dominated the American Jewish and non-Jewish reporting of the meetings.[46]

Silver was no mechanical spokesman for official Zionist policies, and he frequently agitated national leaders with his free-wheeling criticisms. I "wish to be a free-lance in the movement," he once told the ZOA president, "tied to no ZOA organization and holding no office." He championed political Zionism, a Jewish State, as early as the 1920s (we have seen that he felt comfortable with the idea of a Jewish state much earlier), against the advice of the establishment leaders who urged him to mute this controversial theme and speak about humanitarian topics. He supported Jabotinsky militantism when it was unpopular with Zionist leaders; and he frequently displeased ZOA officials by blasting the behavior of Palestine Jews in such areas as land speculation, labor exploitation, and unjust economic practices. He called these censures "criticisms of love" (a Talmudic phrase), and they certainly did not mitigate his ability to transform even a non-Zionist crowd into passionate supporters of the Land of Israel and Palestinian Jewish causes.[47]

By July 1937, on the eve of Silver's modest move into the national arena, he dominated the fortieth ZOA convention in New York. According to one observer, he delivered an "impassioned speech against partition," which was the "oratorical highlight of the convention." The partition plan that he attacked belonged to Chaim Weizmann, the president of the WZO, and early reports had predicted easy passage for the plan at the twentieth World Zionist Congress in August. Even the large majority of the American delegation, despite Silver's oratory, favored the plan. Silver's reasoned appeal to the congress delegates not only urged defeat of the partition plan but also opposition to any dialogue with the British about partition. He and Stephen S. Wise, who spoke in an equally impassioned manner against partition, helped carry the congress and it failed to support the partition plan. According to a reporter, "Silver of Cleveland made the most effective argument against partition, ably marshalling his points; yet the silver-tongued Silver made no attempt to stampede the Congress with his unusual oratorical talents."[48]

Although The Temple, social justice, and Zionism encompassed most of Silver's hours during this second decade of his rabbinate in Cleveland, he did manage to find a little time for leisure. He rented a summer home in Chocorua, New Hampshire, for a period of years and enjoyed summers of hiking, fishing, and what he called "who-done-it" stories there. A few years later the Silvers switched their New England summers to Mooselookmeguntick Lake, Haines Landing, Maine, where Abba, by now an avid fisherman, frequently was photographed with large salmon that he had hooked (usually, his son Daniel insists, hooked while "dad was sleeping"). Even more, Silver enjoyed eating and joking—especially at

Cleveland and New York delicatessens with Yiddish-speaking Jews. People vividly recall him at Siegelstein's, down the street from The Temple; with his silken black pompadour thrown back in a mood of hilarity and his sonorous voice cascading over the rumble of the voices and the clatter of the dishes, he could easily stand out. His witticisms in Yiddish were equal to the most respected *bon mots* of his time, and he took a back seat to nobody, contemporaries insist, in his keen interest in the trivia and gossip of the day.[49]

Silver might have found companionship within the profession that so much admired him, but he had little interest in rabbinical camaraderie despite the scores of colleagues with whom he (quite formally) corresponded. He especially received abundant letters from rabbinical colleagues seeking his help in obtaining pulpits. In the years before the Reform movement created a centralized placement system, a phone call or a letter from a distinguished rabbi to a congregational search committee made an enormous impact. While Silver regularly told men whom he would not recommend that "I have made it a rule not to recommend men for any rabbinic posts," he consistently lobbied congregations on behalf of friends or colleagues whom he felt particularly qualified for a position and occasionally urged a congregation not to consider a particular candidate. To Chicago's South Side Hebrew Congregation in 1930 he wrote that "Rabbi B. is not the sort of man that I would recommend to any congregation," while he sent Springfield, Illinois's B'rith Sholom two letters in 1928 urging them to interview (and then to hire) a colleague. Every year he intervened on behalf of someone, although he rejected ten pleas for help for every one he agreed to support. More than anything else, Silver's letters suggest, his low opinion of the Reform rabbinate deterred him from rendering more vigorous support.

"By and large," he wrote a friend in 1943, "our Rabbinate is less informed than the average Jewish layman. Some of them simply do not know what is going on in the world about them. They do not study. They do not read. They are just pompous loud speakers for stale platitudes."

Of course, such a generalization does an injustice to numerous men in the rabbinate while at the same time it does accurately describe some of his colleagues. Silver had almost no desire for intimacy with his rabbinical colleagues (or with anyone else that he knew outside his family, for that matter), and though his prestige and prominence would elevate him to the presidency of the Reform rabbinical association (from 1945 to 1947), he remained aloof from his colleagues, most of whom he (rightly) considered his intellectual inferiors.[50]

Chapter
Four

Dr. Silver has every qualification to take him far in politics. He probably would have gone places too had he chosen politics instead of the pulpit.

—Leo Sack, February 1944

Silver was more thorough, more analytical, more thought provoking [than Stephen S. Wise]; he was very cold-blooded—warm and hot as he could be on the platform he was very cool in his own retreats, in his own study, in his own counsel, cool, calculating, ruthless, in arriving at conclusions and also in dealing with his opponents.

—Israel Goldstein, 12 September 1973

I have never sought any office in my life.

—Abba Hillel Silver, Tel Aviv, 25 April 1951

Silver's rise to the heights of American Zionist political leadership during the critical years immediately preceding the birth of the State of Israel has its genesis in the twenty-first World Zionist Congress. Although they met in Geneva's splendid Opera House, the mood in mid-August of 1939 was anything but festive. The British Parliament had approved Secretary for Colonial Affairs Malcolm Macdonald's White Paper but three months earlier—a document that limited Jewish immigration to Palestine to seventy-five thousand over the next five years, announced an end to Jewish immigration after 1 March 1944, and greatly restricted the purchase of land by Jews in mandatory Palestine. Further, the several hundred delegates at the congress knew that war was imminent, that Jewish life in Europe was in serious jeopardy, and even that passage home to their respective countries might be seriously threatened.[1]

Silver himself, according to Emanuel Neumann, already had a sense not only of the impending war but of the resulting shift in Jewish political decision making from the European centers to the United States. When Neumann, in a conversation in Geneva both he and Silver independently recalled, urged Silver to aspire to national leadership in Zionist affairs, Silver responded that a war would surely break out, that America would become the center of gravity in world affairs, and that he, Silver, would aspire to leadership. Neumann took this quite seriously and, delighted with the prospect of Silver's active involvement in national affairs, began to lay the groundwork for such aspirations to be realized.[2]

Nevertheless, Silver's outspoken defense of a moderate response to the British did little to increase his popularity at Geneva. Whereas most delegates urged resistance to Britain—active terrorist actions or passive, Gandhi-like, noncooperation—Silver in a late-night speech on Saturday 20 August pleaded for cooperation. His theme did not come as a complete surprise, for he had articulated it clearly to the press on the eve of the conference. His argument was simple: the British government could not long withstand public pressure to alter the White Paper, and hence it was only a "temporary document." In the meantime, he proposed to the delegates (in an "impassioned" speech, according to a *New York Times* correspondent, and interrupted frequently by hecklers) that "we must continue our cooperation with the mandatory government so as to avert chaos in Palestine." He urged the delegates to "do nothing which might bring the Jewish people into conflict" with Britain, for they would need every possible ally in the battle against Nazism.[3]

This moderate approach, though in sympathy with Chaim Weizmann's own position, was a minority position at the conference and it was highly unpopular. One delegate, Berl Katznelson, called

Silver's speech "a stone thrown at the refugees wandering on the seas, a stab in the back." A cynical reporter for a Yiddish newspaper thought that Silver, ever the fundraiser, knew that affluent American Jews would not contribute to a program that defied law and order; hence the method in his madness. Whatever the response to the content of his speech, Silver's oratory did not go unnoticed. The *New York Times* correspondent noted that Silver "has a broad-shouldered build like Paul Muni; he uses his hands like Stokowski; and the rounded phrases of his baritone-voiced oratory would do credit to a Shakespearean actor." Years later, reflecting back on that speech, Silver admitted that "to this day I wonder whether I was wrong then." Despite his ambivalence, the congress ultimately rejected demands for resistance or noncooperation with the British and, while vigorously rejecting the White Paper, it agreed to follow David Ben-Gurion's (later) succinct formulation: "We shall fight the War as if there were no White Paper, and the White Paper as if there were no War."[4]

An equally momentous decision of the Twenty-First Congress, at least in its long-term importance, was the decision to lessen the impact of imminent European chaos by strengthening American Zionism with the creation of the Emergency Committee for Zionist Affairs. A twenty-four member executive, representing the four leading Zionist organizations in America (the Zionist Organization of America, Hadassah, Poale Zion, Mizrachi), elected Rabbi Stephen S. Wise chairman, but as late as the summer of 1940 the emergency committee still did not even have a full-time secretary and it offered little coordination to its constituents. The committee's Department of Public Relations and Political Action did, however, sponsor the effective formation of an American (read Christian) Palestine Committee and a Christian (read clergy) Council on Palestine in 1941, and in 1942 it coordinated several responses to the 1939 White Paper and the *Sturma* (a refugee ship) tragedy. Emanuel Neumann and a brilliant assistant, David Petegorsky, headed the public relations department, yet in spite of their vigorous efforts as late as 1943 "the Emergency Committee for Zionist Affairs had no Washington Bureau, nor could it boast of a single resident representative there."[5]

Petegorsky quit early in 1942, having summed up everything that was wrong with the committee in a lengthy memorandum. It began by describing the emergency committee as a "defective organization and administration which makes effective and intelligent action virtually impossible" and concluded by charging that the group "failed to present a substantial and constructive program [or] to give Jewry inspiring and dynamic leadership." Neumann's resignation followed shortly, "in angry protest against its inadequacies and what seemed to me its unforgivable inactivity." Chaim Weizmann, attending an executive meeting on the eve of Silver's ascension to control of the organization, publicly expressed his disappointment at how little the emergency committee had accomplished.[6]

It was Chaim Weizmann (1874–1952), rather ironically, who came to America in 1942 with the suggestion that Silver head the emergency committee and who pursued this idea with Silver and other Zionist leaders, including Stephen S. Wise, Nahum Goldmann, Emanuel Neumann, Meyer Weisgal, Henry Montor, Irving Miller, and Louis Lipsky—all of whom either wrote to or directly approached Silver. Whether he was in or out of office, Chaim Weizmann led the Zionist movement from 1917, the year of the Balfour Declaration, until just after World War II, when Ben-Gurion would dramatically replace him. Gifted with an uncanny ability to simplify complex problems and to convince his listeners (even if they were skeptical) of the correctness of his solution, he proved irresistible to numerous political leaders, while at the same time he found himself frequently at odds with countless Zionist colleagues. Weizmann dined with Silver in New York, met Silver privately in Chicago, corresponded with him, and made a visit to Cleveland early in 1943. The wzo president wanted to take Silver "out of [his] beautiful Temple, and away from the quiet life [he was] leading in a devoted community, and inject [him] into the maelstrom of American Zionist politics." Weizmann sought to de-termine in his meetings with Silver whether he was seriously com-mitted to intense involvement in worldwide Zionist affairs and willing "to enter a fight if it became necessary." He quickly (and correctly) concluded Silver was fervent and tough, and after his ascension to power he noted the "great gifts of devotion, courage and eloquence" Silver would bring to the position. Later, though, Weizmann would reflect on the "regrettable error" he had made in this choice.

Rabbi Stephen S. Wise told Weizman early in 1943 how glad he would be if Silver "were to take over the too onerous duties of the chairmanship of the Emergency Committee," for he knew "Silver could do the work and do it exceedingly well" because, among other reasons, he was "a younger and stronger man." He concluded his letter to Weizmann enthusiastically: "I would most cordially wel-come him. . . ." But by the summer Wise had a change of mind, and he reluctantly agreed, only under strong pressure from Emanuel Neumann and Israel Goldstein, to share authority. Silver had ex-plicitly warned both Wise and Goldstein that he expected "a con-centration of the political work in my hands," and only then would they "get my wholehearted cooperation," and threats such as this clearly incensed Wise, who had initially hoped that Silver would "inject new life into Zionist work in the U.S."[7]

In August 1943, while vacationing with his family in Maine and only after prolonged negotiations, Silver agreed to co-chair the American Zionist Emergency Council (formerly the Emergency Committee) with Wise. On 9 August in Wise's New York City study Silver signed a formal contractual agreement with Wise—closely inspected by his attorney—which explicitly gave Silver control of the political work of the emergency council (now forty-eight in number) and chairmanship of the executive committee. The agree-ment was formalized on 25 August 1943 with his unanimous elec-tion by the AECZA as its co-chairman and his unanimous election by the executive committee as its chair.[8]

At the executive committee meeting, Silver in an emotional speech expressed his willingness to devote "all the time necessary" to his new tasks. He realized that "many nights [were] to be spent on trains," and he pledged himself "to make sacrifices," expressing his readiness "to move to the East if necessary." He explained to his executive colleagues that "I like to be frank," something none needed to be reminded of, and that "my bark is worse than my bite," something they surely hoped would be true. He promised "to work out some definite lines of cooperation with Dr. Goldmann" and quickly signed a memorandum of agreement with Goldmann defining the roles of the Jewish Agency and the AECZA. Finally, in what must have come as a surprise to the group, he made his first (and we believe only) public announcement "that I and Mrs. Silver hope to settle in Palestine after the war is over"! While Silver would continuously and unambiguously champion American Jewish *aliyah* (immigration) to Palestine and then to Israel, there is no other evidence that the Silvers ever seriously considered making a permanent move to the Jewish national home.[9]

If there were any who didn't know of Silver's years of hard knocks in local Cleveland and Ohio state politics and wondered whether or not the Cleveland rabbi, whose bread-and-butter audience were dignified listeners dressed in their Sunday best, could operate in the bare-knuckled, street-tough politics of American Zionism, his ascension to power dispelled any doubts. He quickly demonstrated, as Nahum Goldmann noted, that he could "arise and fight" with the best. From his vacation retreat in Bald Mountain, Maine, he directed a full-scale battle plan to take control of American Zionism, while at the same time maintaining the appearance of a reluctant candidate, "ready to serve if called upon." "I have never sought any office in the gift of the Zionist movement, nor do I seek any now," he cabled Charles J. Rosenbloom, "but I have never refused to serve the movement in any appropriate capacity, nor would I withhold such service at a time like this."[10]

Rosenbloom of Pittsburgh and Joel Gross of Newark, together

with Emanuel Neumann, a brilliant political tactician, launched a "draft Silver" movement in late July ("Zionist Community for Dr. Abba Hillel Silver as President of the ZOA") aimed at securing for Silver the presidency of the ZOA when it convened in Columbus, Ohio, in September 1943. The sponsoring committee unleashed a barrage of press releases and letters and "vigorously mobilized delegates" during July, and Silver was kept informed several times daily of the attempt to persuade him to "put aside all other Jewish communal obligations in order to accept the leadership of the two movements in America" at a time when American Jewry "faced the greatest crisis in its history." The effect, according to Israel Goldstein, "was electric."[11]

Israel Goldstein, the nearly unanimous choice to win the presidency before Silver's campaign, was, according to Meyer Weisgal, "livid" and "frightened to death." His supporters were certain that at the very least a bitter convention fight would ensue in a contest between Silver and Goldstein. Elihu D. Stone wrote Goldstein that "Silver would be a formidable candidate," and, together with many others, he warned Goldstein to "avoid" a contest with Silver. Goldstein, as well as his primary supporter, Rabbi Stephen Wise, began to make a series of phone calls, and to send telegrams and letters to Maine immediately after the national press releases, trying to discover what type of deal Silver might be willing to conclude. Silver, who had little interest in heading the ZOA, authorized Neumann to conduct all negotiations for him, and by the end of July Goldstein had offered Silver (what he really sought) the chair of the AECZA (Wise would be removed) if he stopped the "draft" movement. Silver agreed to consider it, although he instructed Rosenbloom to "vigorously prosecute the draft movement in the meantime" and told Neumann he wanted "the centralization of political authority in my hands and their whole-hearted cooperation in this arrangement."[12]

By 3 August, as the "draft" movement built up an enormous head of steam and the Goldstein forces became aware of delegations all over the country announcing their support for Silver, Goldstein and Wise offered Silver the chair of the AEZCA Executive Committee and chairmanship of the ZOA Political Committee if he agreed to permit Wise to retain the chairmanship of the AEZCA. Silver told Wise on the phone that he rejected this offer as insufficient, told Goldstein on the phone that "I will accept no less than all three positions," and instructed Rosenbloom to quickly release a statement that he was "entirely [sic] at the disposal of the forthcoming Zionist convention and shall be proud to accept its call for service." Wise, according to Neumann, "stormed against you, charging that you seek to destroy him"; he did write a letter (never mailed to Silver) calling Silver's "*hubris* incredible." At 8:30 P.M. that same night Wise and Goldstein called back and added co-chair of the AEZCA to the previous offer and Silver agreed to order the "draft" movement halted and to endorse Goldstein's candidacy because he, Silver, had won all three of his initial private demands. He agreed that Wise could "issue a statement of unity" if they all "initialed a memo of agreement." The latter was concluded on 9 August in New York and included a list of twenty-four names (Wise, Silver, and Goldstein each submitted eight) to be included in the ZOA executive to be initiated by all three men.[13]

This was not the end of the story, however, as Silver continued to direct a far-flung movement to bring as many pro-Silver delegates as possible to Columbus for the convention so that he could also chair the ZOA Political Committee. Neuman and others warned Silver that Goldstein's followers were "determined to resist to the limit any attempt to implement the third part [Political Committee] of the agreement." Silver's "organizational work proceeded energetically" throughout August; he even took Goldstein to dinner and urged him to welcome more Silverites into ZOA leadership positions and to give him the additional chairmanship. Goldstein claims to have told Silver that he will never have "enough power" and that he, Goldstein, "had done all I could." On the eve of the convention Neumann could inform Silver that "we shall have a powerful block *in force* in Columbus to support the accord and ensure the full implementaton in letter and spirit." He was correct; Silver did in fact have "enough" power; he had it all.[14]

Silver's national appeal had received a tremendous boost with his sensational appearance at the Biltmore Conference of 1942. Not that he was a novice when it came to gaining international recognition (even if that was highly controversial as in 1939) or national leadership. His "passionate eloquence" and "oratorical gem" against the partition of Palestine at the 1937 World Zionist Congress brought "hundreds to their feet"; "though he exceeded his time limit," one observer wrote, "the congress kept on clamoring for him to go on." He was national chairman of the United Palestine Appeal for several terms in the late 1930s and early 1940s (in 1942 he was reelected to his fifth one-year term) and was one of the three founding national chairmen of the United Jewish Appeal in 1939. Nevertheless, it was at the Biltmore Hotel that he electrified the national and even world Zionist leadership (David Ben-Gurion and Chaim Weizmann were present) with his speech on behalf of statehood.[15]

The six hundred or so delegates at the extraordinary Zionist or "Biltmore" Conference of May 1942 at last stated unequivocally and militantly what American Zionists had implied for years—that "Palestine be established as a Jewish Commonwealth." The delegates unanimously adopted this plank as well as the preceding seven points of the Biltmore Declaration and thus firmly committed themselves to a Jewish state. They also reaffirmed Weizmann's leadership of the Zionist movement.[16]

Silver's address to the delegates struck a chord as militant as any of the others the conference heard, and his strident militancy was not out of tune with his fellow Zionists. Not that this was the first time he had proclaimed that nothing short of an independent Jewish state in Palestine would be acceptable to the Jews of America; fifteen months before the Biltmore Conference at a national gathering of the United Palestine Appeal in Washington, D.C.,

Silver told two thousand delegates at the Hotel Willard that the aim of Zionism was a Jewish state; four months prior to the conference he told a national audience on the Columbia Broadcasting System that Zionism demanded a national homeland for the Jewish people in Palestine; and a few days later he repeated essentially the same speech to the national conference of the UPA and called for a Jewish national homeland and a free Jewish nation. Silver's militancy and explicit political Zionism, for some years too strong for American Zionist leaders, now found sympathetic listeners as the challenge of the hour grew clear.[17]

At the Biltmore Silver launched a vigorous attack on all those who opposed political Zionism, arguing that "the ultimate solution of the Jewish problem must finally be sounded, and the ultimate solution is the establishment of a Jewish Nation in Palestine." He demanded a massive effort to achieve this end. Rejecting philanthropic, humanitarian, and cultural programs for Palestine (the heart of American Zionism), he challenged Zionists to propel statehood to the highest priority on the Zionist agenda.[18]

Something else about Silver besides his passionate commitment to Jewish statehood impressed Weizmann in particular, and that was his decision to visit war-torn England at Weizmann's invitation in the spring of 1942, two months before Biltmore. Accompanied by Weizmann, Silver addressed packed throngs in theaters in England and Scotland, focusing his talks on the immorality of the British White Paper. Posters and ads heralded his talks and newspapers printed enthusiastic reviews of the previous lecture. In an eight-day period ("a terrible grind," according to Weizmann) he lectured in Glasgow, Newcastle, Southport, Liverpool, Manchester, Harrogate, Leeds, Birmingham, and, of course, London, and Weizmann seemed immensely grateful. He summed up the "whirlwind tour" by telling Rabbi Silver that "you came, you saw, you conquered." To his colleagues in the Zionist movement he was equally enthusiastic: "Dr. Silver's trip was a signal success—he was brilliant in his speeches—simple, impressive and carrying deep conviction to very fastidious and critical audiences."[19]

Within days of Silver's elevation to the top leadership of the emergency council in August 1943, he took advantage of an opportunity to excite with his oratory and to evoke enthusiasm for Zion or, more precisely, for the Biltmore program. Immediately after the Zionist movement affirmed the Biltmore Declaration, the emergency council initiated plans for the convening of a democratically elected Jewish conference, which, they hoped, would demonstrate that organized American Jewry as a whole endorsed a Jewish state in Palestine. The American Jewish Conference opened at New York's Waldorf-Astoria Hotel on 29 August 1943 with more than five hundred delegates present. One hundred twenty-three, representing sixty-five different national Jewish organizations, were joined by 379 elected by secret ballot in seventy-eight communities and 158 regions of the United States.[20]

Not all the delegates, of course, were Zionists, and not all were enthusiastic about the Biltmore program that endorsed Jewish statehood. Wise, acutely sensitive to those non-Zionists sympathetic to Zionist efforts to abrogate the White Paper but opposed to political Zionism and perhaps afraid that a statehood resolution would embarrass the American government, explicitly urged the delegates not to adopt the Biltmore program's final plank. Other Zionist leaders who addressed the conference intentionally failed to take a position on the endorsement of a Jewish state, with the expectation that this issue would be ignored and that the conference would maintain a spirit of unity. In fact, the new co-chair of the emergency council was not even allotted speaking time by the Zionists— even on Palestine Night.[21]

Late on the evening of 30 August, the American Jewish Congress, however, an organization with which Silver had no connection but which was filled with militant Zionists, surprised the conference by sending Silver to the platform under its aegis. Silver responded by delivering one of the most celebrated and perhaps most significant speeches of his career. "He rose," according to Louis Lipsky, in words similar to those used to describe Silver since his teens,

> from his seat in the second row on the platform. He moved somewhat clumsily and with uncertain steps in the direction of the speaker's desk. He leaned his hands on the desk and braced his shoulders. Then his voice rang out resonant, fresh and arrogant. He was the debater, the pleader, the rebuker. He was interested in making a case and winning it and used all the arts of the advocate who wanted to convince and win a verdict. [22]

Silver urged the acceptance of the classic program of political Zionism—"the cry of despair of a people driven to the wall, fighting for its very life"—grounded in the promise of the Balfour Declaration to establish a Jewish home in Palestine. He destroyed in the strongest possible words the plan of moderate Zionists to leave the commonwealth/statehood issue off the agenda for the sake of "unity" ("We are asked not to relinquish our convictions but at the same time not to express them"); he rejected, equally forcefully, the notion that generous financial contributions to Palestinian causes were sufficient, and demanded, "to continuous bursts of momentous applause," that the conference endorse the Biltmore program on behalf of the "overwhelming majority of American Jews." He urged the delegates, as he concluded his explosive message "to thunderous applause," to "stand by those who have given their tears and their blood and their sweat to build for them and for us and the future generations, at long last, after the weary centuries, a home, a National Home, a Jewish Commonwealth, where the spirit of our entire people can finally be at rest as well as the people itself." A Jewish state then, Silver fervently believed, would be the ultimate "rescue" achievement and the only convincing response to the "millenial tragedy" of Jewish persecution. [23]

Silver had clearly brought the conference face to face with the main issue—the Jewish commonwealth. The reaction to Silver's presentation was electrifying. Nahum Goldmann, who strongly disliked Silver, often calling him "the Almighty" in his letters to friends, and who may even have been a leading voice in the effort to omit any mention of statehood, called it "not only oratorically brilliant but one of his most effective speeches." Emanuel Neumann, a devoted friend of Silver, recalled that "it is impossible to describe the electrifying effect of Silver's speech, which swept the Conference like a hurricane[;] there was repeated and stormy applause, the delegates rising to their feet in a remarkable ovation." There is some truth to Neumann's claim that the speech won "the battle for our 'extreme' position . . . hands down," and there was considerable truth to his assertion that Silver's "magnificent performance and great triumph at the conference was one of the highlights of his career." Louis Lipsky observed that "the electric excitement it created seemed to bind every syllable uttered by the speaker to the nervous system of every listener. It was the climax of a great moment." And Samuel Margoshes, whose columns appeared in the Yiddish press, described it as one of the greatest Jewish addresses in modern history. It clearly established him as the dominant spokesman for American Jewry.[24]

Translating this feverish enthusiasm into a resolution was the task of the conference's Palestine Committee, fortuitously chaired by Silver, who remained silent throughout the three committee sessions of speeches, discussions, and votes. The committee's primary goal seemed to be to avoid any minority resolutions from being approved, for instance, a resolution that would have supported everything but a commonwealth, and this proved quite easy as Zionists quickly neutralized non-Zionists. The final resolution, approved sixty-two to two by the committee, called for "the fulfillment of the Balfour Declaration and of the [League of Nations] Mandate for Palestine whose intent and underlying purpose . . . was to reconstitute Palestine as the Jewish Commonwealth."[25]

Silver presented the resolution on 1 September, and when he finished the first paragraph dealing with the Jewish Commonwealth, reported an observer, "the whole audience rose and exploded." The resolution also condemned the White Paper and demanded its abrogation, and only four of the five hundred or so delegates voted negatively. After the vote was announced, another wave of excitement filled the hall and led to the repeated singing of "*Ha-Tikvah,*" the Zionist anthem. The Palestine resolution of the American Jewish Conference was a tremendous personal victory for Silver and clearly gave enormous momentum to his new task, though it did not alter by one iota the continued opposition to the drive for statehood by the few non-Zionists who understood "rescue" almost exclusively in terms of opening Palestine to Jewish immigration.[26]

The American Jewish Conference stood as the emergency council's most significant accomplishment to date, but its most important tasks were ahead. It was to these that Silver gave his attention after mid-August 1943 and these to which he would give enormous amounts of time, effort, and passion. By the end of August, after a preliminary survey, discussions with members of committees and staff, and a study of schemes for reorganization, Silver prepared a plan of operation for the AZEC. His vision and organizational skills would leave a decisive imprint on the character, policies, and program of American Zionism in its most critical years.[27]

With the goal of Jewish statehood reaffirmed by the conference and a strong demand for immediate rescue of European Jews recorded, Silver, who was given virtual control of the political operations of the AZEC with his unanimous election as chairman of the executive (formerly office) committee and the political committee, turned his attention to molding American public opinion. Several Zionists involved with the emergency council agreed that, as Harold Manson put it, "it was the handiwork of Dr. Silver—a highly efficient and sensitive instrument, completely responsive to his technique and style."[28]

Silver immediately convinced the United Jewish Appeal to allocate significant additional sums of moeny to the emergency council (more than $500,000 for 1943–44, five times that allocated in 1942–43, and, by 1945–46, $723,000); he enticed the extraordinary administrator Henry Montor to leave the UJA and serve as the executive director of the council; he initiated the process of establishing local emergency councils (eventually there were at least 150) throughout the country to bring the causes of the Jews to civic clubs, editors, clergymen, and politicians; he established fourteen working committees, an accomplishment that impressed even Nahum Goldmann; and he wasted no time in convincing his former associate and then senior rabbi of Collingwood Temple in Toledo, Leon Feuer, to take a leave of absence from his congregation and direct the critical Washington branch of the emergency council. The executive committee of the AZEC quickly approved these moves, and Silver and Montor began to fill key organizational positions with some of the most dedicated and experienced Zionist administrators in the country, including Harry Shapiro of the United Palestine Appeal (who succeeded Montor when the latter left the emergency council in 1944 to return to the UJA), Isaiah ("Sy") L. Kenen, Harold Manson, Shulamith Schwarz Nardi, Benjamin Akzin, Emanuel Neumann, Abe Tuvim, Elihu Stone, Leo Sack, and Marvin Lowenthal.[29]

The emergency council had two fundamental goals, carefully articulated by Silver, Feuer, and others in 1943 and 1944. One was to inform, educate, and pressure congressmen, government officials, reporters, editors, and others in responsible positions to do something about rescuing the remaining Jews of Europe, and the other was to convince these same people of the need to open the shores of Palestine, the most logical rescue haven, to Jewish refugees (that is, to abrogate the White Paper), thereby building popular support for the creation of a Jewish state therein.[30]

These twin programs of rescue and rebirth were passionately announced by Silver and vigorously pursued by his hand-picked associates in the emergency council. Nevertheless, by the end of 1943—given "a situation which we cannot help"—Silver doubted that any serious rescue solution other than opening Palestine was possible.

Most world Zionist leaders had reached similar conclusions about rescue by the time Silver moved into emergency council leadership, if not earlier. Nahum Goldmann, in letters written during the spring of 1943, noted the abundant rescue efforts of American Jewry ("all over the country—we really tried") yet felt that "all our efforts have been unsuccessful; we have achieved nothing substantial; and I have my doubts as to whether we will be able to later on." With even greater despair than he revealed at Biltmore a year earlier, Goldmann appeared "heartbroken that we have not achieved more" and certain that "we have to reckon with the destruction of the major part of European Jewry." Other leaders such as Weizmann agreed with Goldmann.[31]

Despite his reservations about rescue possibilities, Silver utilized the pulpit, the lectern, personal visits, and the press to articulate these objectives. He wrote letters to editors of newspapers across the country when a local emergency council leader sent him an anti-Zionist editorial, he wrote letters to individuals when they wrote to him about rescue or Zionism, and he wrote regular columns for the Yiddish and Anglo-Jewish press. His diaries and speeches confirm Leon Feuer's conviction that Silver's "single-minded devotion to the task is simply indescribable." Feuer worked closely with him as he "traveled constantly, addressed literally hundreds of meetings, interviewed scores of prominent personages, and fought like a tiger to make the cause and his judgment of events prevail."[32]

One aspect of this devotion consisted of Silver's weekly trips to Washington, D.C., during 1943–44. Feuer and his aides, Leo Sack, a retired Scripps-Howard Washington correspondent who "knew and had access to virtually everybody of importance in Washington," and Elihu Stone, a friend of many New England congressmen, would arrange Silver's schedule and Silver spent Monday through Wednesday or Tuesday through Thursday of nearly every week of October, November, and December 1943 as well as February, March, and May of 1944 in the nation's capital. He left a pocket diary-calendar of his meetings as well as typescript summaries of his conversations, and one can quickly see that his desperate concern for European Jewry, his passionate desire for a Jewish state, and his strong disgust with the White Paper dominate his conversations. He met senators and representatives, cabinet officers and undersecretaries, the British ambassador, and even the president (9 March 1944).[33]

Most of his days in Washington were filled with these appointments as well as with press conferences and meetings with Zionist leaders and emergency council personnel, and one can select nearly at random a representative schedule. On 12 October 1943 Silver discussed rescue strategies with Nahum Goldmann from 8:30–10:00 A.M.; he pumped Justice Felix Frankfurter from 11:00–12:00 about the attitudes toward Jewish statehood held by Roosevelt ("he has not given it much thought," Frankfurter told Silver) and various officials in the Near East Section of the State Department; at 12:30 P.M. he called on Congressman Emanuel Celler, who had been working on a statement opposing the White Paper and who stressed to Silver the State Department's sympathy with the White Paper and the sense that "only heroic measures" would change that support; at 2:00 Silver thanked the Danish ambassador for the rescue of Danish Jewry by the Danish king and people; and from 3:00–4:00 he met with Roosevelt's close confidant, Judge Samuel Rosenman, and stressed his great disappointment with the administration's efforts at rescue and statehood and urged Rosenman to "become our spokesman, occupying as [you do], one of the few key positions in the world today in one of the most decisive hours in Jewish history."[34]

That same day, from 5:00–6:00, he met with Peter Bergson, organizer of the Hebrew Committee of National Liberation and the Emergency Committee to Rescue the Jewish People of Europe (see chapter 5), who told Silver that he, Bergson, and his friends, constituted the Palestine government-in-exile. Silver reminded Bergson of the unsuccessful effort two years earlier to unite their rival organizations, urged that another attempt be made, denounced the vitriolic campaign that had been conducted against Bergson before he, Silver, took over the leadership, and concluded by explaining to Bergson why his group had "failed completely." Finally at 6:00 P.M., he spoke on the telephone to Senator James Mead (D–N.Y.), who assured Silver that "Palestine should be given to the Jewish people" and that Palestine "did not concern them [the Arabs] at all." When Silver was in Washington, his schedule usually followed this pattern—with a diversion in February to testify in Congress in support of the Palestine resolution (see chapter 5)—and even after Congress had adjourned in the summer of 1944 Silver kept just as busy with lobbying in Chicago for a Palestine plank in the Republican platform.[35]

Concomitant with his Washington lobbying, with his correspondence, phone calls, memos, and meetings, Silver took control of every aspect of the emergency council's planning, purchasing huge amounts of radio time for presentations by stage and screen celebrities, flooding the White House, Congress, and the State Department with thousands and thousands of letters, coordinating mass rallies at Carnegie Hall or Madison Square Garden, and arranging conferences of Christian leaders concerned about rescue and statehood. He spent considerable time in the emergency council office, praising workers for what they had accomplished and exhorting them to do more. One staff member recalls that "nobody on earth was a better head of an organization, a greater inspirer of the people he worked with, or more appreciative, kind, or nice—and we adored him." Most crucial of all his creations were the local emergency councils, coordinated in New York by Montor and then Shapiro and in Washington by Feuer (under the close watch of Silver).[36]

It was the emergency councils, working ceaselessly in nearly every city of political consequence, that kept the larger goals of the AZEC before the eyes and ears of American citizens, and (even though perhaps they accomplished little in the rescue area because it was already too late) ultimately they built up enormous popular backing for a Jewish state. "At a single telephone call," Feuer noted, "they went immediately into action." Samuel Halperin observed that

> In the 1944 Zionist campaign for the abrogation of the White Paper, more than 3,000 non-Jewish organizations—unions, Kiwanis Clubs, YMCA's . . . and Farm Granges—passed pro-Zionist resolutions, circulated petitions, and sent letters and telegrams to the Administration and their congressional representatives. In Meriden, Conn., alone, whose entire Jewish population did not exceed 1,500 persons, more than 12,000 letters on the subject of Palestine were reportedly dispatched to President Roosevelt and the State Department.[37]

Silver repeatedly instructed emergency council professionals to put pressure on government officials from the "bottom-up—by massive, pressure politics" and personally wrote some of the copy sent in a steady stream to the local emergency councils. The result of all this careful organization was, according to one historian, "one of the strongest pressure groups that has ever existed in American history."[38]

Chapter
Five

Al tivtechu b'neddivim—
Put not your trust in princes.
(Psalm 146:3)

—Abba Hillel Silver, 1944

The Biltmore Conference had radicalized the Zionist movement in America by initiating militant protests against the British White Paper of 1939 and by late 1943 by organizing concerted efforts to convince the United States to commit itself to a Jewish state in Palestine as soon as the world war ended. Silver intentionally charted a course that pushed the American Zionist Emergency Council into the forefront of making militant demands and vigorously lobbying for a Jewish state, and as 1943 ended and 1944 began, relegating to a subordinate role European Jewish rescue activities. For Silver the facts were plain; the Nazis had already murdered almost all the Jews of Europe; the most appropriate response to this massive extermination was an autonomous Jewish state; and only political leverage, not humanitarian arguments, could move congressional decisionmakers to action. These decisions energized his efforts in Washington but also brought him into contact with Jews whose priorities and tactics differed from his own. Some of them, angry and resentful, would keep him busy defending his tactics to his colleagues while at the same time he vigorously pursued political leaders.

Late in 1943 Silver proposed to the executive committee of the AZEC that sympathetic congressmen be induced to introduce pro-Zionist resolutions in Congress (he even drafted a model resolution) and that both political parties be persuaded to include similar planks in their platforms for the 1944 presidential elections. In a letter to Weizmann, Silver pointed out how little faith he had in "quiet diplomacy" (a reference to Stephen S. Wise), "a few powerful people" (a reference to FDR confidants) or "our 'good' friend" (a reference to Roosevelt)—as the president "will not move on his own accord, inspired by the moral righteousness of our cause." Rather than moral arguments, he told Weizmann, we will use "voting power" and "pin our hopes" on the "pressure of five million Jews in a critical election year." Silver concluded that congressional resolutions and political platforms were part of the "pressure" necessary to secure "a Jewish Commonwealth in Palestine," to rescue the remaining European Jews, and to persuade the British not to end Jewish immigration completely after the White Paper five-year period of restricted immigration came to an end. Thus the AZEC undertook to engage many local contacts as well as to initiate several weeks of preliminary discussions with congressmen such as Emanuel Celler, Sol Bloom, and Adolph Sabath.[1]

On 27 January 1944, Representatives James A. Wright (D–Penn.) and Ranulf Compton (R–Conn.) introduced identical resolutions supporting "the establishment in Palestine of a national home for the Jewish people" and "Palestine as a free and democratic Jewish commonwealth," while on 1 February Senators Robert Wagner (D–N.Y.) and Robert Taft (R–Ohio) did the same in the Senate, after the secretary of state informed Taft and Silver that he had no objections to the resolution. The House resolution went to Representative Sol Bloom's Committee on Foreign Affairs, and the initial memoranda from AZEC lobbyists to Silver were filled with great expectations, despite Bloom's preference for avoiding any hearings. A dimunitive, colorful showman, a music publisher and real estate operator from a poor, Orthodox Polish-Jewish home before he entered politics as a Democratic congressman from New York City in 1923, Bloom (1870–1949) was a hardly less garrulous, flamboyant, and publicity-seeking politician in his early years. Amiable and accessible and identifiably Jewish inside and outside of Congress, he would serve as a representative until his death, and he became a faithful New Dealer and staunch interventionist whose seniority made him head of the House Foreign Affairs Committee by 1939. Bloom had considerable sympathy for refugees but less sympathy for a Jewish state. Enormous pressure, largely exerted by local emergency councils, led to House hearings that opened on 8– 9 February and continued on 15–16 February 1944. The Zionists as well as the anti-Zionists (including Jews) were ready to testify; the latter arguing against the resolution primarily on the grounds of dual allegiance (American Jews would be accused of having two "homes") and heightened anti-Semitism (anti-Semites would be able to say to American Jews "Go back to your homeland").[2]

Silver together with several other prominent Jewish leaders testified at the hearings in favor of the resolution. He began his hour of testimony on 8 February in a room "packed with several hundred people [while] many persons who could not get into the crowded room filled the adjoining rooms and, standing on chairs, watched the proceedings." He argued that Jewish nationalism had been a continual thread in the history of his people and then attacked the White Paper, which would expire in one month, for preventing "tens of thousands" of refugees from finding a place of rescue. He argued on behalf of the resolution largely on the grounds that the surviving Jews would leave Europe in "waves," while existing nations would only accept "trickles." The Jewish people, he told the congressmen, "desperately needs Palestine for its homeless millions now and after the war," and the "reconstitution of Palestine as a Jewish commonwealth would be . . . an act of historic justice." Silver, in his debut as a congressional pleader, brought twenty-six typewritten pages of testimony. But, as always, "he looks only at the Committee when he talks and employs gestures," one observer noted; "all listen because there is nothing monotonous about this man."[3]

There is ample evidence that the House (and even the Senate) were very sympathetic to these arguments and that substantial majorities in both chambers supported the resolutions, but that the president, the secretary of state (Cordell Hull) and the secretary of war (Stimson) opposed them. The latter were convinced that the British government and other American friends would be angry (the Allies were contemplating an attack on the Nazis through the Balkans and angry Arabs at their rear would be a nuisance) and American oil interests in Saudi Arabia would be jeopardized. Cordell Hull explained:

> At the State Department we felt that the passage of these resolutions, although not binding on the Executive, might precipitate conflict in Palestine and other parts of the Arab world, endangering American troops and requiring the diversion of forces from European and other combat areas. It might prejudice or shatter pending negotiations with Ibn Saud for the construction of a pipeline across Saudi Arabia, which our military leaders felt was of utmost importance to our security. And it would stimulate other special interests to press for the introduction of similar resolutions regarding controversial territorial issues relating to areas such as Poland and Italy.[4]

Army Chief of Staff General George C. Marshall, at the request of Stimson, Stettinius, and Roosevelt, testified against the resolutions in an executive session of the Senate Foreign Relations Committee on 23 February and 4 March; John J. McCloy, assistant secretary of war, and other officers did the same, emphasizing the need to avoid Senate hearings, to postpone consideration of the resolutions, or, in the words of Edward R. Stettinius, Jr., the under secretary of state, "to kill the resolution by executive session testimony." Despite the pressure, the Foreign Relations Committee scheduled hearings (albeit behind closed doors), but the senators not only were aware of the War Department opposition (on 9 February Senator Connally read Secretary of War Stimson's letter of 7 February ["our war effort would be seriously prejudiced"] to the committee), but Roosevelt had convinced, without Silver's knowledge, several Zionist leaders to testify in favor of postponement. The Senate immediately tabled the resolution and when the opposition of the secretary of war was made public on 17 March (Bloom released Stimson's letter of that very day, which stated that "further action on [the resolution] would be prejudicial to the successful prosecution of the war") the House Committee on Foreign Affairs voted 11–3 to do the same.[5]

Thus the administration convinced a Congress probably overwhelmingly in favor of the resolutions to table them; nevertheless, Roosevelt met with Wise and Silver on 9 March 1944 to assure them of his eventual support ("when future decisions are reached") for a Jewish national home "for hundreds of thousands of homeless Jewish refugees." FDR meant literally, however, in the "future," and this public statement, clearly opposed to British policy, was not followed by any action other than the administration's secretly informing the Arab leaders (13 March) that no decision on Palestine would be made without consulting them. Roosevelt had, in Hull's words, "talked both ways to Zionists and Arabs."[6]

Unaware that Roosevelt was working both sides of the street, Silver brushed aside the objections to his "pet project" and used FDR's statement as a catalyst for emergency council mobilization. The response included a giant rally at Madison Square Garden on 21 March 1944 (to permit the "heart of America" to be heard "in this, our struggle") with Silver as the featured speaker and a successful campaign to gather an "avalanche of communications" in Washington. This was the month (March) when, according to the White Paper, Jewish immigration would end, and Silver hoped that enormous "pressure" would move Congress to ignore the administration's signals to postpone action on the resolutions. The Senate Foreign Relations Committee had promised Silver and other emergency council leaders that in two to three weeks the committee would reconsider its postponement, but the "avalanche" of public sympathy could not move a Congress in the midst of a world war when the War and State Departments presented a unified opposition. [7]

Nevertheless, the record of the emergency council after just a few months of Silver's leadership is quite clear. The campaign for a Palestine resolution and especially, that against the White Paper was intensive and well-organized. The voices of American Jews from all over the country were heard in Washington through thousands of resolutions addressed to the State Department, to congressmen, and to other government officials; Christian public opinion was aroused in numerous ways; and scores of editorials in newspapers commented favorably on the emergency council program. In addition, the local community contact groups or emergency councils personally visited most U.S. senators and representatives at home in their own states and districts during the Christmas holidays. Silver aggressively and quite systematically pushed these programs, beginning in September of 1943 when he took over leadership of the AZEC. [8]

Silver was not the only Zionist leader actively lobbying in Washington and throughout America in 1943 and 1944. During the war years, Peter Bergson (b. Hillel Kook, 1915), a Palestinian Jewish militant who had come to the United States in 1940 to represent the underground Irgun Z'vai Leumi interests, founded a chain of organizations that vigorously lobbied for Jewish statehood, for the Jewish underground army in Palestine, and especially for efforts to rescue the Jews in Europe. His organizations, largely for fundraising, operating outside the American Zionist establishment, included the American Friends of a Jewish Palestine (1939–41), the Committee for a Jewish Army (1941–43), the Emergency Committee to Rescue the Jewish People of Europe (1943–45), and the Hebrew Committee of National Liberation and American League for a Free Palestine (1944–45).

Bergson formed the emergency committee at about the same time that Abba Hillel Silver took over the major political work of the emergency council, following the Emergency Conference to Save the Jewish People of Europe, which was held in New York 20–25 July 1943. The conference, desperately trying to reach out to the remaining four million European Jews who had been "singled out for mass destruction as a people,"recommended with abundant concrete suggestions that rescue be seen as a "specific problem . . . not as part of the general refugee problem," and that the United States create a "specific governmental agency" to save the surviving Jews of Europe "from annihilation prior to the cessation of hostilities."[9]

Silver's first meeting with Bergson following his rise to leadership in the AZEC took place at Washington's Dorchester House on 12 October 1943. There Bergson described to Silver a League for a Free Palestine—what would become in the following year the Hebrew Committee of National Liberation and American League for a Free Palestine. Bergson and a few others would constitute themselves the "government-in-exile" of a "Hebrew nation"—a "nation" under enemy occupation that needed to be set free. Silver expressed some sympathy for Bergson's plan—after all, though Bergson spoke of Palestine already as a nation like Holland or France, they shared similar goals. Silver reminded him of earlier efforts by the emergency council leadership to "join our activities," and urged him to again consider how "to integrate our work." And Silver added one more thought: the "sensational and dramatic techniques" of Bergson's previous organizations had "failed as completely as the conservative procedure of the other groups" in effecting "the rescuing of European Jewry."[10]

Silver had several other meetings with Bergson as well as with his lieutenants in the next few months, most of them quite cordial and occupied primarily with discussions of joint action. Silver not only proposed joint projects, but he tried to convince Bergson to join the AZEC; on one occasion he apologized for the vitriolic campaign conducted against Bergson before he took over the leadership. Silver's notes and personal letters on these meetings do not, however, confirm Nahum Goldmann's conclusion that Silver, "though he was not a Revisionist, was more sympathetic to their [Bergsonites] activities and often condoned them." Goldmann himself was not sympathetic to Bergson, calling him a "public calamity" and "a criminal joke," always "ready to betray the fundamentals of Zionism for publicity."[11]

Silver was always courteous and dignified, but he had little or no public sympathy in 1943 for the military arm of the Bergsonites, the Irgun, or for terrorists in general. He frequently noted that the Bergsonites "had been repudiated by all sections of American Jewish public opinion," that they "represent nobody in this country," that their "Hebrew embassy" in Washington was "fake," and that even in Palestine they represent only a "small terrorist group which has been outlawed and which the official Zionist bodies in Palestine have condemned." Letters to congressmen and others both from Silver personally and those sent under his signature by the emergency council insisted to persons in responsible positions that the Bergsonites "should not in any way be encouraged."[12]

Silver's notes from a phone call with and his personal letters to Senator Robert Taft (in June 1944) offer a typical response to Bergson's activities. Bergson had asked Senators Styles Bridges (R–N.H.) and Taft to submit a letter either to Stettinius or to Roosevelt on "the rights of the United States in Palestine." Silver at some length urged Taft not to cooperate with Bergson, largely because of the duplication of efforts involved. Silver pointed out that he himself had read such a statement on rights into the record during the hearings on the Palestine resolution when he had testified before the Committee on Foreign Affairs (on 8 February) and that it had received only a negative response from Cordell Hull. Silver felt certain it would do so again ("the effect of such a statement would be very bad") and that it would nullify the assurance contained in the statement Roosevelt had made after his meeting with Wise and Silver on 9 March. Silver, however, saved his most important reason for last: Bergson "will exploit the fact that [his] letter was sent as proof of [his] political effectiveness in

Washington, and, by contrast, the ineffectiveness of the official Zionist bodies."[13]

This rebuff of Bergson in Silver's communications with Taft came immediately after Bergson had founded the Hebrew Committee (in May 1944), had hoisted the "Zionist flag" over this same embassy on Massachusetts Avenue in Washington, and had arbitrarily divided the world's Jews into, on the one hand, the Jews of Palestine (Hebrews) and the stateless Jews of Europe, and on the other hand all other Jews. This last stratagem and his distinctively nonsectarian and nonpartisan appeals perhaps helped Bergson attract the support of several famous Jewish intellectuals in addition to the support of several well-known political and entertainment figures, because it affirmed the American character of his supporters who, being sensitive to potential charges of dual loyalty, wanted to be clearly distinguished from the "Hebrews." But Bergson's notion that the Hebrew nation in Palestine should be "free and independent of all other Jewries in the world" not only appealed to American Jewish assimilationists but represented a complete denial of classical Zionism's essence—*kelal Yisrael* or Jewish peoplehood.[14]

At the same time that Silver was communicating with Taft, the official publication of the AZEC warned emergency councils across the land about the Bergsonites, who "have hoodwinked Washington circles" with "new costumes and a new lingo." Reminding local council leaders that "all responsible Jewish organizations have by now disowned, condemned, and excoriated them," the editorial continued with a strong letter of denunciation from Senator Robert Wagner.[15]

The crux of the conflict was that the various Bergson organizations challenged the authority and policies of the emergency council, in much the same way that Nahum Goldmann and Stephen S. Wise challenged the individual authority of Silver. By means of full-page ads in major metropolitan newspapers, spectacular rallies, rabbinical delegations, entertaining pageants, intensely serious national conferences (like the Second Annual National Conference to Save the Jewish People of Europe in August 1944), and vigorous lobbying in Congress, the various Bergsonites had made many friends in Congress and saw some hope of Congress passing one of their resolutions. It surely did not hurt that the Bergsonites were "suave, multilingual, entertaining conversationalists, graceful on the dance floor, and with an aura of international mystery about them."[16]

Although Bergson was, according to Leon Feuer, the emergency council representative in Washington, "working for the same objective," Feuer viewed the Bergsonites not as supportive and constructive but as a "troublesome problem" and the agents themselves as "pesky nuisances." On one occasion he called them "illegals," another time he referred to them as "an insignificantly small pistol-packing group of extremists," and he waged the most aggressive campaign of any emergency council official to discredit Bergson and his organizations. The council made an effort to send its own representatives to emergency committee and Hebrew committee meetings during 1943–44, and summaries of these meetings were drafted and mailed to Silver.[17]

The correspondence of Silver, Wise, and the emergency council staff reveals that the Zionists kept careful track of the "well-intentioned, innocent *goyim*" whose names appeared in Bergsonite ads and appeals, and both Silver and Wise sent mailings and made personal appeals urging them to disassociate themselves from Bergson's organizations. In addition, newspaper articles carefully placed by emergency council public relations staffers announced the resignation of prominent leaders from the emergency committee.[18]

In addition, Silver and Wise made special efforts to explain to congressmen, State Department officials and newspaper editors that Bergsonites had "been repudiated by every responsible Jewish organization in the United States and Palestine" and by the "overwhelming majority of Jews" as well. Silver encouraged Representative Bloom to meet Bergson, certain of Bloom's reaction. Bloom wrote Silver that he found Bergson a "very dangerous man, absolutely unscrupulous, who is imbued with an illusion that he has been designated by God to save the Jews of Europe." Bloom warned Silver of Bergson's contempt for the AZEC and his "nerves of iron" with which he disregarded "conscientious scruples." Utterly fearless, Bloom concluded, he is "a fanatic [and] dangerous man" with "enthusiasm . . . brilliance . . . imagination . . . and sincerity." Senator Wagner also vigorously opposed Bergson and occasionally offered press releases to Yiddish and Anglo-Jewish newspapers denouncing the Bergsonites.[19]

The AZEC prepared, updated, and mailed extensively numerous memoranda, press releases, and fact sheets to sympathetic journalists who were encouraged to write exposés. All the literature made a common point: what was the need for another organization under Mr. Bergson's direction when its ideas and programs were being effectively pursued by other well-established and well-recognized bodies? This was the heart of the conflict: a rival organization, manned by aggressive leaders with many friends in Congress, offered spirited competition to the AZEC. Having labored long and hard for rescue and statehood, the AZEC was convinced that there was room for only one organization to pursue these twin goals effectively.[20]

Notwithstanding Silver's close association with Feuer and his leadership of the emergency council during its vigorous obstructionist phase, coworkers from the period under discussion do not recall Silver's strong opposition to Bergson. To the contrary, nearly all of them are convinced that in his heart he secretly approved of Bergson's militancy and of his supporters in Palestine and that he cleverly managed to compromise his own feelings with the demands his more moderate Zionist supporters placed upon him.

Nahum Goldmann recalled Silver's sympathy for and approval of Bergson and applauded Silver, who was caught "between his political position in American life, where he was often on the progressive side, and the stand he took on Palestine, where he endorsed the most prominent right-wing leaders." Samuel Katz, who worked on the London *Daily Express* until the summer of 1945, recalled that although Silver had a "fierce and unrelenting hostility" to Bergson, he "was sympathetic to the Irgun. Notwithstanding his routine denunciations of 'terrorism' to which on suitable occasions he felt he had to give expression, he did little to hide his true feelings and opinions." Doreen Bierbrier, who carefully studied the AZEC, concluded that "the vitriolic campaign against the [Bergsonites] tapered off under Silver's leadership, and [they] rejoined the AZEC early in 1945." And even Bergson himself, whose own grace in conversations with and letters to Silver equalled that of the rabbi, wrote to Silver as if they were intimate friends whose differences were those of a devoted couple. "The Hebrew Committee of National Liberation," he began a letter in October of 1945, "is exceedingly pleased with the recent energetic drive which has been conducted under your leadership by the AZEC."21

Silver appears to have done precisely what he so disliked in President Roosevelt; he "played both sides of the street." To those he wanted to know him as sympathetic to Bergson, he gave one impression, while to those charged with aggressively sabotaging Bergson's operation he gave other signals.

About the same time that Congress was considering the Palestine resolutions and Silver was dealing with the Bergson threat, the Democratic and Republican party platforms for the 1944 presidential election were taking shape. Silver informed the executive committee of the emergency council as early as March that he sought strong Palestine planks in both party platforms; and immediately afterward he and Feuer began to lobby congressmen. Some of his Zionist colleagues felt that the Republican Party should be ignored, because it would be tactically unwise to pressure the Roosevelt administration so shortly after the president had promised a Jewish national home. Silver argued both that a promise was only a promise, not a fact, and that pressure would be more likely to lead to the fulfillment of such a promise than would the present situation

Dinah Silver, mother of Abba Hillel Silver

Moses Silver, father of Abba Hillel Silver

Silver in 1914 as a student at the University of Cincinnati

Silver in 1919 near Verdun in France

The Temple, Cleveland, Ohio

*Virginia Horkheimer Silver,
Abba's wife*

Silver in 1938

Silver with Chaim Weizmann in England in 1942

*Silver, with Rabbi Stephen S. Wise, after meeting with
President Roosevelt in 1944*

*Silver giving the invocation
at the 1944 Republican
National Convention.
Rep. Joe Martin,
convention chairman,
is at the right*

*Daniel, Abba,
Virginia, and
Raphael Silver
in 1945*

Louis Lipsky, Silver, Stephen S. Wise, and Nahum Goldmann in 1946

Silver addressing the United Nations in 1947. Andrei Gromyko (USSR) is next to Silver; Emanuel Neumann, Golda Meir, and Moshe Sharett are behind him.

Silver, in front passenger seat of first car, being welcomed in Israel in 1951

Silver, at dedication of Kfar Silver, in Israel in 1957

Silver with President John F. Kennedy in 1963

Silver with David Ben-Gurion in 1963

Silver in his study in 1963. Photo: Karsh, Ottawa

in which the president, certain of the Jewish vote, did not have to do anything concrete to assure it.[22]

By this time Silver had a very extensive political schooling in local, state, and Washington politics and, as Harold Manson has put it, he "knew the American political system from the inside." Although a supporter of neither party in 1932 (he argued then that both Republicans and Democrats had failed to propose serious solutions to the nation's staggering economic problems), he quickly became a fan of Roosevelt, who a few months after taking office appointed Silver to a National Citizens Committee of the 1933 Mobilization for Human Needs. In March 1934 he lauded FDR's first year in office; in 1936 in a sermon evaluating Roosevelt's "achievements and failures," Silver found mostly the former; and he implicitly supported Roosevelt (and explicitly supported his program) on the eve of the 1936 election.[23]

But after seven years of support for Roosevelt, Silver believed that the country needed a change; eight years was enough for any person to serve the nation. Hence, more than seven months before the 1940 election Silver urged FDR not to seek reelection, and three months before the election Silver endorsed Wilkie for president, though only because "the tradition of rotation in office . . . is a sound one" and not because of objections to Roosevelt's policies. With Roosevelt well into his third term (in February 1942) Silver could still praise him: "a man of great vision, shrewdness and insight, who better than any other statesman read the trend of his times and understood the implications of the rise of Nazism and Fascism." However, beginning in the spring of 1942 with the Biltmore Conference, Silver challenged Roosevelt's promises to the Jews about rescue and statehood. Although Silver avoided endorsing the Republicans (he supported neither political party publicly while serving as a national Zionist leader), the GOP had heard enough of Silver's attacks on Roosevelt to invite the rabbi to offer an invocation at their 1944 convention in Chicago.[24]

Silver first met with Ohio Senator Robert A. Taft (1889–1953), chairman of the platform committee and one of the cosponsors of the Senate Resolution earlier that year, in Taft's office on 26 April 1944. The son of President William Howard Taft, Robert was a Cincinnati attorney, a U.S. Senator, and three times an unsuccessful candidate (1940, 1948, and 1952) for the Republican presidential nomination. A hard-working, extremely intelligent but uninspiring conservative senator with few close friends, Taft came to the Senate in 1938 and immediately joined the conservative opposition to Roosevelt's domestic economic and foreign policies. Dubbed Mr. Republican, he would become arguably the most powerful man in the Senate during his second term (1944–50). At the 1944 meeting with Silver, Silver raised the issue of a Palestine plank and Taft not only suggested he would have much to do with drafting the platform but that he was quite sympathetic to such a plank. Indeed, three weeks earlier he had told Silver "I am grateful to you and your friends for interesting me in the Palestine matter; there is [no] more vital problem." Taft urged Silver to talk with Governor Dewey, the front-runner for the nomination, and the governor and the rabbi met on 1 June in New York. When Dewey read the Senate resolution at their meeting, he expressed his strong approval. Concomitantly, Taft informed Silver that he was drafting a Palestine plank along the lines of the Senate resolution, which Silver could see before Taft left for the Republican National Convention in Chicago. Finally, he urged Silver not to agitate publicly for such a plank, as it would only awaken enemies.[25]

Silver, a bit nervous about what Taft was drafting, sent him his own version of such a plank on 9 June. The response was positive, and the chairman of the Republican National Committee invited Silver to deliver the invocation at the 27 June convention session. Silver arrived in Chicago, however, a week before he was to give his invocation on 20 June in order to lobby members of the resolutions committee who were to begin meeting the following day. Silver was joined by the top staff of the emergency council (Manson, Sack, and Stone) and took a room at a hotel far from the headquarters of the convention. He worked hard "not to give the impression of a lobby" and not to "arouse any possible opposition on the part of anti-Zionist forces."[26]

Taft gave Silver the names of the members of the Committee on Foreign Affairs and of the Drafting Committee; Silver called Governor Dewey in Albany and urged him to contact his campaign manager in Chicago and ask him quietly to inform the committee members of Dewey's support. Dewey did so, and at the same time Manson, Sack, and Stone quietly met with them. Silver left Chicago on 22 June confident of smooth sailing, but when he returned on 26 June he found that opposition to the plank had emerged after he left Chicago and numerous changes in the wording had been suggested. Two alternate drafts were circulating; one Silver called "completely negative and worthless," while the other omitted reference to a Jewish state or commonwealth, the heart of the plank. Silver offered Taft another version and told Dewey that he, Silver, would leave the convention immediately if either "negative resolution" were approved.[27]

At this point (26 June) Silver sought advice from Stephen Wise, who responded that a plank without "commonwealth" was better than no resolution at all. Two hours later John Foster Dulles, Dewey's political adviser, telephoned with yet another draft of the plank (he urged, among other changes, deleting "unrestricted immigration"; Silver rejoined with inserting "unrestricted Jewish immigration") and the alarming information that, despite Silver's strong objections, the plank would also condemn Roosevelt for not insisting that Britain carry out the provisions of the Balfour Declaration in its mandate.[28]

This Dulles-Dewey version of the plank, with a concession to Silver on the "unrestricted immigration" matter, went before the Resolutions Committee and the Drafting Committee after midnight that evening. There more opposition developed; Senator Danaher (R–Conn., who had given the emergency council trouble all year in Washington) objected to the "commonwealth" clause and to telling Great Britain what to do in a matter that did not concern the United States. His objections caused the plank to be tabled and on Tuesday morning 27 June when the committee adjourned there was no Palestine plank.[29]

The entire Resolutions Committee met again at 10:00 A.M., and Silver, Manson, Sack, and Stone kept busy in the preceding hours by telephoning everyone on the committee they believed to be a supporter. It became clear as the meeting commenced that the emergency council could choose a resolution without "commonwealth" or none at all. Silver, after consultation, sent a memo to Senator Taft, who was chairing the meeting, and, gambling that the Republicans desperately needed the Jewish vote, demanded either "commonwealth" or nothing at all.[30]

Shortly after noon Silver learned that despite continued opposition from Senator Danaher, the Resolutions Committee had approved a Palestine plank and instructed the Drafting Committee to make the final revisions in response to the objections raised. Then, at 3:00 P.M., Senator Taft gave Silver and his colleagues the final draft:

> In order to give refuge to milions of distressed Jewish men, women and children driven from their homes by tyranny, we call for the opening of Palestine to their unrestricted immigration and land ownership, so that in accordance with the full intent and purpose of the Balfour Declaration of 1917 and the Resolution of a Republican Congress in 1922, Palestine may be constituted as a free and democratic Commonwealth. We condemn the failure of the President to insist that the mandatory of Palestine carry out the provision of the Balfour Declaration and of the mandate while he pretends to support them.[31]

The final draft of the Palestine Resolution was a victory for Silver and the emergency council, despite the plank's condemnation of Roosevelt—a criticism that Silver told Dewey he opposed even though the Republicans, not the Zionists, authored it. The Republican Party had for the first time ever given unequivocal support to the Zionist program of establishing Palestine as a "free and democratic Commonwealth." The plank was the result of months of lobbying by Silver and Leon Feuer, together with Senator Taft, a fellow Ohioan, for the goals of Zionism and of the patient efforts of Silver and his colleagues at the convention. But when Silver presented a report to the executive committee of the AZEC on 10 July and asked it to endorse the platform, several members castigated Silver for the attack on Roosevelt. As active Democrats, they were embarrassed by the association that would be made between themselves and the plank. This reaction depressed Silver, as he confided to Emanuel Neumann, because it confirmed his belief "that many of the members of the [Executive] Committee are far more involved and committed in one way or another to the Democratic Party than they are to Zionism, and that in the case of a conflict of loyalties, they will sacrifice Zionist interests." He expressed special displeasure with Stephen Wise, who critized the attack on FDR but never expressed gratification with the heart of the resolution.[32]

Nevertheless, the emergency council "hailed with satisfaction" the "section of the Palestine Plank" (as opposed to all of the plank) on a Jewish commonwealth. Led by Rabbi Israel Goldstein, who disagreed with Silver on most issues, the AZEC demanded and got a special session of the ZOA executive to consider a response. Silver lobbied vigorously with his friends in the ZOA not to do anything that would repudiate the emergency council's efforts with the Republicans, and his supporters decisively voted down a motion to disassociate the ZOA from the Republican attack on FDR.[33]

The Democratic National Convention met in July in Chicago and Stephen Wise assured Silver that he would use his longstanding Democratic connections and friendship with the "chief" to "take care of the matter." Wise convinced Representative John McCormack (D–Mass.) to allow him despite Silver's objections to appear at a public hearing before the Committee on Resolutions that

McCormack chaired. This led, however, to an invitation to the leading anti-Zionist rabbi, Morris Lazaron, to appear as well, and Silver chastised Wise for seeking publicity ("a public appearance is the last thing we want") providing Lazaron with a public forum, for not agreeing to work quietly in private, and for opening up the possibility of "repudiating the Emergency Council should we testify, and then no plank is adopted." Wise responded that Silver was completely wrong; the advantages of his appearance ("I spoke as I never spoke before") were great enough to override the possibility of minor negative consequences.[34]

Wise refused to retract his request for public hearings. The Democrats tried to keep Wise and the other AZEC leaders who were present in Chicago largely in the dark about drafts of a Palestine plank ("It's all so confusing and distressing," Wise wrote a friend, "I can't break through a cordon of bell boys") and even whether there would be such a plank at all. "My information," Wise pleadingly wrote FDR, "Is that either no plank concerning Palestine is to be adopted or that the Platform will include a plank which is utterly inadequate." Representatives McCormack and Celler leaked enough bits of information to emergency council staff for the latter to inform Silver on 19 and 20 July that 1) there would be a Palestine plank despite some opposition, and 2) it would be acceptable. Silver urged Wise to go beyond his statement that he would not support the Democratic campaign if there was no Palestine plank and say that he would denounce the party, and Silver explained to a reporter from Washington as he so often did that rumors that he would "stump for Dewey" and "attack . . . the President" were irresponsible. Silver vigorously stressed the absolutely nonpartisan character of the Zionist movement: "I have never stumped for any presidential candidate," he said, and added that he could not do so "if I am to continue to work for Zionism in Washington."[35]

The Democrats finally approved a plank and Silver not only warmly congratulated Wise ("you may be proud of your major contribution") but noted with pleasure that the Democrats outdid the Republicans by supporting a "free and democratic Jewish commonwealth" and "unrestricted Jewish immigration and colonization." Convinced that it was "not the good will of individuals that counted for us," he told the AZEC that "the demonstration of mass public opinion" carried the planks. With both Dewey and Roosevelt strongly endorsing their respective planks calling for a Jewish state in Palestine, the AZEC little more than a year after Silver took control seemed on the verge of a magnificent victory.[36]

Chapter Six

Silver in many ways was a very simple man. There was really no grey area, nothing in between, in political or personal decisions. It was really *Entweg* or *oder, Kinderlach,* you want me, I'm here. You don't want me, I'm not here.

—Harold Manson, 4 November 1971

Mr. Cleveland is out gunning for you in a big way.

—Miriam [Cohen] to Nahum Goldmann, 1 March 1944

When Silver entered the room, Wise began to tremble. I was color-blind to this. I always laughed at Silver.

—Nahum Goldmann, 12 April 1975

I was told yesterday that Silver had in conversation alluded to me as senile—my co-chairman. How charming it all is. Working for a great people is to work by the side of the littlest men.

—Stephen S. Wise to his wife, 1943

In the end Silver crushed Wise and Dr. Goldman.

—Arthur Lourie, 9 June 1975

At various times from 1943 to 1945 Silver clashed vigorously with other Jewish leaders, especially Stephen S. Wise and Nahum Goldmann, as well as less stridently with officials in the Roosevelt administration. Much of the conflict revolved around conflicting procedural strategies in Washington, the level of confidence in Roosevelt's promises, the relative weight of rescue activities versus statehood efforts, and the perception that Silver was anti-Democratic (or even pro-Republican). But some of the conflict is attributable to the personalities involved. Silver, Wise, Goldmann, and others who emerged as central players in the mid-1950s had strong egos, overpowering personalities, debating greatness, fighting spirits, and deep commitments to the correctness of their approaches. Silver's enormous capacity to enjoy life, to laugh and to make others laugh, and even to question himself, remained at home in Cleveland. His "enemies" in Washington saw only his tough and uncompromising "leadership persona." And they resented him for it.

On 20 December 1944 Silver announced his resignation as co-chairman of the AZEC and as chairman of its executive committee. This resignation was the culmination of weeks if not months of difficult dealings with Stephen S. Wise, his co-chairman, and came in the immediate context of a second try at steering the Palestine resolutions, tabled the previous spring, through Congress.[1]

The drama began when Silver, meeting with Senator Taft in Washington twice in early September to discuss the resolution, suggested a letter of inquiry from Taft to Secretary of War Stimson to learn the War Department's present attitude. Henry L. Stimson (1867–1950) was a New York attorney who served as secretary of war (1911–13) under President Taft, secretary of state (1929–33) under President Hoover, and secretary of war (1940–45) under President Roosevelt. Should the response be encouraging, Taft seemed eager to assemble the Foreign Relations Committee again, and Taft informed Silver on 12 September that he had written to Stimson and that Wagner had talked with Stimson as well. While awaiting the reply from Stimson, Silver discussed reintroducing the resolution with several congressmen and arranged for AZEC executive personnel, together with Senator Wagner (1877–1953), to meet with Assistant Secretary of War McCloy. The son of poor German immigrants who grew up in a New York City basement tenement and entered New York State Democratic politics in 1904, Wagner was elected to the U.S. Senate in 1926 and reelected four times. He played a critical role in drafting and sponsoring New Deal legislation, especially the National Labor Relations or "Wagner" Act, which created the National Labor Relations Board. Senator Wagner, like Senator Taft, was a strong supporter of a Jewish state in Palestine throughout World War II. McCloy told Wagner and the Zionists on 20 September that the War Department was not yet ready to withdraw its objections to the resolution, but he said that he would discuss the matter further with Stimson, as he himself had become quite sympathetic to the resolution, though he thought supporters could wait a "few weeks" until the war ended.[2]

Then on 10 October, Stimson removed one obstacle by informing Senator Taft, who had badgered him throughout the summer and fall, that military considerations no longer stood in the way of the Wagner-Taft Palestine resolution. On 15 October the president, in a letter sent through Senator Wagner to the zoa convention, endorsed the Palestine plank in the Democratic Platform. On 30 October the azec with Silver in the chair unanimously agreed to move ahead with "activities in behalf of our resolution" and, if there was no opposition from the State Department, to push for reintroduction of the bill in Congress. Silver, Nahum Goldmann, and Wise met therefore with Edward R. Stettinius, Jr., the secretary of state, on 9 November. A prematurely white-haired corporation executive (executive vice-president of General Motors and chairman of the board of United States Steel) with dark eyebrows, a handsome, tanned face and a quick smile, Stettinius resigned from U.S. Steel in 1940 to devote himself full-time to government activities in the Roosevelt administration. He chaired the War Resources Board, directed lend-lease, and in September of 1943 FDR appointed him undersecretary of state and then in December

1944 after the resignation of the ailing Cordell Hull, secretary of state, from which position he would become one of the architects of the United Nations.[3]

Wise's account of this 9 November meeting, his statement five weeks later that "Dr. Silver had acted in grossest violation of decisions of the Executive Committee," and his conclusion that "Dr. Silver . . . overrode the objections both of Congressman Bloom and Sen. Wagner and had invited defeat in the Senate Committee" are contradicted by the minutes of the AZEC Executive Committee, Stettinius's account, and records of the Department of State.[4]

The three leaders asked Stettinius if, now that Stimson had removed the military objections and the president had endorsed the Palestine plank of the Democratic Platform, they could urge reintroduction of the bill in Congress. Stettinius agreed to discuss the matter with the president and he did so the next day. On 15 November 1944 the secretary of state telephoned Wise to say that "the President feels that putting the resolution through now would just stir things up," and the executive committee as well as the full AZEC discussed this reply on 21 November. Silver argued that the emergency council should make a powerful effort to change Roosevelt's mind, while Wise argued that the matter should now be left alone. The emergency council finally decided "that efforts should be made once more to obtain clearance from the president, through Senator Wagner, and perhaps others," though Wise expressed reluctance about seeing Senator Taft rather than Senator Wagner (Taft, he felt, was unlikely to be able to see Roosevelt) and hesitation about including Silver and perhaps another executive committee member in a meeting with Senator Wagner.[5]

Wise went ahead on his own (as did Goldmann) and met with Stettinius, and the latter informed Wise on 2 December 1944 that the president still opposed reintroducing the resolution. Stettinius noted in his *Diaries* that Wise was "very happy about it," and there is no doubt that Wise was disinclined to do anything to change the mind of Roosevelt. In fact, Wise and Goldmann made vigorous efforts to convince Senator Wagner and Representative Sol Bloom to postpone consideration of the resolution, while Silver had come to Washington to make every effort to get the State Department and the president to change their opposition to the resolution. Senator Connally had told Silver that "State and the White House do not want action on your Resolution; I know this authoritatively; you are being doubled-crossed." Wise's intensive efforts to foil Silver were reflected in Representative Bloom's complaint to Rabbi Israel Goldstein that he did not know what to do ("poor little me," he moaned) because American Jewry spoke with many voices: "one moment Rabbi Silver tells [me] to go ahead with the hearings, and the next Rabbi Wise tells [me] to delay."[6]

Notwithstanding Wise's entreaties, the Senate Foreign Relations Committee opened hearings on S.R. 247 (Wagner-Taft), and the House Foreign Affairs Committee did the same on H.R. 418 (Wright-Compton). In fact, the House easily reported the resolution out of committee on 29 November 1944, and there was strong support once again in the Senate as well. Senator Wagner, whom Silver met with one day after coming to Washington, told Silver that he had no intention of seeing the president to persuade him to remove his objections, but that he looked forward eagerly to his own testimony on behalf of the resolution before the committee the next morning. So did Senator Taft, who also made a strong plea for the resolution before the Foreign Relations Committee on 29 November. The committee, however, voted 11–5 to delay action one week, because Senator Connally insisted they must know for sure whether State opposed the resolution.[7]

Thomas T. Connally (1877–1963), a Texas attorney, state legislator, and county prosecutor, was elected to the House of Representatives in 1916 and reelected five consecutive times until 1928 when he was elected to his first of four consecutive Senate terms. A member of the House Foreign Affairs Committee for twelve years and of the Senate Committee on Foreign Relations from 1929, Connally took over the chair of the latter from 1941 to 1946. Connally pleaded for the secretary of state to testify and Stettinius agreed to do so as soon as possible. Immediately after the 29 November vote, Senators Wagner and Silver decided to try to persuade Stettinius, and through him the president, to support the resolution. Wagner wrote a letter to the president on 2 December reminding him of his 15 October endorsement of a Jewish commonwealth in Palestine. The decisive meeting with Stettinius was set for 4 December 1944, two days before Stettinius's testimony.[8]

When Silver and Wagner arrived in Stettinius's office, Stettinius showed them to their great surprise a telegram from Wise sent on 3 December and intended ("in confidence") only for Stettinius and the "chief." Wise, on behalf of his "many associates," said that the American Jewish community would not be displeased if State and the president continued their opposition to the resolution, and that the president could count on Wise to defend him. This message reiterated a cable Wise had sent Stettinius on 1 December in which he promised to support the president if he continued to feel "postponement necessary." (On 21 December Roosevelt wrote to Wise and expressed his appreciation for Wise's efforts.) Silver felt that this telegram "exposed our nakedness, revealed our division and confusion of counsel . . . and sealed the fate of the Palestine resolution," though Stettinius politely listened to the arguments of Wagner and Silver, explained how the Palestine resolution would embarrass Roosevelt when he met with Churchill and Stalin, promised Silver he would talk to Roosevelt about a written statement on the resolution and, according to Silver, even assured them he would not appear before the Foreign Relations Committee.[9]

Two days later, however, on 6 December, Stettinius testified "on five minutes notice." Speaking very vaguely, he said that the president, "from the standpoint of the general international situation at this time" (meaning the opposition of Arab governments), did not want the resolution passed. Nevertheless, the Senate Foreign Relations Committee (and Silver) wanted a response in writing from the president, and its members told Stettinius they would wait two more days and then vote. Stettinius did not return to the committee on 8 December, nor did the Senators hear directly from the president, but the secretary of state returned to the committee on 11 December, immediately after talking to Wise, to tell committee members of strong Arab opposition and to release a statement from the Department of State (not from Roosevelt) that "passage of the resolution at the present time would be unwise from the standpoint of the general international situation." (A few days later Roosevelt told Stettinius that "you handled that well in my absence and I hope I don't have to hear about it again for awhile," and Wise communicated this to Silver after he met with Stettinius.)[10]

The Senate was stopped by the State Department's opposition of 11 December, though two-thirds of the Senators present at the meeting signed a statement of support for the resolution and made clear that were it not for the Stettinius/Roosevelt opposition they would have approved it. Officially, however, that same day the committee voted 10–8 for postponement, and the resolution was dead in the House as well. Wise and some of his followers began immediately to plan how to make Silver the scapegoat for the failure of the resolution.[11]

This was not the first occasion on which Silver met interference, nor his first resignation. Several months earlier Nahum Goldmann, who was the Jewish Agency representative in Washington since the summer of 1943 when Weizmann opened a Jewish Agency office and who was a close ally of Wise, had embarrassed Silver and the AZEC by acting both as the head of an independent political bureau in Washington and against the emergency council's wishes.[12]

Goldmann, who would later refer to himself frequently as "the last aristocrat," negotiated for several decades with the world's greatest leaders. A statesman without a state and a tremendously egocentric man, he impressed countless heads of state when he negotiated skillfully as if he actually represented a legal, corporate entity rather than diaspora Jewry. A close friend of Stephen S. Wise, who possessed numerous passports for his work in Washington, Europe, and Palestine, Goldmann played a lone hand in his Washington lobbying and considered himself one of the leaders of the American Jewish community.

The first conflict with Goldmann took place in November 1943 when Silver learned that Goldmann had met with Samuel Rosenman (on 3 November) and Representative Bloom (on 22 September, 6 October, and 29 October) immediately following visits and phone calls from Silver, despite the agreement signed a few months earlier by Goldmann that he would not make contacts in Washington "without first apprising Silver." For Silver this created "an impossible situation," and he told Goldman he would inform the emergency council that "there cannot be two independent political bureaus working for Palestine in the United States" and that he would not allow Goldmann to "unilaterally define the scope and authority" of his work. Goldmann wrote Silver a blistering (but true) letter, chiding him for "the impression that every conversation in Washington constitutes a state affair," accusing Silver of seeing government officials without consulting Wise, himself, and the emergency council, and explaining to Silver that "it is not possible every time a situation arises to phone to Cleveland to ascertain your views on the subject."[13]

Silver responded to Goldmann with considerable anger and sarcasm and reminded him "that while it is not possible every time a situation arises to phone to Cleveland to ascertain my views, you haven't been particularly burdened with such long distance conversations to my best knowledge." The truth, of course, was that they tried to avoid conversations with each other; Silver tried to have Henry Montor—with whom he was in daily contact—communicate for him with Goldman, while the latter was himself none too eager to speak with Silver outside of AZEC meetings.[14]

The second conflict with Goldmann took place in December 1943 when Goldmann preempted Silver and met with Lt. Col.

Harold Hoskins, a Roosevelt envoy to the Middle East. Goldmann explained to Silver that he would never have done this had not Hoskins "telephoned several times saying that he wanted to see me" about his mission to Ibn Saud. Two months later in February 1944 Goldmann convinced Rosenman, just as Silver and some AZEC leaders were negotiating with Rosenman for a meeting with Roosevelt, to include non-Zionists at the meeting. One of Weizmann's closest associates, indeed, his factotum in the United States, Meyer Weisgal, recalled that "Nahum Goldmann worked one side of the street, the Emergency Council worked the other; occasionally they bumped into each other in the dark."[15]

With this "bump," Goldmann greatly angered "Mr. Cleveland," as he often referred to Silver in letters, and Silver, according to Goldmann's office assistant, was "out gunning for you in a big way." Ever since Goldmann had first informed Silver early in 1943 that he was initiating "discussions about our plans for the future of Palestine with my friends in Washington," he tried to keep AZEC leaders informed of his meetings with the secretary of state and other high officials. Nevertheless, he neither asked permission of the AZEC executive committee nor paid attention to its requests when various members, including "Mr. Cleveland," urged him to accept its discipline. And, to make his situation worse, he liked to boast to people that the secretary of state "saw me first and then saw Silver."[16]

Goldmann had promised Silver in writing immediately after Silver took over the executive committee of the AZEC that "all previous arrangements concerning our respective functions would be maintained; all public relations and propaganda activities are the task of the emergency council." Silver did not forget this promise and wrote to Chaim Weizmann shortly after the Rosenman affair about Goldmann's usurpation of AZEC territory. He reminded Weizmann of Goldmann's agreement to "consult me before going to our government officials and to send me reports of such visits, neither of which has been done." Weizmann distributed funds to the Washington office of the Jewish Agency, which Goldmann

125

headed, and though he was a close ally of Goldmann, he seemed an appropriate person for Silver to ask for help. In a letter dated 1 May 1944, Weizmann apologized to Silver for any "personal embarrassment" Goldmann's work had caused, urged the "fullest co-ordination between the Emergency Council and the Agency office," and suggested that a little "goodwill and harmony" between the two leaders would solve the problem. Neither man, however, ever really tried to meet the other half way. [17]

The final conflicts were twofold. First, Goldmann sent an insulting letter to Silver in May 1944 that suggested not only that Silver had "bullied" Wise but that "it would have been easy to ascertain, before the [Palestine] resolution was introduced, that the War Department would regard it as untimely and it would have been wiser not to introduce it." Second, Goldmann met on 9 August and 14 August 1944 with Stettinius—meetings about which Silver was told nothing in advance and after which Silver wrote Goldmann "a personal word expressing my own astonishment and amazement that such decisions intimately related to my Zionist duties here should have been taken without consultation with me." Goldmann wrote Weizmann, Wise, and Silver that Stettinius had told him the Palestine resolution must be postponed, and he told Silver that the resolution should not be introduced again "unless the Administration definitely promises not to raise any objections." To Wise and Weizmann he criticized Silver strongly and hoped they could "deter [him] from using the same tactics again to try to obtain what is unobtainable." [18]

Silver, exhausted ("I am weary of it all") and unable to function effectively, resigned from the emergency council in August 1944, noting that

> the continued functioning of two Zionist political bureaus in Washington creates an impossible situation. [I] brought the matter up on several occasions previously but nothing has been done. [I] cannot continue in this fashion and [am] submitting [my] resignation. [19]

It took numerous appeals and much stroking from the highest levels of the Zionist leadership as well as promises from Goldmann "to behave" before Silver would return to the leadership in September 1944.

At best, however, there was only a superficial truce between these two proud, talented, energetic, persuasive men with strong personalities and equally strong egos. In June 1944 Goldmann noted, "my relation with Silver are [sic] unchanged . . . I do what I do and, at the moment, he isn't doing very much." Goldmann hit the mark; only if one of the two was preoccupied with other matters or was on vacation was there "less opportunity for friction." Aware of this, Goldmann took advantage of any opportunity "to get him [Silver] out"; he asked Weizmann how to "get rid of him," or at least to "arrange a set-up whereby he should not be in control but share the responsibility with Wise and myself." Goldmann would eventually accomplish this, but not until 1949.[20]

Wise, of course, accomplished both much sooner, though only temporarily. A tall, proud, dignified, sincere rabbi, already a legendary orator and world personality by the time of World War I, Wise had been deeply committed to the Jewish people and Zionism for half a century when Silver moved into his territory in 1943. Silver largely ignored Wise's advice and scorned his influence with Roosevelt; Wise, in response, became bitter and jealous. In his last few years of life, burdened with cancer, he tried his very best to fight for the issues, not his position, but his deep hurt over his rejection by Silver and his allies left him without the enormous kindness and love with which he had engaged in his earlier Zionist activities. His interference in the Palestine resolution affair went deeper than merely behind-the-back (and some open) machinations (private meetings, secret communications, unauthorized phone calls, ad hoc committees) in order to embarrass Silver. Early in 1944, after a meeting between Roosevelt and Wise and Silver had been arranged, Wise convinced the president to postpone it (the meeting never took place) because Wise had to be on the West Coast and he would not allow Silver to see Roosevelt alone for fear of losing his special relationship with the chief executive.[21]

In November and December 1944, on at least three occasions, Wise tried to manipulate the emergency council to convene meetings without Silver present or to call meetings without leaving the requisite time between the call and the meeting. In October, without Silver's being aware of it, Wise arranged for a private interview with Roosevelt. Both Lipsky and Neumann joined Silver (who spoke of a "spiritual rottenness in the movement") in denouncing Wise before the executive committee. Further, Wise's continual campaigning in September and October for Roosevelt and subsequent defense of and apology for him angered Silver, whose strong commitment was to an emergency council and a Zionist movement not tied to either political party. "Our Court Jew," he told the press after his resignation, "has always shielded, defended and apologized for an Administration with which he is politically entangled." Earlier, during the presidential campaign, he wrote to Neumann that he had seen an ad in the *New York Times* in which Wise was "going on the 'stump'" for Democratic candidates. Silver could not reconcile Wise's campaign speeches for Roosevelt "with the position of neutrality on American politics which our Emergency Council and our leaders are supposed to maintain" and noted that he consistently refused to endorse or campaign for any candidate "on the ground of my position as Executive Chairman of the AZEC."[22]

On this issue Silver spoke and wrote often. While his enemies called him a Republican, Silver quite accurately denied this accusation. A dedicated and activist liberal, he never spoke on behalf of Wilkie's candidacy nor did he advocate Roosevelt's defeat in 1940. In 1944 he once again voted for President Roosevelt, despite his public criticisms of his foreign policy. On the eve of the 1946 gubernatorial and congressional elections he still refused to endorse either party or any candidate, insisting that "I belong to no Party; I serve the interests of no political party." Public criticism of Roosevelt's actions vis-à-vis the Jews and a Jewish nation was not identical with membership in the Republican Party, but was, in the words of Silver, *yesurin shel ahavah,* constructive criticism by one who cared deeply. [23]

It was clearly Silver's perception that as the emergency council, which had been virtually moribund under Wise's sole leadership, began to show new life and to get results in 1934–44, Wise began to reassert his primary position and to treat Silver as a secondary and even negligible officer. Most of all, Silver did not trust Roosevelt, and Wise's close alliance with and enormous confidence in the president (he addressed his letters to the president to "Dear Chief" and "Dear Skipper" and received personal responses from Roosevelt) gnawed at Silver, who was convinced that only mass pressure on Congress not "backstairs diplomacy" would ever move Roosevelt. Just before his second resignation in December, Silver expressed his feelings about Roosevelt this way:

> The President is not sold on Palestine. He does not understand our movement. I doubt whether he has read a single memorandum which we have sent to him. He entertains towards our movement the same attitude of general good will and uninvolved benignancy which he entertains towards a dozen other worthy causes, but having no intention of pressing for them vigorously on the international scene. Engrossed as he is in a global war, he cannot be counted on to go out of his way for us unless he is goaded and prodded into it by the pressure of public opinion and by a real and earnest insistence on the part of a determined and not easily appeased Jewish community. [24]

It was Silver's deep feeling that Roosevelt had done next to nothing for the Jewish people during the past few years and that the "Court Jew," as he often called Wise, had always shielded, defended, and apologized for an administration with which he was politically entangled.

Silver despaired of carrying out emergency council policy in a situation where the "duality or multiplicity of leadership resulted in confusion and frustration," and he was "persuaded that had the conduct of our affairs been left in my hands, we could have . . . persuaded the President to change his mind and had the resolution adopted by the Congress of the United States." Unable to work effectively with "Dr. Wise acting on his own, without the authority of the Emergency Council (in fact in clear contravention to the instruction of the Emergency Council)," he accused Wise of "treating the Zionist movement as a piece of personal property and bitterly resenting any new leadership which threatens his monopoly." On 20 December 1944 Silver resigned again and set off the "Silver-Wise Affair." Joining him were, among others, Harry L. Shapiro, the executive director of the emergency council, and Harold Manson, the director of information of the emergency council, supporters of Silver who told the *New York Times* that Silver's resignation was "irrevocable." Silver, although he confirmed his resignation, refused to discuss details of the resignation with the *Times* or any reporters and the stories in the press (except some of the Yiddish press that made Silver the "people's choice") largely reflected the views of Wise and his associates. The most succinct and insightful analysis of the "political fight" came from Goldmann. He noted that Silver and Wise could not get along with each other because of "personal reasons and because of differences as to tactics."[25]

The emergency council quickly elected Wise chairman (on 28 December) and on 2 January 1945 reorganized the structure to give him and his followers complete control of emergency council policy. Disappointed Zionists throughout the United States, however, insisted on Silver's recall to the leadership, and several of his supporters formed the American Zionist Policy Committee (with an office and a small staff) to organize these pro-Silver leaders and propel them into action. They generated, as Melvin Urofsky has correctly observed, "a constant stream of newspaper articles, speeches and testimonial dinners," whose "unprecedented" quantity "shocked" one Zionist "beyond comprehension" and almost all of which Silver collected in his files.[26]

Typical is the letter Philip Slomovitz, editor of the Detroit *Jewish News,* wrote in April 1945 to Rabbi Leon Fram, president of the Zionist Organization of Detroit and a strong Silver supporter:

> My position in support of the resolution urging that Doctor Silver be recalled to the leadership of the Zionist Emergency Council is well known. It is, therefore, a source of deep regret to me that I shall be unable to attend tonite's meeting.
>
> During the thirty months of my presidency of the Zionist Council of Detroit, I have had occasion to learn methods and procedures in Zionist policy. My associates and I on the Zionist Council have learned the meaning of firm action under Dr. Silver as compared with the weakness which preceded his administration, and which has again set in. The crisis which has been brought about by the most deplorable internal conflict had put an end to that firmness which was needed to protect the Zionist position.
>
> Those who know anything about the conflict which has set in our ranks know that the purge of Dr. Silver was preceded by a purge of some of the ablest men within the Zionist Organization, and that the entire issue was one of the selfish political motives which ought not to be tolerated in our movement.
>
> We had begun a militant policy of guaranteeing the security of the Zionist Movement. The elimination of Dr. Silver introduced a period of despair which gave encouragement to the Arabs and has encouraged the enemies of Zionism in a hostile State Department—in spite of the support we have received from both political parties and the over-whelming voice of our Congress.[27]

The anti-Silver group in the AZEC lost little time in distributing pamphlets and memos accusing Silver of having run the emergency council as the *Fuehrer* and asking if "his dictatorship is marching on?" Wise called Silver "reckless" and "irresponsible," as well as a "demagogue," while Robert Szold, a former ZOA president, noted

131

that "people mistake Silver's braggadacio and the capacity to insult and call names, for courage." The telegrams, resolutions, and rallies with which Silver and his supporters flooded the country forced the Wise faction of the emergency council to establish a peace committee and to explore with Silver his return to leadership. Though the offer from the executive committee on 13 July 1945 again involved serving as co-chair with Wise, real power clearly lay with Silver, who during several meetings with his opponents refused anything less than chairing the executive committee and controlling the key appointments. It was, as Emanuel Neumann noted, a "whopper of a triumph."[28]

Silver and Wise had known each other for many years before this conflict came into the open, and, as one might expect from two men with such strong senses of their own self-importance, their relationship had suffered difficulties since 1917. Wise's second letter to Silver on 7 May 1917 complained with scarcely veiled spite that although he, Wise, had written "a few days ago" to congratulate him on the offer from The Temple in Cleveland, I have had no word from you in reply, but I know you are a very busy man and your word, however deferred, will be welcome when it comes." Wise followed this gentle reprimand with an appeal to Silver's "conscience and judgment," accusing him (wrongly) of disguising his strong Zionist commitment in order to secure the Cleveland pulpit. Reminding Silver that these "words of counsel" came from "a man so much older than you," he joined Silver to retrieve his "self-respect."[29]

Over the next two decades, however, Wise not only became convinced of Silver's devotion to Zionism but praised Silver frequently in letters and interviews as "a remarkable man . . . a most ardent Zionist . . . a powerful, passionate [speaker]." As early as 1916 Wise wrote that Silver was "one of the strong, earnest, gifted young men in the . . . Jewish ministry"; in 1920 Wise told an Indiana reporter that Silver "is the finest orator I have ever heard" and wrote to Silver after he spoke at the New York City Free

Synagogue that his lecture "stirred the congregation to its depths"; in 1924 he wrote to Silver that his Carnegie Hall lecture (on 27 May) was "the most remarkable address I have ever heard." He was no less generous in his praise a few days after ousting Silver and taking complete control of the AZEC, calling Silver, with amazing hypocrisy, one of the "most gifted and brilliant men in American Jewish life."[30]

In addition to the reasons set forth, some of the tension that erupted between Silver and Wise as the emergency council took on a revitalized role after September 1943 may have resulted from the simple fact that, as Wise noted in 1917, he was "a man so much older than [Silver]." When Wise appealed to Silver in 1943 to take over much of the emergency council he indicated that "the burdens of the office exceeded my physical capacity" (he had cancer) and that "I am tired." Nonetheless, he also believed—rightly—that the office was his by right of service and achievement in the American Jewish community. So when the critical events of the fall of 1944 unfolded, Wise could not remain uninvolved ("I was not then prepared," he noted in 1945, "to accept the role of retirement."), and his eagerness to make a contribution to American Jewry took a form that Silver, quite understandably, could not tolerate.[31]

Silver's inability to function under such circumstances was not necessarily inevitable, but his personality was not one to easily take direction from others or to operate in a subordinate role. In virtually every area of his professional career he chaired the committees, directed the staffs, or acted alone, and he had done so with extraordinary organizational skill. It was not of course true, as Nahum Goldmann claimed, that Silver "could only function when he had absolute authority," nor do "authoritarian" and "autocratic," terms used by one historian of this period, seem to describe his mode of operation. Though Silver sought control (full control, in fact) of the AZEC, he was not a dictator; he took elaborate pains to encourage open debate and closed votes and to have a mandate from the AZEC for each of his actions. He could not, on the other hand, work together with another strong leader of another organization who openly sought to preempt him or with a former strong leader of his own organization who would neither yield power gracefully nor compromise his confidence in Roosevelt. Goldmann did perceive correctly that Silver "lacked the gift of working under someone else and in collaboration with people who felt themselves to be on an equal footing with him," and Wise insightfully noted that "one strange mistake was made by Dr. Silver, namely, that I was to serve as the nominal head of the Emergency Council—as an 'elder statesman'—and that he was to be its only leader."[32]

Wise quite properly felt himself to be an equal, and although his physical condition by 1943–44 might have dictated a less active role, after four decades of outstanding leadership of American Jewry he could not sit this one out. And Silver, when asked to be something less than the manager (a position rightfully his), did not easily join the team. Goldmann in a letter to Weizmann hit the mark when he said that Silver "is not the kind of man with whom one can make compromises—either he wins or he loses." Silver believed Wise had a "hysterical prestige-complex," while Wise viewed Silver as a "dictator" and his leadership as a "regime." Each accusation had some truth in it, but the larger truth was the great unlikeliness that these two giants of American Jewry—with egos as large as their roles and radically different approaches to Zionist political tactics—would ever share a leadership role. Indeed, even after Silver's return to AZEC the dislike of the two men for each other continued and is traceable in numerous documents. Goldmann was quite correct when he noted several months after their "reconciliation" that "the Wise-Silver situation does not get better." It never did.[33]

Chapter Seven

I fight hard but I always fight fair.

—Abba Hillel Silver, 27 January 1948

[Silver] is vain . . . something of a megalomaniac, but
. . . I feel that if you turned a little of your charm on to
him, you could get him into your pocket.

—Lord Inverchapel,
16 November 1946

Silver was the Jewish people in its virility. [He] was like a
bull in a china closet.

—Rose Halperin, 27 July 1974

On 31 August 1945, shortly after succeeding the deceased president, and against the advice of the State Department, Harry S.
Truman wrote the new Labor Party Prime Minister, Clement Attlee, and urged Great Britain to permit one hundred thousand
Jewish refugees to enter Palestine. Truman combined a deep sympathy for the suffering of the displaced persons in Europe, a sincere
desire to take a step toward Jewish statehood, and a strong sense
that on the eve of mayoral elections in New York this would be
politically popular. There is abundant evidence for the latter conclusion, and one analyst wrote that "Among informed non-Jews
. . . pro-Zionist opinions were virtually as prevalent as among Jews
in general."[1]

Truman did not pluck the figure one hundred thousand out of the air. Earl G. Harrison, a deeply respected dean of the University of Pennsylvania Law School, former commissioner of Immigration and Naturalization, and the American representative on the Inter-Governmental Committee on Refugees, suggested this figure in his well-publicized late summer report on the atrocious conditions of the D.P. (displaced persons) camps, and the Jewish Agency in Palestine had petitioned Whitehall earlier for precisely this number. It was in fact Silver together with David Ben-Gurion who had unsuccessfully presented the request for one hundred thousand immigration certificates to the Colonial Secretary, George Glenvil Hall, when they were in London for the Zionist Conference of August 1945, a conference at which Silver on 3 August unleashed an unusually militant speech. Hall, according to Chaim Weizmann's account, was quite sympathetic to the request, acknowledging the Jewish refugee dilemma but pointing out that Labor had only been in power two weeks. Others, however, note Hall's shock and disgust. Whatever Hall's real feelings were, Harrison's report only added support to this request, for on a "purely humanitarian basis with no reference to ideological or political considerations," he wrote Truman, the surviving Jews perceived "no acceptable or even decent solution for their future other than Palestine."[2]

In July, prior to leaving for Potsdam to meet with Stalin and Churchill, Truman had received the results of a widespread and well-organized petition campaign: a petition on Palestine signed by governors of thirty-two states and a similar round-robin bearing the signatures of 197 members of the House and forty-one Senators. Surely this stimulated Truman's comment to Churchill in a letter of 24 July that "there is a great interest in America in the Palestine problem; it continue[s] to provoke passionate protest from Americans." And upon his return to America on 16 August Truman told the nation that "we [the United States] want to let as many of the Jews into Palestine as it is possible to let into that country." At the same time, however, the Arab states were privately given the standard assurance that Truman's plea to Attlee represented no fundamental alteration in U.S. policy toward Palestine. Silver applauded Truman's entreaty to Attlee: "all through the years of the war," he told a Zionist convention, "and until 31st of last year . . . nothing whatsoever, but *absolutely nothing*, was done by our Government in behalf of our cause."[3]

The British understandably feared that one hundred thousand Jews would only be the start of an immense Jewish immigration to Palestine and that this would suddenly turn British policy from pro-Arab to pro-Jewish. For them, the White Paper of 1939 still dictated their actions; they were strongly opposed to open or mass immigration in the fall of 1945; hence the British never seriously considered Truman's one hundred thousand request. Silver dates his own rejection of "Weizmann 'moderation'" to this fall, though he had clearly assumed a mantle of militancy much earlier. What he did clearly determine at this time in his own mind was both the utter hopelessness of achieving rescue for the D.P.s or Jewish statehood with the British in control of Palestine, and he became consistently hostile and nasty when discussing Great Britain's policies or its officials. Even Menachem Begin, no easy man to please, noted about this time that Silver made a "great impression" on him and strongly supported the need "to fight the British by extra-legal means."[4]

At the very least, Silver felt that Weizmann's methods were useless and, worse, often quite dangerous. He referred to Weizmann's statements in the fall of 1945 as the "soft appeasement line" and sought means to control Weizmann when he arrived in the United States in November, lest he "confuse our people and our Government." Silver wanted Weizmann to cease acting the role of the "wise and patient statesman" and to become instead "forceful and aggressive." The real danger, Silver believed, was that political leaders and the press would embrace the quiet Weizmann as the Zionist moderate and paint Silver and his colleagues as "extremists." This tactic, successfully used in Great Britain, would vitiate what for Silver was "the classic demand of Zionism—Jewish statehood" and that dictated the need to cease the postures of "moderation and patience." Silver had concluded even before this time that only "forceful resistance" would succeed, a "desperate" but single alternative.[5]

Nevertheless, Weizmann and Silver maintained cordial relations and communicated frequently. On 16 September, the same day that Attlee wrote to Truman asking for more time to respond to both the short-term problem of the refugees and the larger problem of Palestine, and, most importantly, when he rejected the request for one hundred thousand on the grounds that putting Jews "at the head of the queue" would be "disastrous for the Jews," Weizmann phoned Silver with the full contents of Attlee's cable. Despite the rejection, the British were certainly sensitive to the human tragedy of the D.P.s. But while they debated how to respond to the humanitarian dilemma of the refugees, and while Attlee and Truman as well as their ministers and secretaries corresponded privately about Palestine, Silver as chairman of the emergency council together with Stephen Wise kept the pressure on Truman.[6]

On 23 September Silver and Wise released a statement that said that Attlee's counteroffer to Truman, to transfer some thirty-five thousand Jewish refugees to North Africa, was totally inadequate, and that Truman should prevent this "shameful injustice." A few days later the emergency council ran an ad in dozens of newspapers calling on Attlee to open Palestine to all Jewish refugees and to establish a Jewish state there. On 29 September Silver and Wise argued their case directly to Truman at the White House and the next evening twenty-two thousand people filled Madison Square Garden for an emergency council rally, while forty-five thousand more demonstrated simultaneously outside.[7]

Ironically, Silver was aware of two striking facts in August and September of 1945: one, that there were barely fifty thousand Jewish D.P.s in Western Europe, and two, that the Jews of Palestine had not the means to absorb even these fifty thousand! Even more crucial, he knew that if the "British and American governments did grant us a large number of certificates without a decision on the major issue of a Jewish State," it would be "a severe political blow!" What Silver meant in this letter to a Zionist colleague was that Attlee and Bevin and Truman and Byrnes could have admitted all the Jewish immigrants and instantly deprived the Jews of their fundamental argument for a Jewish state! The solution? For Silver it was simply to continue to teach Americans, Jews and non-Jews, about political Zionism. This meant, in effect, to minimize the philanthropic and humanitarian arguments ("Save Jewish Refugees") and to stress Jewish statehood. This had been of course Silver's own emphasis for some time, but he more explicitly articulated it to his coworkers in the Zionist movement after the summer of 1945 by urging them to assert the political will of a nation in the making rather than plead for compassion. [8]

Silver also continued to resent the efforts (he called them "interference") of Nahum Goldmann, whom he called "the floating Jewish ambassador in Washington." He felt that he and the emergency council, exclusively, ought to handle lobbying with the administration, and he made "difficulties" for Goldmann, who complained frequently and bitterly about it to Palestine leaders. Their conflict would peak the following summer, after the Anglo-American commission of inquiry had submitted its report and Goldmann arrived in Washington with an alternative from the executive of the Jewish Agency. [9]

But in the early days of October 1945, Ernest Bevin, the dominant figure in Attlee's cabinet and the architect of British Palestine policy while he was foreign secretary (1945–51), first proposed a joint Anglo-American investigatory committee to the cabinet. By the middle of the month the suggestion was being discussed favorably in Washington. The British government hoped to educate Americans on Palestine realities (the impossibility of using Palestine as the only solution to the Jewish refugee problem) and to convince them (or others) to take some D.P.s by proposing that the

United States and Great Britain establish a joint committee to study the displaced persons issue and the "absorptive capacity" of Palestine and "other countries outside Europe." Despite strong appeals from Wise and Silver that all the "facts are already well-known" and that what were needed were "immediate concrete measures," a very strong letter from Silver and Wise to the president ("there is no need of further commissions and inquiries"), and Truman's own suspicions that the British were just delaying the decision, the president responded positively to the committee, though he (successfully) demanded that Palestine be the center of discussion and that the committee report within four months. [10]

Truman's acceptance, of course, was preceded by the usual assurances from the secretary of state to the Arabs (made on 18 October), who had strongly criticized Truman's appeal for refugee admissions to Palestine, and by instructing the secretary to release the Roosevelt–Ibn Saud letters of spring 1945 that assured the Arabs that nothing would be done in Palestine without their agreement. Bevin accepted these conditions and announced the committee's establishment in the House of Commons on 13 November 1945 with incredible optimism: "I will stake my political future on solving this problem. . . ." On the same day Truman also announced the formation of the committee; Stephen Wise and Silver following an AZEC Executive Committee meeting on 14 November immediately wired him that "it was with the deepest regret that we learned of the acceptance by our government of the British proposal," and Silver for the next week daily denounced the proposed committee and the U.S. government ("it has fallen into a carefully prepared trap") to the press. [11]

The Anglo-American committee began hearings in Washington on 4 January 1946. Silver, who firmly believed that Bevin was "determined to liquidate the Balfour Declaration" and that the committee was little more than a "British strategy to prevent Jews from entering Palestine" (after all, he pointed out, several government commissions had already "inquired"), refused to testify and urged Zionist leaders in America and then in Jerusalem to do the same. He argued to his colleagues that the committee would not bring the solution one step nearer, as it could only ascertain well-known facts. He agreed with Albert Einstein who testified on 11 January and told the committee that it was a "waste of time." In November and December prior to the start of the hearings when American Zionist leaders discussed the proper response to the proposed committee, Silver vigorously pursued the boycott suggestion. He argued that Bevin's ultimate purpose was to destroy the Jewish national home, that Truman was "giving the Jews of America another double cross" because he "lacked the determination" to confront Attlee and Bevin, and that nothing would be gained by cooperating with the "enemy." The moderates, however, in America and then in Jerusalem triumphed, and Silver remained one of the few Zionist leaders to refuse to talk to the Anglo-American committee of inquiry.[12]

Despite Silver's boycott, other emergency council officials including Wise and Emanuel Neumann as well as world Zionist leaders such as Weizmann and Ben-Gurion, did testify, and Silver received lengthy reports of the committee's proceedings from Emanuel Neumann and Arthur Lourie, both of whom not only followed its hearings from London to Paris to Cairo to Jerusalem to Geneva but used code names in their "top secret" reports of lunches, dinners, and teas with committee members ("I have lunched with Harvey [Buxton], dined with Gray [McDonald], and had tea with Frances [Crum].") On 30 April 1946 after secret deliberations in Switzerland (carefully monitored by the Zionists) and private briefings for Attlee and Truman, the unanimous report was released to the public. Its conclusions included the recommendations that one hundred thousand Jewish refugees be immediately admitted into Palestine and that a binational state (NOT a Jewish state in the whole of Palestine), dominated neither by Jews nor Arabs, be established in Palestine.[13]

On the same day the report became public information, Truman announced that he had accepted the committee's recommendation to admit one hundred thousand Jewish refugees into Palestine, though he said nothing about the other nine recommendations except that they "require careful study." This made Attlee furious, for Truman had not consulted him at all before his announcement (despite Attlee's and Bevin's pleas that he do so) but laid "heavy burdens on us without lifting a little finger to help." Bevin too made the same claim; repeatedly he stated that the American government accepted only one-tenth of the report and ignored the rest. Attlee scuttled the committee's report within a day of its proclamation by stating (on 1 May) that "it would not be possible for the Government of Palestine to admit [100,000] immigrants unless and until [illegal armies] have been disbanded and their arms surrendered." In addition, the prime minister emphasized in the same speech to Parliament that the report would only be considered "as a whole," which one insightful M.P., Sydney Silverman, immediately understood (correctly) to mean that no part of the report would be implemented.[14]

In the final days of the committee's work in Switzerland, Truman was informed of the emerging recommendation to admit the one hundred thousand Jewish refugees and expressed his approval. On their return home in late April, two pro-Zionist American members of the committee, Bartley Crum and James McDonald, met with Silver in New York (28 April) and showed him the report. Why with Silver? Crum told him that "the man whom the Colonial Office and the Foreign Office fear most in the world is Rabbi Silver," and his support for the committee's report was crucial. Crum had spoken with Nahum Goldmann a few days earlier and probably heard from him how Silver would react, for Goldmann wrote Wise as the Anglo-American committee wrapped up its work that "our friend Abba will be burning to start protesting." Silver told McDonald that the report was "both bad and sad [and] a complete repudiation of the Zionist program," and told both of them that he would denounce the report because it rejected a Jewish state. Crum and McDonald explained to Silver that such a response would only turn Truman against the Zionists; why not, they suggested as a compromise, urge Truman to accept the recommendation about the one hundred thousand and postpone a decision on the rest? Crum suggested this same strategy (successfully) to Truman, who agreed to allow the Zionists (Silver and Neumann) to draft his response. They did so in Silver's handwriting; the AZEC as well as the administration made some changes the next day (29 April); and the statement was then released on 30 April.[15]

The emergency council, which clearly grasped that the report presented the Zionists with a dilemma, wasted no time in issuing a statement highly critical of all items in the report except the one hundred thousand recommendation—for which they carefully praised Truman's positive acceptance—because the report rejected "Jewish rights and aspirations." Silver urged local branches to stress the positive aspects and vigorously to attack the negative parts of the report: "Let's begin talking about a plan of action in our communities," he told AZEC local leaders, "not merely in relation to Congress but on the national scene [and] present this emergency to the American public." When Bevin and Attlee made their opposition to even the one hundred thousand quite clear, Silver suggested another in a long line of mass protests. It took place just a few hours after Bevin had told a Labor Party conference at Bournemouth that the United States had pushed Britain to allow the one hundred thousand Jews into Palestine to guarantee they would not come to America! The Madison Square Garden rally on 11 June 1946 featured Silver, and he responded to the British by reminding them of the $3,500,000,000 lend-lease loan pending in Congress (to prevent the collapse of the war-shattered British economy) and urging Americans to write their congressmen and inquire whether British pledges to repay a loan are any more to be trusted than a "shocking record of broken pledges" to facilitate a Jewish state.[16]

Thousands of Jewish Americans, keyed up by the Bevin statement, responded with letters and telegrams to Washington urging that approval of the loan be linked to the one hundred thousand visas, and the intensity of lobbying by the administration suggested concern over passage of the loan. But once again Rabbi Stephen Wise played a critical role, despite emergency council orders to the contrary, and he told Congress in response to an appeal from presidential adviser David Niles that the loan should be approved. Representative Sol Bloom, chairman of the House Foreign Affairs Committee, with the rabbi's permission read Wise's letter to the House on the second day of debate (8 July 1946). The Washington correspondent for the *Boston Herald* later wrote that "the most clear-cut factor in the shift of attitude was Stephen S. Wise's statement," and according to Silver, Wise "demoralized and scattered our friends in Congress."[17]

With Truman's 30 April 1946 acceptance of the one hundred thousand recommendation and lack of interest in the rest of the report, Bevin and the British grew steadily more angry at the Jews (Bevin rarely distinguished between Zionists and Jews and greatly exaggerated Jewish, or what he called "New York Zionist," political power in America), at the Americans, and particularly at Truman. James McDonald, the non-Jewish Zionist who had served on the Anglo-American committee of inquiry, felt that Bevin's "bitterness against Mr. Truman was almost pathological: it found its match only in his blazing hatred for his other scapegoats—the Jews."[18]

Frustrated by the lack of cooperation offered by the Jews (whether in Palestine or in America) and determined to maintain British control in the Middle East, Bevin met with Truman's understanding for his exasperation. The president early in June assured the British that the United States would transport the one hundred thousand Jews to Palestine and he appointed a cabinet committee on Palestine (and "alternates") to conduct discussions with the British (at their request) on how to implement the Anglo-American report. Early in July after meeting with Wise, Silver, and Goldmann, Truman issued a press release (2 July) reaffirming his commitment to Palestine, his hope that there is "no delay in pushing forward with [the 100,000]," and assuring Britain of American "technical and financial responsibility" for the homeless Jews. The pressure was on, but Attlee and Bevin, perhaps above all else, were eager for American cooperation and thus they were open to negotiations on the ten points of the report.[19]

The American delegation, eager to gain British acceptance of the report, was headed by Henry F. Grady (1882–1957). A native San Franciscan who received a doctorate in international finance from Columbia University (1927) and taught international trade at the University of California at Berkeley (1928–37), Grady had also made his mark in government work as a technical expert in commerce and diplomacy before the age of forty. He served as an assistant secretary of state (1937–41) under Roosevelt and took on one difficult special diplomatic assignment after another, including in 1946 supervising the Greek elections. From Greece he went to London as Secretary of State Byrnes's representative on the cabinet committee on Palestine. He found himself in London in July 1946, listening to a plan of the Colonial Office (to be known as the Morrison-Grady plan after Herbert Morrison introduced it in the House of Commons) which the British hoped would gain American acceptance. It was a complex proposal, almost identical to the provincial autonomy plan that Sir Douglas Harris of the Colonial Office had submitted anonymously to the Anglo-American committee months earlier, which had been rejected. To simplify, it would establish an autonomous Jewish province (with fertile land, extensive citrus farming, much of the coast, and a port) and an autonomous Arab province, though the British would have retained crucial powers (such as control over immigration) as the "administering authority." It was to be a binational state (a jointly administered Palestinian state, with Arab and Jewish parity, rather than either a Jewish or an Arab state) under a trusteeship; it had within it the basis for possible partition (Secretary of State Byrnes could not figure out how provincial autonomy or binationalism differed from partition, and he was not alone; for there were multiple partition

plans, some of which shaded into provincial autonomy and binationalism, but all of which challenged an uncompromising Zionist
sovereignty.). Finally, and, imperative for American cooperation—
it would have required no United States military or administrative
participation. Grady's delegation unanimously agreed to the program (24 July) and Attlee telegraphed Truman that he was thrilled
by the "cooperative spirit" of the Americans who had reached
agreement with the British in less than two weeks.[20]

Alas, the one hundred thousand were linked in the proposal to
the complicated constitutional procedures of provincial autonomy
or binationalism or cantonization or federalization (depending on
which analyst one reads!), and both Jewish as well as non-Jewish
pro-Zionists in the United States immediately attacked the scheme.
Within one day of Grady's cable to Washington, Silver was lobbying
vigorously in Washington to convince cabinet members to urge
Truman to reject the plan and the AZEC had begun to mobilize its
supporters. The executive of the emergency council urged Crum
and McDonald to see Truman and denounce Morrison-Grady,
easily convinced Robert Taft and Robert Wagner to denigrate the
report in the Senate (Taft called it a "cynical plan," Wagner a
"deceitful device"), and according to Silver's report of a long conversation with David Niles, quickly sold Washington on the notion
that the "Grady report was a British product." In spite of these
feverish efforts and despite Silver's denunciation of Morrison-Grady
as a "conscienceless act of treachery" because of its "ghettoization of
the Jews in their own homeland," Truman, lobbied just as hard by
the State Department on behalf of Morrison-Grady, remained prepared to approve it after a whole week of intensive pressure.[21]

At a cabinet meeting on the morning of 30 July, lunchtime
arrived with the president prepared to accept the Morrison-Grady
plan, and only a telegram from Secretary of State Byrnes (meeting
with Attlee in Paris) suggesting that acceptance would have dangerous domestic consequences convinced all members of the cabinet except Acheson (representing the State Department) to oppose

the proposal when they resumed their "long meeting" after lunch. Truman, according to Dean Acheson's memorandum of the 30 July meeting, decided that he could not support the recommendations because of the "intensity of feeling in centers of Jewish population in this country." Silver, monitoring the cabinet meeting (probably via David Niles), was taken by surprise and he described Truman's decision as "a sudden, almost miraculous, last minute shift," though it clearly was linked to a lack of popular support, that is, to considerations of domestic politics. The AZEC, according to Acheson, had effectively mobilized public sentiment against Morrison-Grady, and there seemed to be little congressional support for it either. Truman could only buy time by announcing that he was recalling Grady to discuss the entire matter further and by telling Attlee (on 12 August) that the plan had little public support. [22]

Provincial autonomy was further doomed when Grady and his delegation met with members of the Anglo-American committee early in August. The latter were angry that their report had not been reaffirmed in the July conference, that the Americans had sold out to British imperialism, that the Jews would be ghettoized in Palestine (they would not be allowed in the Arab province), and that the crucial matter of the one hundred thousand was buried within a complicated scheme of administration. American support for Morrison-Grady had collapsed and with it any hopes for either a binational state or partition in Palestine. [23]

Two months later Truman, under considerable pressure from Zionist organizations disappointed with his modest accomplishments and eager to preempt Dewey's scheduled speech to the United Jewish Appeal a few days later, released a statement on the eve of Yom Kippur (4 October 1946). In this "Yom Kippur statement" he moved considerably further in the direction of partition by supporting "the creation of a viable Jewish state in control of its own immigration and economic policies in an adequate area of Palestine instead of the whole of Palestine." Zionists including Silver prepared Truman's statement, although the Department of

State added some critical words that made the president's position only a compromise between the Zionists and the British. The American press nearly everywhere clearly noted (wrongly, but to the Zionists' delight) that Truman had affirmed partition and a Jewish state.[24]

Attlee responded to Truman's statement with a furious letter because Truman had refused the prime minister's earnest request that Truman "postpone making [his] statement at least for the time necessary for me to communicate with Mr. Bevin," and he boldly denounced Truman for "refusing even a few hours grace." Truman had curtly told Attlee "Sorry—I cannot wait"; and Attlee told Truman he was "astonished" at Truman's impulsiveness."[25]

Silver and Wise, too, despite their role in helping to craft the statement immediately attacked the president. Their basic accusation was that pronouncements offered no substitute for actions and that hundreds of thousands of Jewish refugees still remained trapped in European camps (the number of D.P.s in Western Europe had increased dramatically in 1946). Silver called the statement "a political move to appeal to the 850,000 Jewish votes in New York" on the eve of congressional elections, and he argued that it "was harmful and not advantageous" because "statements will not bring Jews out of the concentration camps." Although Jewish labor leaders claimed that Silver had attacked Truman to win Republican votes for the 5 November elections, there is no evidence to support this. In fact, the dual attack by Silver and the Democratic Party loyalist Stephen Wise belies the conspiratorial theory; but in addition Zionist leaders offered vigorous defenses of Silver's motives.[26]

Partition did not emerge *de nouveau*. A decade earlier the British Peel Commission had recommended partition, and Silver inside and outside the United States had vigorously opposed it. At the fortieth ZOA convention in June 1937, Silver in an impassioned speech denounced the suggestion. A month or so later, despite Weizmann's support of partition and predictions that the World Zionist Congress would accept partition overwhelmingly, Silver (together with Stephen Wise) not only urged its rejection but argued against even discussing it with Great Britain. Never, he argued, begin negotiations with your absolute minimum demand, and his arguments led one reporter to call his speech the "best address" and "the most effectively argued" at the congress. When he returned from the congress, two thousand people came to The Temple to hear Silver blast partition yet again. [27]

The Anglo-American committee also considered and clearly rejected partition, though there is evidence that a variety of Jewish leaders, including Ben-Gurion, might have found it acceptable. In part this was because partition was a very ambiguous term meaning different things to different people. Silver and Wise, in fact, had supported partition at the World Zionist Congress of 1937. And, of course, the Anglo-American committee's proposal for a binational state (where Jews and Arabs each had an autonomous entity within one state) was in many minds not so far removed from the partitioning (two self-governing states) of Palestine. [28]

Truman's "Yom Kippur statement" has been widely acknowledged as being the result of the administration's accepting Nahum Goldmann's vigorous summer lobbying for part of Palestine—rather than all—as the Jewish state. Early in May Nahum Goldmann told the AZEC that he had reluctantly concluded that since "we have practically no support for the establishment of [all of] Palestine . . . as a Jewish State" the Zionists must "be ready to make territorial concessions." Goldmann found little or no support for this willingness to agree to partition because the AZEC leadership reflected Silver's militant demand for what he called, in response to Goldmann, "an undivided Palestine." Nevertheless, the Jewish Agency executive meeting in Paris late in July and early in August of 1946, overwhelmingly by a vote of ten to one approved a resolution calling for discussions of partition with British and American officials, and sent Goldmann to Washington to present the resolution to government decision-makers. Nothing the "floating ambassador" had done previously would enrage Silver as much as this mission, and he attacked Goldmann with all the tools at his command. Goldmann himself clearly knew the challenge of his mission; a few hours before leaving Paris he asked Stephen Wise for his "blessings as a Rabbi and a friend."[29]

Goldmann, as he promised Ben-Gurion in Paris, dutifully met with Silver immediately upon arriving in New York City on 6 August (at 4:30 P.M.), and they flew together to Washington to meet with other AZEC executive members that same evening (at 9:00 P.M.). Silver was aghast at the Jewish Agency Executive's decision because, as he told Goldmann, once partition was suggested by Goldmann it became the Jewish position and it was, by definition, unacceptable to the Arabs, who insisted (as Silver did for a Jewish state) on all of Palestine as an Arab state. Furthermore, why open up the discussions with something that perhaps, if they became desperate, might be a minimal or compromise position? Desperate to find a compromise with Goldmann on 6 August and the next day at a meeting of the AZEC executive, Silver got Goldmann to agree both privately and publicly that he would not initiate partition discussions in Washington, but "indicate a willingness to discuss the subject" if the administration introduced it. That very day, however, Goldmann had already begun a series of meetings with government leaders to inform them "in confidence" of the complicated partition resolution.[30]

A meeting with Dean Acheson on 7 August was followed by numerous other top-level contacts (Bartley Crum, David Niles, John Snyder, Robert Patterson, the Cabinet Committee on Palestine, Lord Inverchapel, and others), and within a few days the Jewish Agency partition plan reached Truman's desk. On 10 August Bartley Crum phoned Silver to tell him that Truman was sold on the plan and Goldmann, somewhat gloatingly, called to give Silver the same news. Goldmann's letters suggest some delight in embarrassing Silver and he wrote Weizmann immediately about his triumph. On 12 August Goldmann told a reporter that the "members of the Cabinet group with whom [I] conferred separately were particularly interested in the document as offering a practical solution to the present impasse," and he presented the *New York Times* with a detailed map of the partition areas. Goldmann later claimed that Truman had accepted the plan on 9 August after he, Goldmann, had won over everyone else.[31]

Silver's reaction was swift, dramatic, and unyielding. He opposed the resolution, the manner in which Goldmann had carried it out (not only his duplicity but his not including Silver in his meetings), the "interference" of the Jewish Agency on "his" turf (in violation of a contractual agreement Goldmann and Silver signed in 1943), and his discovery that the Jewish Agency Executive had voted against Goldmann's taking Silver with him when he lobbied in Washington. Goldmann later explained that many government officials, disliking Silver, would have been reluctant to see Goldmann if the militant Silver had tagged along, and that "I could never have achieved what I did achieve in those hectic days except by being able to move alone . . . in man-to-man talk." Goldmann concluded this letter to Bartley Crum with the naive hope that "one day Silver will understand this."[32]

Silver's disgust with Goldmann essentially revolved around the latter's refusal to solicit Silver's cooperation, his refusal to inform Silver of whom he wished to see in Washington, his secret cables to high officials in the administration, his refusal to invite Silver to accompany him, Silver's basic opposition to compromise, and Silver's monumental ego. Silver wrote to a friend in Paris during Goldmann's secret lobbying that "he has acted secretly on his own," and naturally Silver rejected any "responsibility for the outcome of [the] mission"—but he clearly wished he could have taken credit for lobbying the administration if compromise would ultimately have been necessary. When Silver heard that Truman had told Bartley Crum that although he was impressed with Goldmann's arguments for partition the president "wondered why Hillel Silver was not with him," his spirits were lifted. Nevertheless, he resigned from the Jewish Agency Executive, telling Ben-Gurion that Goldmann's "deceitful actions" and "duplicity" caused his move.[33]

Silver also told Ben-Gurion that Goldmann's "inept and willful" mission was a "disaster." For whom, one wonders? For Silver far more than for the Zionists? Not only was it a disaster, he continued, but he was able "to avert [a] disastrous decision favoring the [Morrison] Grady committee proposal." The truth of course was that Silver's lobbying did help prevent Truman from endorsing Morrison-Grady, but Goldmann undertook his mission after Morrison-Grady's fate had been decided by the administration and "the procedure followed by your emissary" [Goldmann] had no relationship to Morrison-Grady's rejection. Truman, in fact, liked the Jewish Agency plan very much, Goldmann surely deserves the credit, and the British had almost no interest in partition or anything other than Morrison-Grady.[34]

Silver used every possible opportunity during September and October to denounce Goldmann and his involvement in partition, and his personal opposition became the official position of the Zionist movement in America when its members rejected partition at the forty-ninth annual convention in late October and gave Silver a huge vote of confidence by reelecting him president. Silver used his blazing hot opening address to continue the condemnation of Goldmann and his partition plan. The convention supported his denunciation and nearly every mention of Goldmann's name "provoked hisses and boos." Silver was delighted, for on the eve of the convention, Goldmann at a press conference indulged in a sustained and vicious attack upon him. Nevertheless, Silver's bitter attack on Goldmann seemed both unnecessary and unmerciful, the conversion of a personal feud into an apparent principled argument that did not rise above personal resentment. And how ironical that Silver in his speech declares his own support for, or at least his willingness to consider, a partition plan which provided uncompromising Zionist sovereignty and little territorial loss.[35]

Bevin, decisively rejecting the Jewish Agency partition plan in late August and early September, came to the United States and met with Silver in November. On the eve of his two meetings with Bevin (14 and 20 November), Silver permitted himself an expression of hope for the one hundred thousand still stranded in Europe: "For the first time I have come to feel that there is a determination on the part of [the British] to see this thing through—at least as far as moving the refugees is concerned."[36]

In their first meeting, Bevin emphasized his support of "the whole of Morrison-Grady," though Silver concluded that Bevin "does not seem to have a clear plan in his own mind" and that "his confidence in the Morrison-Grady Plan seems to be pretty well shaken." Silver then, so it is said by Lord Inverchapel in his summary of the second meeting, suggested partition to Bevin, despite his own personal opposition to it and that of the Jewish Agency. According to Inverchapel, who was present, Silver sought a word of encouragement from Bevin so that he, Silver, could go to the upcoming World Zionist Congress in Basle and champion a winning cause. Is this true? Did Silver's militant opposition to partition, publicly expressed for a decade, yield to the realities of political opportunity?[37]

This seems unlikely, because Silver's own detailed memorandums of both conversations as well as Inverchapel's official report of the 20 November meeting deny that he supported partition. There is, however, contrary evidence: Dean Acheson's summary of his conversation with Inverchapel in which the latter reports to Acheson on what Silver said to Bevin. However, for days before and after his meetings with Bevin, the militant Silver, whom Bevin called the most intransigent of the American Jewish leaders, continued to take the extreme position of demanding a Jewish state in all of Palestine. He argued for a Jewish state in all of Palestine in a meeting with Senator Arthur Vandenberg on 14 November (the same day he met with Bevin) and in a speech at the General Zionist

Confederations conference prior to the opening of the congress. And he went to Basle where the World Zionist Congress would open on 9 December to demand an "undivided and undiminished" Palestine. This he did in two long, meticulously constructed and impassioned attacks on Goldmann, the Jewish Agency Executive, and especially on partition (delivered on 10 and 19 December).[38]

It is hard to determine how successful Silver was at the wild Basle conference in which Emanuel Neumann interrupted Weizmann's 16 December speech with a shout of "demagogue" after Weizmann had belittled Silver's Zionist efforts among Cleveland Jewry; Ben-Gurion spoke for and against partition in the same speech, and he was at once Weizmann's chief supporter and chief opponent; this future leader of the Jewish state, according to Eliahu Elath, called Silver the *Fuehrer;* Wise actually did describe Silver as a "dictator" and described Silver's supporters as "bandits"; Weizmann was not reelected president (Goldmann in a letter to Wise blamed this on Silver); and Silver's enemies circulated rumors that he was vigorously seeking the presidency. (These rumors had been circulating among Zionist leaders earlier in 1946). Undaunted, Silver delivered three major addresses: one in English to the congress, one in Hebrew to the General Zionists, and one in Yiddish to the political commission![39]

Goldmann in his memoirs claims that he won on partition and Silver lost on the issue of all of Palestine at the congress when the Silverites unsuccessfully tried to insert "inside Palestine as a whole" in a resolution reiterating the Biltmore Program. But this "gratifying" victory was not much of a victory; Goldmann suffered enough defeats for him to recall Basle on one occasion as "one of my most disagreeable political experiences," while his friend Wise on one occasion described those days in Basle as filled with "trickery and treachery everywhere," and, another time, "replete with the most skilled and conscienceless manipulation that has ever emerged from a public relations cesspool." The seventy-seven-member Zionist General Council put Silver and Neumann (and a majority of

General Zionists) on the new nineteen-member coalition Zionist Executive, they elected Silver chairman of the powerful political commission and chairman of the American section of the Jewish Agency Executive (Ben-Gurion headed the Jerusalem section of the executive), and they yielded to his stubborn opposition to Weizmann by ousting the latter from leadership. It is difficult to determine winners and losers under such circumstances.[40]

Stephen Wise did not suffer defeat well, however. Silver's maximalist demands and his repudiation of Weizmann's regime and compromising policies led Wise upon his return home to resign as vice-president of the zoa (Silver was the president) in protest over Silver's power—or, better, his abuse of it. He agreed with the writer in *The New Statesman and Nation* who accurately described Silver as "an ambitious politician whose primary aim was to oust Dr. Weizmann from the presidency and to challenge the whole policy of Anglo-Jewish cooperation," and Wise felt general disgust with a congress at which he was largely an anachronism. He felt this loneliness strongly, and he described the Congress quite faithfully in his "press conference" of Saturday evening 3 January 1947 at the meeting house of the Free Synagogue, as "a collection of personal habits and rancors and private ambitions." Few were sympathetic to Wise: the Detroit *Jewish Chronicle* called his response "the bleating of a frustrated old man," the *Jewish Spectator* called him "a bad and revengeful loser," the Yiddish *Jewish Morning Journal* described Wise as a "prima donna." Silver himself refused to respond to the charges.[41]

Even in November and December and the early winter of 1947, Bevin and Attlee still hoped that a binational state could win the support of the Americans, a prerequisite for any further acceptance. Bevin did, however, threaten Silver at their 14 November 1946 meeting that if the Zionists would not cooperate with the Arabs and British, the Palestine problem might be dumped on the United Nations. Bevin felt confident that the pro-Arab majority in the United Nations would at least endorse a "unitary" or a binational state, more or less like the Morrison-Grady plan, and he knew that there was no chance of Arab endorsement of Truman's partition plan because the Arabs demanded nothing less than Palestine as an Arab state.[42]

Bevin, however, like Attlee, did naively hope that the Arabs might favor binationalism or provincial autonomy as a compromise; the Arabs knew that Morrison-Grady was possibly a step towards partition, which was for them a totally unacceptable solution. At the very least, then, the British were desperately struggling in the fall of 1946 to discover any solution that might satisfy both Arabs and Jews, which might protect British interests in the eastern Mediterranean, and might win the support of the British and American publics. Despite pressure from numerous British government officials, Attlee and Bevin adamantly rejected Truman's "Yom Kippur statement," if for no other reason than that it had no chance of acceptance. This was true, it turned out, even among the Jews, as the British learned in a meeting at the Colonial Office on 11 February 1947 that David Ben-Gurion and Moshe Shertok attended. No matter, wrote the third Jewish delegate at the meeting, how "absurd and fantastic . . . and unreal and impracticable [our demands] looked," partition was out of the question. Fixed on the idea of an independent binational state and failing to find support for it, the British would find no alternative but to ask the United Nations for help. This was done with some confidence in the outcome; the General Assembly would not meet until the fall and every Arab state had a seat in it. As Arthur Creech-Jones, the colonial secretary, put it in the late February parliamentary debates over the proposal: "We are not going to the United Nations to surrender the mandate."[43]

With Bevin's announcement to the House of Commons on 18 February that the government had decided to turn to the United Nations for help, Silver and the AZEC reacted vigorously. Even before the formal announcement Silver called five hundred delegates from local emergency councils to Washington for a strategy session (the Extraordinary Zionist Emergency Conference), since the General Assembly would not meet until the fall and hence the 250,000 or so displaced European Jews (the late 1946 figure) would languish for at least another year. Various proposals emerged at the meeting—most encouraging the leadership to lobby vigorously with the American representatives at the United Nations on behalf of the refugees and a Jewish state—while delegates lobbied their representatives and senators singly or in groups.[44]

Silver, shortly after the conference ended, launched a public attack on Bevin who after the decision to go to the U.N. charged in the House of Commons that Truman's concern with "local elections," despite honorable British intentions, prevented a solution to the Palestine problem. Silver responded by calling the accusation "as mendacious, misleading and insulting a statement as ever issued from the lips of a British Foreign Secretary," and he argued that Britain had no serious intention of relinquishing its mandate in Palestine.[45]

He was probably wrong about this; a broad spectrum of the British Parliament, cabinet, and public desperately sought a way to withdraw from their very expensive, debilitating, and hopeless occupation of Palestine. Nevertheless, concomitant with his verbal lashing of Bevin, Silver spent extensive periods of the week in Washington with elected officials, State Department officials (especially Loy Henderson, the director of the office of Near Eastern and African Affairs, Secretary of State Byrnes, and his successor, George Marshall) and with AZEC leaders, as all reports indicated that only the United States (among the Big Five) had not yet agreed to the emerging proposal that a special U.N. committee study Palestine prior to the September opening of the General Assembly.[46]

On 11 March 1947 Silver left New York for an emergency meeting of the Jewish Agency Executive in Jerusalem where an extensive lobbying campaign (program and tactics) was put into operation. He convinced the executive to allow the American branch of the Jewish Agency to present the Jewish people's case before the U.N., but the executive rankled Silver by adding Gold-mann to the six-man U.S. delegation selected to prepare the case. When Silver returned to the United States on 31 March he found the AZEC machinery finely tuned; the fourteen resolutions approved by the Jewish Agency Executive had already been sent to the chairmen of all local emergency committees.[47]

Britain's formal request to the U.N. on 2 April asked for an extraordinary session of the General Assembly in order to establish a special committee to make recommendations to the regular ses-sion of the General Assembly in September. Silver asked the U.N. on 22 April to allow the Jewish Agency—recognized by the League of Nations as the Jewish spokesman for Palestine—to represent the Jewish people at the special session on Palestine, which would convene on 28 April. On the eve of this opening session Silver talked with one hundred correspondents at the American section of the Jewish Agency office in New York and used this press con-ference to urge the United States to support the establishment of a special committee on Palestine composed of disinterested mem-bers.[48]

Silver considered neither the State Department nor the president as "intent on our cause," and since the U.S. position at the U.N. would be crucial, he announced that the AZEC would try to "con-vince the President and the State Department that they should champion our cause" and continue to present the Palestine case to the American people as well. The AZEC launched an "Action for Palestine Week" early in May, complete with newspaper ads, radio broadcasts, public rallies, resolutions, letter-writing campaigns, and speeches by scores of the two hundred active lecturers on the circuit. The U.S. government agreed to the special committee and Silver claimed the "major cause of the U.S. delegation's position" to be the "work done by the Emergency Council in stimulating Amer-ican public opinion."[49]

The General Assembly appointed an eleven-nation steering committee on Palestine and agreed to permit (again, largely as a result of U.S. pressure) both the Jewish Agency for Palestine and the Arab Higher Committee to present their cases to the fifty-five-member political committee. Silver also attributed the decision of the American delegation to support the appearance of the Jewish Agency for Palestine to the Emergency Council's mobilization of the American people.[50]

Flanked by Nahum Goldmann and Moshe Shertok, on 8 May 1947 Silver presented the case on behalf of the Jewish people. "Reading carefully" from a ten-page prepared text, he delivered, according to the *New York Times* correspondent, an "eloquent, even-tempered, thirty-minute address" filled with "logical cogency, statesmanlike restraint and moving warmth of emotion." He urged the Special Committee on Palestine, which appeared certain to begin its "fact-finding" immediately, to visit Europe and Palestine, believing that if the committee members saw the tragedy of the Jews still trapped in Europe they would strongly support a Jewish state.[51]

Thanks in large part to the wise and firm leadership of Senor Aranha of Brazil, who presided over the plenary sessions, and Lester B. Pearson of Canada, who handled the rugged sessions of the political committee, the two-week special session of the United Nations General Assembly moved smoothly. By a vote of forty-five to seven the General Assembly established a Special Committee on Palestine (UNSCOP) which was to submit a report to the General Assembly by 1 September 1947. Silver's address, dignified and persuasive, left a strong impression on many of the delegates who would make up the UNSCOP.[52]

The UNSCOP held its first meeting at Lake Success on 26 May and three weeks later arrived in Jerusalem for a five-week visit, having yielded to Arab pressures not to visit D.P. camps but having agreed to permit a Jewish Agency Liaison Office to accompany it. The Arab Higher Committee boycotted the committee, though the UNSCOP met Arab representatives in Beirut after leaving Palestine and heading for Geneva to prepare their report. Zionist representatives lobbied the committee members in Geneva as intensely as they had done in Lausanne in 1946; David Horowitz, a gifted economist and Histadrut official, reported that he spent "hour after hour over the maps" with the alternate Swedish member of the committee and that he was strongly assisted by Moshe Shertok.[53]

On 31 August the report, with an introductory section and eleven recommendations, was completed and signed, though the AZEC knew that the American response would begin to be formulated weeks before the report became public. During July and August Silver lobbied high executive officials and legislative leaders wherever he could find them, and the American Christian Palestine Committee under the aegis of the AZEC organized rallies, forums, and especially letter-writing campaigns that yielded thousands of letters from concerned Christians urging Truman to support a Jewish state.[54].

The UNSCOP agreed to the termination of the Mandate, to independence for Palestine, to admission of 150,000 Jewish refugees within two years, and to international action to solve the Jewish displaced persons in Europe (then numbering 250,000); it split over whether Palestine should be partitioned into an Arab state, a Jewish state, and an internationalized Jerusalem (seven nations) or established as an independent federal state (three nations). Both plans explicitly rejected binationalism or cantonization and, of course, a single Arab or Jewish state, but only the majority report with seven affirmative votes had any chance of success.[55]

Silver initially opposed the majority plan (for unfairly asking the Jews to give up claims to the western Galilee and Jerusalem) but after returning from the World Zionist Actions Committee in Zurich in early September he subordinated his personal objections and accepted it as a "basis for discussion, a basis for a solution," along with nearly all American Jewish organizations and the American press, while the British and American governments opposed the plan. Loy Henderson and several others with access to Truman vigorously presented pro-Arab arguments against partition and generally in favor of a binational solution. Secretary of State Marshall, sympathetic to the British, probably would have been swayed by Henderson's cogent opposition to a Jewish state had it not been for Truman's strong support for the UNSCOP majority report.[56]

The AZEC and Zionist Organization of America began a torrent of lobbying during September and October that reached every corner of the nation as Zionists sought to demonstrate to the American U.N. delegation and to the government that public opinion was overwhelmingly pro-Zionist. Silver on the eve of the General Assembly's opening described the "next few weeks or few months" as "probably the most critical in the history of our movement," and despite some fears that the majority report might become the "Jewish Report," launched the most vigorous AZEC lobbying effort of his four-year leadership.[57]

The General Assembly met on 16 September and the Palestine question dominated the session despite other international tensions. The General Assembly set up an Ad Hoc Committee on the Palestine Question, composed of all the member states, to consider this issue. The Arab Higher Committee and the Jewish Agency again testified—the former rejecting both the majority and minority reports; the latter accepting the majority report as the "indispensable minimum." Silver again presented the Jewish case, this time (2 October) in a one-hour speech in which he "reluctantly" accepted the U.N. partition plan. Loy Henderson, in a lengthy and persuasive memo to the secretary of state (22 September), had argued that the United States ought not to support either the partition of Palestine or the establishment of a Jewish state therein because either would undermine vital American relations with the Arabs and both were unworkable.[58]

As the State Department Arabists vigorously lobbied the administration against a Jewish state, they especially worked on the secretary of state. George C. Marshall, Jr. (1880–1959), a soft-spoken, extremely self-confident professional soldier, headed the United States army from 1939–45, was *Time* magazine's Man of the

Year in 1944, served as secretary of state for two years beginning in January 1947, and was the only professional military man ever to win the Nobel Prize for Peace (1953). Although best known for his role in developing the European Recovery Program or the Marshall Plan, his tenure as secretary of state paralleled England's dumping of the "Palestine problem" on the United Nations. Marshall yielded to the lobbyists and remained vague about the official U.S. position when he addressed the General Assembly (on 17 September) and he instructed the delegates to remain as neutral as possible. The Zionists bombarded the administration with arguments in support of partition, while the British Colonial Secretary, Creech-Jones, announced before the United Nations (26 September) that the British would not implement any U.N. policy unacceptable to both Arabs and Jews. Furthermore, he announced that the British were prepared to terminate the mandate and planned an "early with-drawal" from Palestine. Despite the refusal of the British to imple-ment the majority report (clearly unacceptable to the Arabs), Truman instructed the U.S. delegation to support it and Herschel V. Johnson, the acting representative of the United States at the U.N., announced this decision on 11 October. The Soviet Union, anxious to break up the British Empire, announced its support of partition (two independent states) two days later.[59]

Zionist pressure certainly played a role in Truman's decision, for he was made constantly aware of how strongly Americans supported a Jewish state in Palestine. AZEC local chairmen stimulated positive press comments on the majority report as the best possible compro-mise early in October; Leo Sack coordinated the furious Wash-ington lobbying; and Silver, noting on 22 October that "with only fourteen U.N. delegates on our side we have got an enormous job ahead of us," wrote personal letters to senators and representatives, lobbied oil executives, foreign ministers, and ambassadors at the U.N., (especially the neutral Latin American delegations), and personally contacted Christian leaders to mobilize their supporters. He analyzed the situation as largely a political matter and urged maximum pressure be put on key senators and representatives as well as on the American people as a whole, for the ultimate goal was to "bring enormous pressure on Truman" and "lobby wavering delegations." One telegraph station in Brooklyn recorded more than twenty-five thousand wires to Secretary of State Marshall, while the emergency council got one hundred thousand telegrams out of Chicago urging Truman to support the majority report in a forty-eight-hour period! Truman acknowledged in his *Memoirs* that "I do not think I ever had as much pressure and propaganda aimed at the White House as I had in this instance."[60]

The AZEC leadership took credit for Truman's decision. Silver told the Executive Committee that the president did not instruct Johnson to support the UNSCOP majority report "because of his devotion to our cause" but "because of the sheer pressure of political logistics applied by the Jewish leadership in the United States." Other leaders, such as Emanuel Neumann and Leo Sack, argued similarly.[61]

With the support of both of the superpowers, partition became a realistic possibility. On 25 November 1947 the Ad Hoc Committee approved the plan twenty-five to thirteen (seventeen abstentions), one vote short of the two-thirds that would be necessary in the General Assembly. Vigorous Arab commercial and diplomatic pressure, as well as Zionist pressure, the latter directed by Moshe Shertok and Silver, now centered on those small or medium-sized nations (especially Haiti, the Philippines, Mexico, Liberia, and even France) whose delegations had abstained, for any of them might be persuaded to support partition. Silver from his suite at New York's Commodore Hotel (the board of trustees at The Temple had awarded him an "indefinite leave of absence") spent three days (25–27 November) in a whirlwind of meetings, telephone calls, memos, and meals designed to convince delegates of the Zionist cause. Seven in fact did yield to the Zionists, including France, Haiti, Liberia, and the Philippines, and on the Jewish Sabbath, 29 November 1947, at a converted skating rink in Flushing, New York, the General Assembly approved partition (officially, Resolution No. 181, 2) by thirty-three to thirteen (with ten abstentions). Although Truman denied his own lobbying between the Ad Hoc Committee and the General Assembly vote, both Nahum Goldmann and David Horowitz as well as Silver argued that Truman's involvement in the last three days played a crucial role in the final vote. Horowitz summed it up best: "The United States exerted the weight of its influence almost at the last hour, and the way the final vote turned out must be ascribed to this fact."[62]

The tablet on which Silver like so many Jews tallied the nationally broadcast vote still survives; as the vote was announced, pandemonium erupted inside and outside the United Nations as Jews and friends celebrated the decision. The Arabs quickly jolted the Jews back to reality: their delegations walked out of the U.N., and one day after the partition announcement they launched an attack on Jews near Tel Aviv. Thus the 29 November vote, in Silver's words, was only "the evening and the morning of the first day," and the rest of the week would be "bitter and painful."[63]

The result was a team effort, bringing together numerous lobbyists dedicated to the cause of a Jewish state, though the AZEC efforts to build public opinion and quickly and effectively channel this sentiment toward Washington loom large. Silver coordinated much of the overall strategy of the political struggle; in Neumann's words, "Silver marshalled our forces and the all-out political offensive . . . that mobilized the sympathies of the American people and insured the support of the American government." Abundant evidence still exists to confirm the extent to which Silver clearly conceived, wisely planned, and firmly executed a strategy that convinced Truman—whom Silver called the "key foreign policy decision-maker—to shape American policy in favor of the Zionists.[64]

Chapter Eight

If we are not careful we might get a Jewish State quite
soon with Silver as president . . . God help us!

—Chaim Weizmann, 3 November 1947

Dr. Silver was not particularly popular among his peers.
He was feared and resented as a loner who was neither
controllable nor amenable to group discipline. . . .
[Henry] Morgenthau and [Henry] Montor resented his
overbearing manner, his determination to dominate, to
control every situation.

—Gottlieb Hammer, *Good Faith and Credit*

It would help if, figuratively, both the Mufti and Rabbi
Silver were thrown into the Red Sea.

—Harry S. Truman, 1948

Silver . . . is the dictator of American Zionism.

—Chaim Weizmann, 1 August 1948

It is more than deplorable that the Rabbi in Cleveland
does not begin to understand all the terrible harm he is
doing to the young State in making its initial steps so
dreadfully difficult and dangerous. . . . He will never be
forgiven for the harm he is doing.

—Chaim Weizmann, 23 November 1948

The United States' support for the momentous decision of 29
November began to erode immediately after the vote was taken and

the British decision, communicated secretly to the United States at the end of November, was made to set the time of the transfer of power for 15 May 1948. Abba Hillel Silver found himself pressed to fight one more battle with the Truman administration, which was deeply embroiled in its own uncertain relationship with a new Europe and watching its relations with the Soviet Union steadily grow cold. The American retreat on partition brought complaints from many friends and allies, not just Jewish organizations, but Silver would spearhead one corner (though not the point) of the arrowhead as he appeared at different forums at different times during 1948. Little that he did had the impact of his work from 1943 through 1947, in part because the singleness of purpose so apparent before the November vote quickly dissipated as numerous agendas unfolded inside and outside the Zionist world and, in greater part, because Silver was more and more only one of the participants (and not always the most important one).

Silver told his close friend and Zionist colleague Emanuel Neumann a few days after the vote that "days, months, perhaps even years of a desperate struggle were ahead," and there would only be that "one night of rejoicing." Within days following the partition decision, vigorous Arab assaults were made against Jewish positions in Palestine, and Secretary of State George Marshall told his staff that the United States might have erred in accepting partition. He expressed his anxiety about a possible United States troop commitment in Palestine and approved the recommendation of Loy Henderson, director of the Office of Near Eastern and African Affairs, to prohibit the export of American arms to the Middle East, that is, to the Jews. With increasingly vocal antipartition noises being heard in Congress and among other government officials, Silver launched another intensive AZEC correspondence campaign designed to win popular support for maintaining the tenuous commitment to a Jewish state in Palestine. According to Vera Weizmann, this campaign opened "a round of political activities of such intensity and complexity as my husband and I had never before experienced."[1]

The events of the winter of 1947–48 regarding Palestine took place against the background of the coup in Czechoslovakia and actual or impending Soviet threats in Greece, Berlin, Turkey and Hungary—threats that might have required United States troop commitments. The crucial events of that winter include Truman's vacillations during the months following the vote; the State Department's move toward a switch from partition to trusteeship (in January and February); the Policy Planning Staff's recommendation that the United States take no "further initiative in implementing or aiding partition" (issued on 19 January); Secretary of Defense Forrestal's efforts to oppose implementing partition, including his appearance before the special subcommittee of the House Armed Services Committee (19 January); the startling suggestion of the American ambassador to the United Nations that, given the tensions in Palestine, partition be postponed, a "cease-fire" be declared, and the U.N. establish a "temporary [indefinite] trusteeship" (on 19 March); the crucial influence of presidential adviser Clark Clifford on Truman's decision-making; Truman's relationship with Chaim Weizmann; and, finally, after this gigantic retreat from partition, Truman's decision in late April to support the Jewish cause in spite of what he termed "extreme Zionists."[2]

The tale does not involve Silver at the very highest level, because Truman adamantly refused to talk with him. Truman's biographer states that the president "despised Rabbi Silver" as a militant Zionist trouble-maker and felt that "terror and Rabbi Silver are the contributing causes of *some,* if not all, of our troubles." Secretary of State Marshall and the undersecretary, Robert A. Lovett, two other crucial policymakers, seemed little more accessible to Silver. Nevertheless, he worked as vigorously as ever both personally (primarily in Congress and at the U.N.) and institutionally (through the AZEC and the American section of the executive of the Jewish Agency for

Palestine) to counter the State Department's efforts to convince Zionist leaders to give up their goal of statehood in the face of militant Arab opposition.[3]

The Silvers left for Palestine on 30 December 1947 to see Abba's parents, to meet with Zionist executive members, and to hammer out, according to the Hebrew press, a "coordination agreement" between the armed Zionist organizations (especially the Irgun) and the Haganah by means of negotiations with both sides. He arrived on 15 January after keynoting a huge Zionist rally in Paris on 8 January, and he spoke at length to his colleagues at meetings on 19, 25, and 26 January, pledging to raise large sums of money and to continue to pressure the U.S. government to support the 29 November decision. Although he met almost daily and for long hours with Zionist political and military leaders, with the executive and with various committees, he spent his free hours with his parents and with reporters, who conducted extensive interviews with him for the Hebrew press. Silver barely escaped an Arab attack on the besieged highways and another attack in the Old City during his stay, and he appealed to His Excellency Sir Alan Cunningham during an hour-long conversation to provide adequate protection for the Jews. This would be his last visit with his mother, who died within a month ("It was a very great privilege of mine to have had the opportunity of seeing her before she passed away," Silver told Moshe Shertok). His father died in January 1949 at the age of eighty-eight. The visit ended, however, well before Silver had planned; he "suddenly terminated his visit," in the words of the American consul general, on 2 February as crises in Washington and at the United Nations led American Zionist leaders to inundate him with telegrams to come home.[4]

He arrived in New York on 5 February and told the American section of the Jewish Agency Executive on 8 February about his trip, his renewed determination to pressure Congress to demand continued support for partition, his plans to work with administration officials who were willing to see him to prevent a retreat from partition, and the desperate need of the Palestinian Jews for money and weapons to defend against expected Arab invasions when statehood would be proclaimed. Meetings with the decidedly pro-Arab Dean Rusk, director of the State Department's Office of Special Political Affairs and subsequently of the Office of United Nations Affairs, with Ambassador Austin (frequently), and with dozens of senators and representatives (especially Fish, Martin, McCormack, Taft, and Vandenberg) kept Silver busy throughout February and March. Between meetings he coordinated the national mobilization of the AZEC and chaired the meetings of the American section of the Jewish Agency Executive (more than thirty executive meetings took place during February, March, and April 1948). On 22 February he presented the U.N. on behalf of the Jewish Agency for Palestine with a twelve-hundred-word indictment of British rule in Palestine. England's so called "neutrality," he argued, disguised a pro-Arab policy. And he lobbied vigorously among Latin American delegations during the days that followed that presentation. Silver's knowledge of Latin American politics, especially at the local level, was extensive, and the memos he sent to these delegations as well as his notes on his endless meetings with their representatives detail his careful attention to those arguments that might prove persuasive. On 5 March, after observing the Palestine debate for nearly ten days, he addressed the U.N. Security Council as the "chief Zionist spokesman" and with abundant evidence argued that the British continually had subverted the 29 November partition resolution. On 12 March Silver addressed the Big Four (U.S., USSR, China, France), arguing that partition constituted an "irreducible minimum" and beseeching the U.N. not to abandon it. The meetings of the American section of the Jewish Agency Executive throughout February and March provided Silver with a trial forum for his arguments, and these lively discussions about U.N. actions would inspire his rhetoric at the U.N.[5]

His letters make abundantly clear the importance he attached to getting to the top policymakers, especially Truman, Marshall, and

Lovett, his frustration at not being able to reach them (an indication that he had now become only one member of the team, and clearly not the captain), and his conviction that "lower-level officials" in the State Department were sabotaging the Palestine resolution with arguments such as that "the United States is sacrificing its interests in the Arab world to Zionist pressure and domestic politics." He relentlessly continued his lobbying with whomever he could find against all attempts to reverse, modify, or defer partition. He explained this commitment to his son Daniel in a letter in early March, noting that it was "impossible to advance our cause in Washington without the support of public opinion or mass action," and therefore he was working "overtime to spur the rank-and-file everywhere to turn the tide."[6]

On 19 March 1948 Senator Warren R. Austin, the American ambassador to the U.N., made a speech retreating from partition and proposing temporary trusteeship, one day after Truman had appeared before a joint session of Congress, and in the wake of the Czechoslovakian crisis had asked for universal military training and a resumption of the draft. Austin, a celebrated Vermont attorney long active in Republican politics, had been elected to the Senate in 1931, reelected in 1934 and 1940, and, thanks to his popularity and influence, had served as assistant minority leader. He had a special interest in foreign policy and demonstrated sufficient skill at it for a Democratic president to appoint him special ambassador and adviser to the acting representative of the United States in the United Nations. At the end of his Senate term in January 1947, the president designated him the representative of the United States on the Security Council. After Austin made his speech, Silver responded with an address to the Security Council denouncing the "shocking reversal" of American policy, the "fatal capitulation" to Arab threats, and making his own threat that the Jews of Palestine would resist trusteeship with force. Convinced (correctly) that State Department policymakers had concluded that partition could not be implemented without force, that the United States would refuse to intervene to enforce it, and that some practical alternative must be found, he went on to argue (as did scores of newspapers the next day) that the United States had essentially abandoned partition on 19 March, Black Friday.[7]

Silver followed this angry retort to Austin with what Joseph Schechtman called a "powerful and closely reasoned indictment" on CBS on 31 March, an address that denounced United States alternatives to partition and urged Americans to support the partition plan with intensified efforts and "to fight, every inch of the way, with full force ahead, to defeat Trusteeship in the Security Council and at the special assembly." He did not and could not know (few did) how Truman felt in early March, though he suspected (probably correctly) that Truman approved of a retreat from partition if and when partition failed, and this growing awareness of Truman's position stunned Silver as well as other Zionist leaders. Only one of them, Chaim Weizmann, had had secret assurances (on 18 March) from Truman that he would support partition, and Truman reaffirmed these promises, again demanding secrecy, on 23 April.[8]

Silver could only guess at Truman's feelings and his motivations, though he intuited enough to sense the danger that the alternatives to partition, presented to Truman by his advisers and approved by the secretary of state, posed to the goal of statehood. In an address to the Political and Security Committee of the General Assembly on 22 April, which one reporter called "the most eloquent I have ever heard," Silver described the "rapid disintegration of the central mandatory regime and the creation of a vacuum in authority" and pleaded for U.N. support for partition, arguing that a Jewish state would arise in May when the British left no matter what the U.N. decided to do. Silver does not seem ever to have doubted either Bevin's absolute determination to leave Palestine on 15 May or the impossibility of Bevin's cooperating with any American plan that would extend the British stay in Palestine. He did, however, continually berate the British in March and April for abandoning to chaos and civil war a country for which Britain had accepted responsibility.[9]

Early in May, as Britain prepared to withdraw all of its seventy-five thousand troops as well as administrative machinery from Palestine—thereby leaving Jews and Arabs to fight a bitter civil war—Silver met with the other members of the American executive of the Jewish Agency as well as the Agency's political advisory committee to discuss (and to reject) the latest efforts of the State Department to delay ("postpone," said Marshall) the momentum toward statehood by means of an immediate truce. Their meetings took place during massive letter-writing campaigns, a Day of Mobilization and Prayer, national conferences, work stoppages, editorials, and rallies. One rally at Madison Square Park, at which Silver bitterly attacked U.S. policy and the State Department and protested the trusteeship plan, drew, according to the chief police inspector's conservative estimate, one hundred thousand people, "the biggest crowd ever in the park." The AZEC carefully designed these events to pressure Truman and his advisers to renew their support for partition and to recognize, when the British pulled out, the new state.[10]

Most pressing to these Zionist leaders was the State Department's support in April and early May of a United Nations–sponsored truce (Security Council Truce Commission), which would have delayed the establishment of a Jewish state beyond 15 May and created the possibility that they would be called upon to wage a second campaign to win U.S. support for a Jewish state. Silver's old nemesis Nahum Goldmann and some other moderate leaders as well argued for support of the truce proposal, for though it meant deferring statehood for a few months, it also meant a chance to regroup Jewish forces. Silver (Dean Rusk called him an "extremist" and his followers the "war party") vigorously opposed the truce and the deferment, making the proclamation of a Jewish state, despite its precariousness, the highest priority and insisting that the opportunity for a Jewish state might be lost forever if it were delayed, because a cease-fire or truce would extend the mandate beyond 15 May. The vote within the Zionist executive mattered little (although three of the other five members voted with Silver), for time was on the side of those who supported partition, complete British withdrawal, and the proclamation of statehood. The mandate expired on 14 May 1948 at midnight Palestine time; eleven minutes later Truman "dumbfounded" the U.S. delegation at the U.N. (with whom he had not consulted) by recognizing the state of Israel (at 6:11 P.M. EST). A few minutes later I. L. Kenen informed Silver of the news. He responded excitedly, "This is marvelous; this is what we've been praying for."[11]

Israel's triumph corresponded with that of Silver and his followers, the "Silverites." At the fifty-first Zionist Organization of America convention in Pittsburgh, two months after Israel's dramatic proclamation of statehood, Silver, Emanuel Neumann, and their supporters reached the peak of their power. After handing a well-organized opposition group a resounding defeat, Silver yielded the ZOA presidency to Neumann, perhaps his closest friend, and optimistically prepared a plan for reorganizing the World Zionist Organization. The opposition, which had organized itself as the Committee for Progressive Zionism just prior to the 1947 convention, included some of the most dedicated Zionist leaders in America: Rudolf G. Sonneborn (1898–1986), Louis Lipsky (1876–1963), Solomon Goldman, and a long-time enemy of Silver from Cleveland, Ezra Shapiro. All of them resented Silver's and Neumann's five years of American Zionist leadership. Their defeat, however, did not destroy them; early in 1949 these self-designated "Progressives" would launch an aggressive campaign that would culminate in the defeat of Silver and Neumann (they called Silver and Neumann "dictators, reactionaries and enemies of the state of Israel").[12]

Silver and Neumann, armed with a strong mandate from American Zionists concerned that the ZOA not be perceived as merely an arm of a foreign power, flew to Jerusalem in August 1948 for a showdown with Israeli leaders over *hafradah* (separation) of the wzo from the state of Israel. The problems connected with Zionist reorganization as a result of the creation of the new state—and especially the relationship between the political leadership of Israel and that of the diaspora (and not just American) Zionist organizations—would occupy world Zionist leaders for some time. Silver understood that the child (Israel) would have to cut itself loose from its mother (the Zionist movement) in order to define a new relationship, and like so many other American Zionists, he wanted to make certain that Israeli leaders did not control the diaspora Zionist bodies as they struggled with the challenges of incipient nationhood.

Silver, leading the American delegation, attended meetings of the Jewish Agency Executive and the Actions Committee of the World Zionist Congress from 22 August to 3 September 1948. The American delegates proposed in part that Israeli leaders be removed from the wzo executive, because it would be awkward if not embarrassing if David Ben-Gurion or some other Israeli political leader directed the affairs of American Zionism as head of the executive. The result, of course, of such a removal would also be to propel American Zionists into the leadership of the wzo, and leaders of the "Progressives" described Silver as determined to oust Ben-Gurion from the executive of the wzo and take over his chairmanship. Silver continually denied any such motivation, and there is no documentary evidence to challenge this claim. [13]

The Americans met with considerable success in Israel, including ousting Ben-Gurion from the Jewish Agency Executive, and Silver returned home in September to resume his rabbinate and continue his busy schedule of lobbying in Washington on behalf of the Jewish state. He continued to chair the American section of the Jewish Agency Executive, served as a member of the executive of the Jewish Agency and as national cochairman of the United Palestine Appeal, and he still headed the AZEC. Upon his arrival home, Silver learned that Henry Montor (1905–82), the professional head of the UPA, had submitted a letter of resignation to Israel Goldstein, the national chairman of the UPA. The letter would set off the "UJA Crisis" and lead a few months later to Silver's sudden and permanent resignation from Zionist leadership and his return to his office and study at The Temple. [14]

Montor had served as the executive director of the UPA for two decades and as the executive vice-chairman of the UJA since its inception in 1939. His letter announced his resignation from the UJA effective at the end of 1948 and from the UPA effective immediately. Montor had opposed Silver and Neumann earlier—usually surreptitiously but sometimes openly as at the "political session" of the fiftieth ZOA convention in 1947, where he blasted Silver's tacit support of the Irgun. The American Zionists' triumph in Jerusalem depressed him. He accused Silver and Neumann of "dictating the present policies of the ZOA" and "strangling the most decent and progressive forces in the State of Israel." What bothered him most, according to a 1949 letter and his later recollections, was that the ZOA took "absolute and undisputed control over every penny raised for Palestine through the UJA" and "regarded the funds for Palestine as their private treasure chest." What probably bothered him at least as much, as he recalled nearly four decades later in private correspondence, was Silver's "arrogance." Both of these problems would constitute the heart of the conflict, which culminated in Silver's departure from the leadership. [15]

Montor in his accusations touched upon a significant change in Jewish fundraising that he and his colleagues—largely the Progressives—sought to achieve. The UPA, which received that portion of funds raised for Palestine through the UJA, had been controlled by Zionists since its inception in 1925 and it distributed its funds through the Palestine Foundation and the Jewish National Fund (*Keren Hayesod* and *Keren Kayemet L'Yisrael*), what Montor called "a pyramided holding corporation." Montor sought an independent UPA, generously stocked with non-Zionist fundraisers, which would control allocations in America and leave Israeli allocations to the

UJA. This would put the UJA in Israeli hands and replace Silver, Neumann, and their Zionist friends with Montor's associates— welfare fund and federation leaders, that is, American Jewish philanthropic leaders who would turn to the UJA not the ZOA for guidance.[16]

By September 1948 Montor's plans for "a separate fund to rival the United Palestine Appeal" had been leaked to Silver's associates. Montor and his friends had decided on the strategy of eliminating the UPA's role as the organization that transmitted funds from the UJA to the Jewish Agency. This would, *de facto*, wrest from Silver's hands the principal source of his power. The strategy was simple: incorporate the Jewish Agency's New York office as an entirely new organization to be called The Jewish Agency, Inc. (or Americans United For Israel). The various federations and welfare funds would then bypass the UJA and recognize instead The Jewish Agency, Inc. as the recipient of funds intended for use in Israel. A few months later, as the plan reached its successful culmination, the executive of the Jewish Agency, usurping the authority of the UPA board of directors, signed an agreement with the UJA beneficiaries (including The Jewish Agency, Inc.) and successfully coopted the UPA.[17]

Silver's and Neumann's coup in Jerusalem occasioned Montor's angry (but carefully calculated) resignation, and concomitantly he joined with the Progressives (now buoyed by the Committee of Contributors) to deprive the UPA of its control over funds, to wrest control of the UPA from Silver and Neumann, and to place fundraising more and more under the control of the emerging class of communal professionals (mostly) loyal to Montor. Montor's arguments may or may not have been "specious" (Israel Goldstein, whom Silver had fought bitterly in 1938 and 1943, used this word and told Montor they were also "baseless slurs"; Montor himself would retract them all in early January 1949), but he clearly felt a tremendous bitterness toward Silver and Neumann, which would grow even stronger in the following months.[18]

Berl Locker, chairman of the Jewish Agency Executive in Israel,

immediately cabled to Montor that the Israeli leadership sym-
pathized with the "Montorites" goal of coopting or circumventing
the ZOA and would even travel to the United States if necessary to
kill the ZOA and build a new organization dominated by non-
Zionists. Locker together with Ben-Gurion viewed the ZOA as a
strong supporter of the General Zionists (a serious political rival in
the upcoming K'nesset elections) and they saw Silver, because of his
prominence, as a potential threat to their own party (Mapai). In
addition, both men worried (unnecessarily) or planted rumors that
Silver was about to go to Israel and head the General Zionist list or
battle Ben-Gurion by seeking the presidency of the WZO. Nahum
Goldmann explained why he together with two other members of
the American section bypassed Silver and wrote to Locker and the
Jewish Agency Executive in Jerusalem asking for its intercession: "I
say Dr. Silver cannot decide it [the choice for campaign chairman];
I cannot decide it; only the Executive can decide." Silver described
both Goldmann's initiative and Locker's cable as "a Montor-Morgenthau move, outside the Jewish Agency's jurisdiction," noting
that "all the rest is *shmooz.*"[19]

Despite the initiative (to which I will return), the Silverites
satisfactorily disposed of the reorganization of the UPA: CJFWF medi-
ators (a conciliation committee) hammered out a compromise (23
November 1948) that reorganized the UPA board of directors and
reaffirmed the traditional role of the UPA and the Joint Distribution
Committee in appointing the UJA chairman. This compromise,
however, did not end the matter. Some of the members of the
Jewish Agency Executive led by Nahum Goldmann unilaterally
decided to negotiate with Montor and his close friend, Henry
Morgenthau, Jr., to convince them to resume their leadership
positions in American Jewish fundraising. From the Israeli perspective, successful fundraising could best be achieved by having out in
front on the national level glamorous names—even if they were
non-Zionists—men of means whose names might automatically
inspire others to give. These men were often non-Zionists and

therefore uninvolved with the Zionist organizations in the United States. Most important to Silver, they were, he felt, men without commitments to maximal Jewish education, to the knowledge of Hebrew language and literature, or to an interest in Jewish culture and learning: They were Jews who perceived Judaism as a church and Jews as members of the Mosaic persuasion.[20]

The most prominent of the glamorous non-Zionists was Henry Morgenthau, Jr. (1891–1962), the UJA general chairman from 1947 to 1949, former secretary of the treasury (from 1934 to 1945) under Roosevelt (at the time the highest office ever held by a Jew in the United States), a gifted fundraiser whose "big gift" keynote addresses had dazzled Jews across the land in 1947 and 1948, and an indefatigable worker (despite the Zionists' nickname, "The Morgue") whose long, volunteer days at the UJA served as a model for campaign workers.

Philip Klaus, a member of the anti-Zionist American Council for Judaism, remembers Morgenthau's 1947 visit to Richmond, Virginia, and the "spiritual exhilaration . . . of the meeting." Morgenthau, as a "central, prophetic figure," created "a spiritual revival," according to Klaus, and he had convinced Klaus to "pledge generously." Montor described Morgenthau's Richmond address on the conflict between personal conviction and communal responsibility as "the longest and most moving personal statement I have ever heard him make," and, referring to his impact on Klaus, noted how Morgenthau "thawed out every frigid person present." Montor insisted that he and Morgenthau were a team and included Morgenthau in the "palace revolt."[21]

By the time the UPA executive had accepted Montor's resignation (on 21 October), he and Morgenthau had organized nearly one hundred Jewish communal leaders—mostly members of the increasingly powerful Council of Jewish Federations and Welfare Funds—into the Committee of Contributors and Workers. The committee leadership consisted of distinguished, veteran leaders of local Jewish communities, including several who held executive positions in national Jewish organizations and had been trying for several years to take Jewish philanthropy permanently out of the hands of Zionists and put it into the hands of communal fundraisers. In November 1948 the ccw announced plans for an Atlantic City conference of national Jewish leaders, to take place on 11–12 December and launch its own 1949 fundraising campaign for Israel. The Progressives supported the proposed conference and demanded that the UPA grant 50 percent representation to communal leaders in a reconstructed organization as the price of not convening the conference together with the ccw. Several Israeli leaders gave their support to the "palace revolt"; for example, Ben-Gurion in a swipe at Silver and Neumann told Montor that he was "content to see the direction of UJA in the hands of non-Zionist lay leaders and professional executives, rather than of ideologically-committed but party-affiliated Zionists."[22]

Hours before the delegates were to leave their homes for Atlantic City, the UPA and ccw hammered out an agreement (on 8 December)—in large part the work of cJFWF conciliators—in which in return for granting communal leaders 40 percent representation, the ccw agreed to cancel its conference. Now only one question remained for Silver, who spent nearly every weekday night during December, January, and February at the Sulgrave Hotel in New York City in order to do battle more conveniently, would Montor return to the fundraising leadership? His opposition to Morgenthau's return to general chairmanship of the UJA represented only a deep resentment of Montor, whose return Morgenthau demanded as a condition of his own.[23]

"Montor," Silver wrote to Israel Goldstein in 1948, "is not to be trusted." Silver felt that Montor intentionally orchestrated "big givers" meetings to exclude fervent Zionists or those who might espouse political Zionism and thus scare away the non-Zionists by mentioning the threatening phrase, "a Jewish state." He also correctly suspected that Montor and Morgenthau with the support of leaders in Israel sought to block appropriations to the emergency committee because of its "political work," demanding a Jewish political state in Palestine; that they threatened the emergency committee with an investigation of its tax status because of its "political activities"; and that they used their positions "to sabotage the UPA." World Zionist leaders such as Weizmann and Ben-Gurion as well as numerous American Jewish leaders who were opposed to Silver's leadership (two Hadassah leaders were in the forefront of this opposition: Rose Halpern and Judith Epstein) voiced strong support in January 1949 for the return of the team.[24]

Silver had threatened Israeli leaders that he would resign from the Zionist leadership if they intervened in this internal affair of who should be the UJA campaign chairman. Nevertheless, the Jewish Agency Executive (twelve members) did intervene in this UPA matter, just as Berl Locker had signaled. The members of the executive left for New York City on 27 January to convene an extraordinary plenary session of the American section of the Jewish Agency Executive, the first ever in the United States. On 9 February in a compromise after days of debate, the Jewish Agency Executive (which included Neumann and Silver) approved the return of Morgenthau and of Montor, with certain controls and safeguards (there would be three executive directors, one of whom [Montor] would be chosen by Morgenthau).[25]

But Morgenthau and Montor demanded greater power (they wanted primary authority to reside with Morgenthau and executive authority to rest with Montor). The executive hesitated, but Silver's final attempt to convince Morgenthau to compromise—a request by the executive that Morgenthau meet with Silver if the latter flew to Florida—was rejected by Morgenthau. "I am prepared to leave by plane tomorrow," Silver cabled Morgenthau, "and welcome such an opportunity." Morgenthau, however, replied that he had nothing to say to Silver, repeating his insistence that Montor control all fundraising activities. At Goldmann's request, the executive then reversed itself and accepted the Morgenthau-Montor team. Silver had been outmaneuvered by his indefatigible Zionist enemies. With this defeat, Silver and Neumann resigned from the Jewish Agency Executive on 15 February, citing the "unwarranted and impertinent intrusion" of the Jewish Agency Executive into American Jewish affairs and announcing that they rejected not only Montor, Goldmann, and Morgenthau but "all that they stand for" as well. It was merely a formality for the UPA board of directors on 28 February to approve the return of Morgenthau and Montor. Silver and twenty-nine followers abstained and fifty-two members of the board voted their approval and sealed Silver's defeat. With Silver gone, Nahum Goldmann took over as chairman of the Jewish Agency Executive, American section.[26]

There is little doubt that in addition to Zionist issues, Silver himself served as a catalyst for much of the opposition that successfuly forced him to resign. Despite five years of dedicated national leadership at great personal sacrifice, a significant number of Jewish leaders inside and outside the United States had grown eager to end what one of them called "the Silver regime." Different people found him arrogant, overbearing, domineering, egotistical, contemptuous, and an enemy of anyone who dared oppose him or one of his ideas.[27]

Perhaps some of these qualities were what helped make him a great leader at a critical hour and an articulate spokesman for the Zionist and Jewish case in world forums, but they also made him a most difficult individual to deal with. From Ben-Gurion and Weizmann, both of whom repeatedly called Silver a "dictator" in 1948–49, to Nahum Goldmann who called him "a foul personality, a nasty character . . . absolutely ruthless to his opponents," to American Jewish leaders who actually hated him, he had accumulated a wide assortment of enemies—especially men and women who wanted to share if not appropriate his power. He did not yield easily, and when he faced an ignominious defeat early in 1949—the return of Montor and Morgenthau coupled with the agreement signed by The United Jewish Appeal and the Jewish Agency, Inc.— he resigned from national leadership only after his opponents (the

Committee for Progressive Zionism) had vigorously denounced him. A month later at the May 1949 ZOA convention, he formally said goodbye, or as Henry Morgenthau, Jr. reportedly noted with delight "a certain rabbi from Cleveland delivered his *swine* song." The ZOA President, Daniel Frisch, put it even more bluntly: "You must understand," he told a colleague, "that Silver is now a dead-duck."[28]

Not completely. Even after his February resignation from the Jewish Agency Executive, supporters launched a "draft Silver" movement to convince him to announce his candidacy for ZOA president. He refused, announcing his intention to support Frisch's candidacy and to resign his AZEC position in September but to remain active in national and international affairs. In his 105-minute address to the ZOA convention on 29 May 1949 Silver provided a detailed summary, with as much eloquence, stinging satire, humorous twists, harsh invectives, and finely spun phrases as the most powerful political addresses of his early career, of his interpretation of the "crisis" of 1948–49. Abe Sachar, president of Brandeis University, noted that "few men have ever surpassed him in the relentless logic of his oratorical offensive" and bemoaned his irrevocable decision to leave the public Zionist arena. Silver had concluded and Virginia agreed that to have "accepted the Presidency of the ZOA again might have undermined my sanity." He was probably right. He had recently informed Sol Freehof that "I have been so busy this season that I really have not been able to check up on myself." He began his "check-up" as soon as possible, as he and Virginia left the United States in July on the *Queen Elizabeth* for a vacation.[29]

Before departing for the French Riviera, Silver had to wrap up the loose ends of a local problem that had irritated him during the UJA crisis. Early in 1947 together with the other senior Reform rabbi in Cleveland, Barnett Brickner, Silver had organized and their congregations had helped finance a third Reform congregation in Cleveland. Known initially as Temple Emanu El in the Making on the Heights, its first rabbi, Alan S. Green, was brought from Houston by Silver and Brickner and generously encouraged to build a new congregation. However, a fourth synagogue, Suburban Temple, brought Silver considerable turmoil.[30]

Suburban was organized by members of The Temple opposed to Silver's Zionism and to the congregation's emphasis on Zionism and Hebrew in the religious school. While Emanu El sought unaffiliated Jews living a considerable distance from either of the two established Reform congregations, Suburban actively sought to lure (Silver and Brickner called it raid) members of the existing congregations away from Euclid Avenue Temple or The Temple. The new congregation even went so far in its advertisements to note the "racial mix" in the older congregations' neighborhoods, and to draw out explicitly the implications of its own name. Suburban's first rabbi, who quit as quickly as he could, described the membership as "un-Jewish, ignorant and wicked folk," and he noted the efforts of the leadership to be an "exclusive and limited congregation with country club appeal." He told Virginia Silver of "the madness, irresponsibility and self-hatred" he witnessed among Suburban's leaders during the first year of his rabbinate. He told Silver in the spring of 1949 that its "anti-Zionist, anti-Israel bias was carried to the extreme of barring Jewish current events (news of Israel) in the school."[31]

Suburban's rabbi told his brother that Silver treated him with "kindness" and "sympathy" (despite the tension of the Montor-Morgenthau struggle), but all through the fall of 1948 and the early months of 1949 Silver and The Temple leadership waged a vigorous battle to prevent dozens of members from leaving. Silver took an "adamant stand" against the new congregation; indeed, the congregation's rabbi told Silver's assistant that "Dr. S. was the only rabbi with guts enuf [sic] to handle these little Jew-haters. He had their number from the start," the disillusioned rabbi noted, "and would not compromise with them." But this refusal to compromise took its toll on Silver; his personal letters during these months reveal his anxiety not only over Montor's fundraising machinations but the vigilance required to keep up with Suburban's activities.[32]

The international and national tensions of 1947, 1948, and 1949 had taken enormous amounts of physical and psychological energy, and nearly everyone who worked with Silver in both the 1940s and 1950s noted the toll that Jewish statehood and Zionist politics had exacted. Elihu Elath, for example, who could not imagine that Silver ever "relaxed" in the 1940s when they lobbied together, was struck by how different Silver looked and acted when they strolled together (in England) in the 1950s. Silver "chatted quietly, walked slowly, laughed vigorously and displayed a quiet calm" when they met; his scholarly research took precedence over Zionist politics when they drank tea together and he peppered Elath with queries about Elath's own day to day activities. Of course, one cannot know for sure if the battles Silver fought from 1943–49 shortened his life, but few people that I interviewed failed to discern a dramatic change in his person during this time. The 1950s would see Silver largely at home, relaxed, and enjoying the honors of an elder statesman while he pursued his early love, writing. He may never have been happier, or so many who knew him then would suggest.

Chapter Nine

I spend Saturday evening at my desk preparing my Sunday morning lecture.

—Abba Hillel Silver, 24 November 1930

Silver was cold-blooded—warm and hot as he could be on the platform, he was very cool in his own retreats, in his own study, in his own counsel, cool, calculating, ruthless.

—Israel Goldstein, 12 September 1973

Silver could laugh volcanically [sic]; the charm of Silver was in his smile.

—Shulamith Schwartz Nardi, July 1986

He was a very cultured person himself [but] he always surrounded himself with an intimate circle of people with infinitely inferior cultural equipment. That was one of the paradoxes about that human being that we never understood.

—Ezra Shapiro, 10 June 1975

A few months before his death in 1963, in celebration of his seventieth birthday, Silver participated in a dialogue with Rabbi Solomon B. Freehof, his classmate and devoted friend. In response to a question from Freehof about the "best achievement of every-thing you have done," Silver naturally selected his contribution toward the establishment of the State of Israel as the achievement

185

he "treasure[d] the most." But he went on to point out that "I never permitted my Zionist activities, even when they were most intense [1943–48] . . . to push aside or to overshadow my activities and my duties as a rabbi."[1]

It is true that Silver's Zionist activities did not overshadow his rabbinical duties; even his AZEC work did not push these responsibilities aside. Much evidence exists to confirm his dedication to his congregational responsibilities, even when his Zionist activities were "most intense." Of course, he defined his rabbinate in such a way as to make "pastor of his flock" a lower priority than "teacher of Torah" ("principally," he told Freehof, "the rabbi . . . is teacher— not pastor, but teacher"), but there is little if any evidence to suggest that he neglected the pastoral needs of those who sought his help. All of his former assistants agree, however, that most congregants did not seek his help; his secretary from 1947 to 1953 recalls that "hardly anyone came to him for pastoral counseling." She believes that temple members perceived Silver's role first as a celebrated national leader who ought not to be bothered with minor troubles, second, as a "teacher of Torah to his people," third, as a celebrant of lifecycle events for members, and last, as a counselor. Silver expressed much the same sense of his rabbinate when he told one assistant "if I had it my way I'd design a synagogue with only a sanctuary and a religious school."[2]

Nevertheless, throughout most of his rabbinate with the obvious exception of the lobbying years, Silver held open "office hours" in his study for one-and-a-half to two hours before lunch. He constantly noted this in his correspondence, inviting congregants and others to drop in on any day of the week. He usually arrived at The Temple about 9:00 A.M., after early morning reading, then opened his considerable mail and dictated letters before meeting visitors. After a robust lunch ("he loved to eat," recalled one assistant) he would devote the afternoon (whenever possible) to reading and reflection. This pattern changed little during his first twenty-five years at The Temple.[3]

One might conclude from his relatively free "office hours," or from the claim made by an assistant who worked with Silver for six years that "he never did any pastoral work," that Silver lacked the personal warmth so necessary for moments of caring and healing. Quite the contrary. While he might have restricted his hospital calls to people who were desperately ill and even felt some reluctance in such areas, literally hundreds of congregants sent personal letters of thanks to Silver all through the 1920s, 1930s, and especially the 1940s, and emphasized his patience, compassion, and gentleness. This "source of unlimited power" to some congregants was also, according to one assistant (1944–48), "absolutely beautiful in pastoral moments." He became "total concentration," this same rabbi would later observe, "as if he could set aside Jewish and world concerns when his healing smile was needed."[4]

Silver himself placed his teaching (and his pulpit served, of course, as a type of lectern) above all else. To him, "teaching young and old the spiritual and ethical doctrines of Judaism" constituted the "major contribution" of his congregational work. Former confirmands from the 1940s vividly remember Silver's dedication to teaching these young people, and his compulsive returns to Cleveland—from Washington or New York—to lecture and to discuss with them (usually on Friday afternoon) some aspect of the history of Judaism.[5]

One confirmand (from the class of 1927) remembers Silver as an "uncompromising lecturer in a class of 114 students" and the "fear" he instilled in the youngsters should they fail to be "prepared with the assignment." He wore formal pulpit attire—cutaway coat, striped trousers, starched collar, black tie—in the classroom, and this, together with his professorial style of addressing all the students by their last names and putting them on the spot with questions about the homework, lent his classes (on Thursday and Friday afternoons) a formal, serious atmosphere. Rigorous quizzes, papers, exams, and ribbons for honors in confirmation classes as well as in all the intermediate and upper grades—with summer sessions for students who did not complete a grade successfully!—added to the students' seriousness of purpose. Indeed, one confirmand from the 1940s, later a rabbi, recalls that not only did Silver urge his confirmands to "spend as much time on their Judaic studies as on their secular ones," but that "his Confirmation exam provoked as much anxiety as the doctoral exam I was to endure twenty years later."[6]

Silver returned home, of course, to his Sunday morning pulpit, which provided him with the opportunity thirty to forty times per year to teach his congregants from 11:15 to 12:00. His sermons were more properly lectures, and many of those from the 1920s, 1930s, and 1940s read as well half-a-century or so later as they must have been received as oral messages then. One rabbi who studied with Wise and served under Silver in the 1940s noted that "Wise and Silver were both golden-tongued; only Dr. Silver's sermons, however, still read." They are pure Litvak—reasoned and poetic. Long and tightly organized; generous in their use of documentation, evidence, literary (especially rabbinic) references, metaphors and analogies; and demonstrating wide-ranging reading and careful crafting, these sermons serve the primary purpose of informing, transmitting, and communicating the Judaic tradition as mediated through the eyes and mind of a Reform rabbi. Rarely bound by the need to moralize or by the designated weekly Torah portion (though it was read at every Sabbath morning service, frequently by someone who had just turned thirteen), Silver combined the polished lecture style of a popular university professor with the passionate conviction and power of a fiery orator whose "voice could glide over the tonal range" and whose "long talon-like but beautifully molded fingers" could "encompass the entire audience."[7]

Saturday evenings at least from the 1920s through the 1940s served as the time for the final preparation of sermons. Although he read and thought about his Sunday lecture throughout the week, Silver waited until Saturday evening to dictate to his secretary the Sunday lecture. Silver's secretary arrived at his home nearly every

Saturday evening for dictation. That same evening the secretary would type a transcript of the sermon; Silver would then more or less memorize it (this continued into the 1950s); the following morning the secretary would sit in the balcony and take down the sermon as delivered; and final typed copies would be produced based largely on the oral delivery but with corrections made from the earlier, dictated copy.[8]

Silver, the rabbi-teacher, took an active interest in the entire educational program of the gigantic religious school. Although an assistant rabbi usually supervised this school, Silver would regularly roam in and out of the Sabbath and even (early) Sunday morning classes. Former students able to remember these visits recall sitting in awe, tense and quiet in his presence. "If anyone was bigger than life," one recalls, "it was Abba Hillel Silver; he was the source of unlimited power." Silver himself, judging from his papers and his assistants' recollections, would travel from class to class in order to make mental notes, mostly about teachers, texts, and pedagogy. "I visited all of the classrooms on Sunday," he wrote one assistant, "and there seemed to be a lack of spirit." "He believed profoundly in Jewish education," an assistant from the AZEC years recalled, and he maintained close contact with (as well as offered frequent critiques of) those responsible for supervising the teachers in the schools.[9]

Silver's copious memos together with the tales of his assistants suggest that every area of The Temple's complex machinery fell under his scrutiny. His first assistant, Leon Feuer, recalled that "there was no question . . . as to who was the boss of the total operation: the rabbi." Silver's "weekly custom" consisted in "inspecting The Temple building, from furnace room to dome, while vigorously singing 'Valencia,' . . . [and] God help the staff if everything was not in place and spic-and-span." He wrote one assistant that "the curtain in Mahler Hall needed a new track," told another that the "leather cushion of the settee outside the Chapel is torn," and wrote a memo about the "marble slab along side of the door in the lobby leading up to the choir loft that has been loosened." He took an even more serious interest in the leadership of the congregation, with the result that some said (not without justification, according to Feuer), that the leaders of the synagogue "simply served as rubber stamps for Silver's policies."

Other powerful rabbis of Silver's generation—Barnett Brickner (1892–1958), Edgar Magnin (1890–1984), Solomon Freehof 1892–19), Stephen Wise (1874–1949), to name but a few—also dominated their synagogue leadership and received rubber stamp approval, but very few congregations had as much "smoothness, efficiency and cooperation . . . with all eyes focused on the main objectives" as did the one that Silver served. The "main objectives" that Feuer mentions, of course, were the rabbi's deep involvement in local and state politics and his even deeper involvement in national and international Zionist activities. The congregation, or at least the board of trustees, took enormous pride in Silver's visibility and strongly endorsed his communal involvement.[10]

Even on the eve of assuming the leadership of the AZEC, while immersed in numerous national activities on behalf of European and Palestinian Jews and "traveling a great deal all over the country," Silver let little slip beyond his control. He told his second assistant, Melbourne Harris, that "I have met several times with the House Committee, the Finance Committee, the Choir Committee as well as quite a number of committees of the TWA [Temple Women's Association] about their program and activities for next year." Little changed two months later, after Silver had accepted the co-chair of the AZEC and began to travel regularly to Washington and New York City and busy himself even further in national Zionist affairs. On the eve of the High Holy Days, "added to the customary activities at this season of the year," Silver agreed actively to direct the congregation's participation in the third war loan drive with the hope, he told one congregant, that The Temple would "raise over a million dollars . . . in war bonds [they actually sold more than three million dollars worth of bonds] and purchase a fleet of ten ambulance planes which will bear the name of The Temple."

Early in 1944 while lobbying in Washington, he wrote to one of the six hundred Temple "boys" serving overseas with the news that he would return to Cleveland to keynote the fourth war loan drive. He kept up a massive correspondence with scores of these soldiers, urging them to "drop me a line and let me know how you are feeling [as] I like to hear from my young friends." His willingness to officiate at congregants' weddings as well as the need to conduct the funerals of those he knew well hardly diminished during 1943–44 and 1944–45, despite his New York and Washington commutes, and in the final year or so prior to the dramatic U.N. vote on partition, Silver's secretary claimed that "never once did I see him neglect his congregational responsibilities."[11]

At the same time that he found it hard to let go, he clearly possessed the ability to delegate responsibility to the various administrative personnel at The Temple. He consistently expressed his "happiness with his staff taking whatever responsibility they were able to" and viewed his function as "frequently checking up on their progress." His associates could, almost unanimously, recall him as "a perfect boss."[12]

Many who did not know him personally also referred to him as "boss." In the home of one congregant, Silver was "portrayed to us children as a religious leader capable of evoking terror in the mayor's office and even in the White House," and one of his secretaries was warned before applying for the job that "Silver eats secretaries alive" and "brings his secretary to tears weekly." Yet those who worked at The Temple and those who entered either of Silver's two rented homes on Lake Erie in Bratenahl or later in Shaker Heights, referred to him as "gentle," "quiet," "shy," and softly humorous." Robert Marx (b. 1927), a youth of about thirteen at the time, joined the Silvers for lunch one Sunday after Solomon Freehof had spoken at The Temple, and his recollections are typical. In the presence of the "powerful man [Silver] from the awesome pulpit," Marx felt like Heinrich Heine, who was in terror at being invited to an audience with the mighty Goethe: the rehearsed speeches went out the window and all he could manage to say was: "Beautiful day, isn't it?" Silver quickly put Marx at ease, quietly laughing and joking with him as his own father might have done at their table.[13]

Nearly everyone recalls Silver's "marvelous sense of humor" away from the pulpit, his affectionate handshakes and hugs, and his love of eating (especially potato pancakes). Silver's humor was abundant: "he would laugh with his whole body," an assistant recalled. Another assistant recalled that "I saw him evoke laughter incessantly, especially with a repertoire of Yiddish jokes." He was no less uninhibited when it came to eating, though he never ate before a lecture. He explained this once to a secretary: "one never eats before a performance." He ate much and he ate well, beginning with his rabbinical school days when he would spend nearly all his biweekly pulpit honoraria on meals in Cincinnati restaurants and continuing well into the 1950s when, according to his assistant, he loved to "raid the icebox." The Friday night dinner, the Sunday midday meal, and almost any occasion with guests present beginning with his earliest years of married life were semiformal affairs, with a cook (who doubled as a housekeeper) and a maid assisting Virginia.

Guests recall an elegant dining room with long, formal meals, and "Ab," as Ginny would call him, softly "quizzing" each of the boys on his weekly studies and activities. "Quietly" is frequently used by those who recall Silver's conversation at home or in a social group of men and women, where he relaxed by playing cards and chatting on the typical topics of social gatherings. Florence Michaelson (Bernstein), a niece who lived with Ginny and Abba during the 1930s after her mother Pearl died (1931), used the word "quietly" often in our conversation, while Leon Feuer, Silver's first assistant, noted that "conversationally, he tended to be rather withdrawn." One son remembers that while "he loved to hear and to tell a good story, he was not somebody who needed to be the center of attention at family meals," while the other felt that his father was "relaxed and easygoing socially with tons of friends with whom he felt close." Earl Stone, an assistant rabbi from 1950 to 1956, recalls a dinner at the Silver home when, on a hot and humid evening, Virginia convinced Earl and the other male guest to remove their coats, but "Ab" refused his wife's request to remove either his coat or vest. Nobody recalls Silver even in July and August without a tie, vest, and coat, sometimes even a straw hat. One son recalls that "I never in my whole childhood or young adulthood saw him leave the bedroom except with his coat and tie on."[14]

Virginia did much more than merely make guests feel comfortable in the Silvers' Bratenahl and Shaker Heights homes. Nearly everyone with whom I spoke in Cleveland and the rabbinical assistant who served at The Temple used the word "gracious" to describe her, but they also emphasized that she advised her husband on most matters connected with The Temple. She was not especially involved in the national and overseas issues that excited Abba, but she was more than just a sweet nice southern lady who never missed Temple services. If Silver confided in anyone, it was Ginny, and numerous people insist that she was "bright as a tack," "vivacious, bright, funny, caring," and that "he would take her advice on many, many a strategy" and "confide in her." There seems no doubt in anyone's mind that "she was a great help to him," though Earl Stone may exaggerate when he says that "she was always the power behind the throne." At the very least, my conversations confirm the observation of one of her sons that "Mom gave him perspective and balance in the home; in the sense of managing their lives, she was terribly important."[15]

Virginia was a typical rabbi's wife during the 1930s and 1940s as her sons were growing and her husband's career became more demanding. She was a wife and mother, devoted to Abba and the boys, shopping for food and clothes, accompanying the boys to their clubs and activities, disciplining them, and not only arranging social events but seemingly providing Abba with most of his male friends by maintaining relationships with the wives. Both sons agree that she subordinated her intellectual instincts to their father, pursuing them only in the two decades of her life after her husband died.

Whatever Ginny's support meant, Silver maintained a strong desire for male fellowship. It would find frequent outlets, though his delight in acting like a kid proved harder to satisfy. Since he loved to eat and *shmooze* with his buddies, best of all was a meal at the Tasty Shop (at 105th and Euclid) with his Zionist cronies, where he could be, according to one of those pals, "one of the boys." Two of his friends, Joseph Silbert (1901–   ) and Jack Skirball, recalled deli lunches and late evening snacks where Abba could satisfy his fondness for food and ribald jokes. He dominated such gatherings, as he did the crowd at Goodman's Barber Shop, where he took his Friday shave and haircut, or card games with his friends. He loved poker, bridge, and gin rummy and regularly insisted that the winnings go to The Temple sunshine (charity) fund. He "collected [and remembered]), one friend recalled, "Yiddish jokes as others did phone numbers." To Skirball, a rabbinical school pal and a long-time friend, Silver was always a "boy." One time during World War II when he spoke in Los Angeles, Silver called Jack from his hotel and they planned a dinner together with Jack's wife. On the way to dinner (in Pomona, outside Los Angeles), Silver saw a street fair and insisted that the Skirballs stop so he might ride on the merry-go-round. According to Jack, "he had the time of his life."[16]

His relationship with his sons was sometimes highly formal; on one occasion (10 October 1947) he dictated a personal letter to his son Daniel Jeremy and told his secretary to type and sign it for him. She did, closing with "Your loving father" and signing "Liz Rice"! In the letter he advised his son about both his rabbinical school application and his desire to study at the Hebrew University in Jerusalem and discussed their summer study together. For years, Abba had studied Hebrew texts with his two sons. "During the summers, one or two weekday evenings, and on Sabbath afternoons," one son (who became a rabbi) recalls, beginning when I was probably six or seven, Dad would call us in one after the other and we would have an hour's Hebrew lesson with him. We would read a little Tanach; later on, much later, Rashi, Targum Onkelos, then on up. . . . In the summers we would go swimming; if we could conjugate a verb or decline a noun, we could climb on his shoulders and dive off. If we couldn't, we got dunked.

In 1947, after the boys returned from college, Abba studied Maimonides's *Book of Knowledge* with Daniel Jeremy (b. 1928) and the biblical book of Ecclesiastes with Raphael (b. 1930). For Daniel Jeremy, thse studies provided him with the necessary background to pursue a rabbinical education, a doctoral degree in medieval Jewish philosophy, and a career of productive Jewish scholarship, while Raphael, who pursued a business career, "looked forward no less than my brother" to the lessons, and recalls Abba pointing out how pleased he was to teach his sons as his father had taught him.[17]

Most of those who knew Abba and Ginny during the years after the establishment of the Jewish state recall how eager the couple was to have grandchildren and how enthusiastically Abba greeted the arrival of those he lived to see. The demands of his people, in Cleveland and overseas, did not leave him as much time at home with his own children as he might have liked in the 1930s and early 1940s, and he worked hard to make up for lost time in the last years of his life. His letters from the early 1960s suggest that his grandchildren brought him as least as much pleasure as his rabbinate, and his family treasures similar memories.

Chapter
Ten

Providence favored me with loving parents to whom a
book was even more precious than a loaf of bread.

—Abba Hillel Silver, 14 July 1963

When Silver's opponents succeeded in driving him out of his
chairmanship of the Jewish Agency Executive early in 1949, he
returned to his Cleveland rabbinate. During the fall of 1949 and the
High Holy Days he began once again regularly to deliver the
Sunday morning lectures that had filled The Temple sanctuary for
two decades or so before he took on the burden of national leadership. In addition, he turned his attention to several scholarly
writing projects he had contemplated for some time, producing at
least one book that would influence a generation of rabbis and other
readers as well.

Silver did not, however, withdraw completely from his Washington lobbying. Indeed, the young state of Israel regularly took
advantage of his friendliness with some officials in the Eisenhower
administration, and Silver was pleased to respond and always did so
with alacrity. As he told Israel's ambassador to the United States
Abba Eban in 1951 (and repeatedly thereafter), "I shall be very
happy to help you in every way I can; if the matter is urgent, I could
come to Washington immediately." While he was *persona non grata*
with Truman, Silver was clearly *persona grata* with John Foster
Dulles (the secretary of state), Dwight D. Eisenhower, Thomas E.
Dewey (the Republican governor of New York) and Sherman
Adams (a presidential assistant). And although his contributions to

the emergence of the Jewish state were probably more significant when Silver was denied access to the Truman White House, his relatively easy access to Dulles, Dewey, and Eisenhower certainly aided Israel as it struggled for survival during its first decade of existence.[1]

Silver's connection with the Eisenhower administration went back to 1949 when he was contacted by then Senator Dulles during a special senatorial election in New York. Dulles ran (unsuccessfully) against a Jew, Herbert H. Lehman (1878–1963), and Governor Dewey had asked Silver to defend Dulles against Lehman's charges that Dulles was soft on Israel. Silver wrote a brief letter delineating Dulles's commitments to Israel and praising his efforts against racial and religious prejudice, and both Dewey and Dulles remained grateful to Silver throughout the following decade. At a critical hour several years later, when Silver had successfully lobbied a reluctant Eisenhower to sell "defensive" weapons to Israel (see below), the secretary of state would remind the president of Silver's defense of him in the senatorial election.[2]

Dewey arranged a forty-five-minute conversation between Silver and Ike at Eisenhower's Morningside Heights residence before the 1952 presidential election, and Silver lectured the Republican candidate on Israel's security needs. To reporters who interviewed him after the meeting, Silver refused to endorse either Eisenhower or his Democratic opponent, Adlai Stevenson, telling the press "I am a religious leader, not a Republican or Democrat." He did use the interview, however, to blast Truman for having suggested a day earlier that Eisenhower was soft in his opposition to the discriminatory (anti-Jewish and anti-Catholic) Walter-McCarran immigration bill. In contrast to earlier decades when Silver had remained genuinely neutral politically, he strongly supported Eisenhower's campaign and permitted the Republican National Committee to use his meeting with Eisenhower in its campaign literature.[3]

Silver's support for Eisenhower went further than just permitting their meeting to be used for publicity. Dewey had asked Silver to draft letters for Eisenhower spelling out his position on Israel (in response to the Labor Zionist endorsement of Stevenson); Silver agreed to an exchange of such letters, which would begin (14 October) with an inquiry by Silver about Ike's position on Israel and continue (17 October) with a response from Eisenhower (written by Silver) to Silver. The rabbi and future president agreed in advance of their meeting that it would be best if Silver refused to endorse Ike publicly lest it be seen merely as a *quid pro quo* for Ike's support of Israel. When a few days after their meeting Stevenson released a statement on Israel (23 October) and Silver applauded both candidates' positions on Israel ("clearly no difference"), the Republican leadership expressed its thanks. The Republican National Chairman told Silver he would be "forever grateful for [Silver's] courageous defense" of Ike; Governor Dewey thanked Silver for his "wonderful contribution"; Ohio Senator John Bricker phoned Silver to express his "profound appreciation"; Eisenhower thanked Silver for his "fine support"; and after the election, Ike invited him to offer a prayer at his inauguration.[4]

Silver's contacts with the secretary of state remained frequent during the 1950s and usually revolved around crises in the Middle East. After Israel's Prime Minister David Ben-Gurion and Israeli Ambassador Abba Eban urged Silver to discuss the reported pro-Arab tilt of the administration, Silver met Dulles on 17 February 1953 and concluded there is "no new line . . . only a new look." Dulles frequently called Silver directly on the phone to seek his advice or invited him to Washington for lunch; he regularly returned Silver's calls promptly if he was in a meeting, thanked Silver publicly ("Rabbi Silver assisted materially in bringing about the resumption of the grant-in-aid to Israel" [28 October 1953], and asked Silver to draft position papers for Dulles's use at National Security Council meetings. In addition, the secretary of state sought Silver's advice on Israeli requests for weapons. He asked Silver on 30 October 1956 during the Suez War to phone Ben-Gurion and ask him to withdraw Israeli troops from Egypt in exchange for a strong public statement of support from Eisenhower. He asked Silver to write Eisenhower's evening radio talk (on 31 October 1956) in response to Ben-Gurion's qualified agreement to withdraw, and after lunching with Silver, he agreed to persuade Eisenhower not to discuss sanctions against Israel in an address on the Middle East. Dulles also frequently met with Silver for reports on the rabbi's visits to Israel, and regularly asked various underlings (especially Christian Herter, the under secretary of state) to discuss the administration's policy on Israel with Silver.[5]

On 26 April 1956 the secretary of state arranged for a meeting attended by Dulles, Silver, and the president that lasted nearly an hour to hear Silver present arguments that could convince an unwilling administration to sell $64 million worth of weapons to Israel. Silver called them "defensive" weapons necessary to "restore the military balance," while Dulles argued, according to Silver, that the preponderance of military strength was with Israel and hence the state had no need for more arms. Silver insisted that only a strong Israel could act as a "deterrent to [Arab] aggression" and that "Zionist pressure" was a pejorative phrase because the truth was that the Jews and the non-Jewish community overwhelmingly supported arms for Israel, not just so-called Zionists; Dulles, now willing to discuss the sale with American allies, reminded Ike of Silver's public defense of the secretary of state in 1949 and the president, according to Silver's account, appeared to grow more sympathetic to these arguments than he had been earlier in the conversation.[6]

Silver's summaries of his meetings with Eisenhower, and his interviews with reporters after these meetings, were quite frank. After a half-hour meeting with the president on 8 July 1953, arranged by Dulles, the rabbi was saddened by Eisenhower's "inadequate" grasp of the "Israeli cause," his lack of clarity on the subject of "whether Israel is a religious or a secular state," and his "confusion about the divisions in American Jewry." Nevertheless, he found Ike's commitment to Israeli security genuine, but he was determined to monitor it regularly. In 1957 after Eisenhower addressed the nation on the Middle East, Silver pointed out negative parts of the speech to reporters and told an administration official (Jack Martin) that the "tone was unfortunate" and that the "positive statements" might have been "couched in friendlier and more reassuring terms." With Dulles, Silver was always friendly and polite but ready vigorously to attack his positions on Israel and the Middle East in general. After several years of such conversations, debates, and letter exchanges, Dulles told Silver that he learned more from him than from all his advisers.[7]

David Ben-Gurion's role in Silver's being ousted from the leadership led Silver to harbor a deep hostility toward Israel's first prime minister, a hostility that took several years to soften on both sides. Ben-Gurion (1886–1973), who devoted more than sixty-five years of his life to active politics, had gained international prominence in Jewry by the early 1930s, when he was elected to the Jewish Agency Executive (1933) and then elected chairman of this body (1935). He spent much of the early 1940s in the United States, close to the White House and deeply involved in Zionist lobbying and intra-party conflicts; after World War II he solidified his position as the leader of the World Zionist Organization and he served as the first prime minister of Israel from its inception in 1948 through 1953, and again from 1956 to 1963. A few months after Silver's removal from the Zionist leadership, on the eve of the fifty-second annual Zionist Organization of America convention, Ben-Gurion wrote to Silver and challenged his Zionist credentials. Ben-Gurion argued in his letter that a Zionist was someone who settled in Israel, and hence Silver might be a friend of Israel but not a Zionist! Silver responded with a historical analysis of Zionism, arguing that the term Zionist has been continuously used to describe those passionately committed to the establishment of a Jewish state, whether or not they planned to settle there themselves.[8]

Later that year, in November 1949, the *New York Times* ran a headline that announced that Ben-Gurion has assailed Silver for trying to sway Israeli policy; Ben-Gurion did indeed blast "Zionists" abroad, though not Silver by name, and while Ben-Gurion denied that Silver was the target, Silver was not so sure. He remained convinced that Ben-Gurion disliked him and felt threatened by him, although he felt there was insufficient reason for either response.[9]

The tension had not abated by 1951 and Ben-Gurion refused a request by Ambassador Eban to invite Silver to Israel as a guest of the state. Silver went anyway from 25 April to 13 May as a guest of the General Zionists, and despite an official boycott of his visit by Mapai leaders (including Ben-Gurion), he was dazzled by his reception. More than one thousand people from all over the country waited for hours to greet him and his late flight. Cheering crowds lined the streets of Petach Tikvah, Ramat Gan, and Tel Aviv as his motorcade left the airport with Silver seated in an open maroon Pontiac waving his hat. A school was announced in his name (Kefar Silver) outside of Ashkelon and the cornerstone set in place, and a speech he gave in Tel Aviv's Mograbi Theatre (on 28 April) was heard by thousands of Israelis, grateful for Silver's role in establishing the state and standing outside the packed auditorium.[10]

Two years later (in April–May 1951) Ben-Gurion visited the United States and logged eight thousand miles on a cross-country fundraising tour to launch Bonds for Israel. He carefully avoided references to Zionism and the Zionist movement lest he alienate non-Zionists (whatever their definition) who might wish to invest in Israel. But on the eve of his departure from New York, he could not control his feelings any longer and he attacked the American Zionist movement. Courting the checkbooks of non-Zionists, he claimed that Zionists did not speak for American Jewry, that the majority of those who contributed funds to Israel had no interest in the Zionist Organization of America, that the American Zionist movement served "as a wall between them and Israel," and, finally, that so-called Zionists should concentrate on education and settling in Israel. This thinly veiled attack on Silver and Neumann and their leadership of the ZOA incensed Silver, and he assailed Ben-

Gurion incessantly over the next few months, noting that Ben-Gurion "whistled many tunes simultaneously [but] the sweet tunes [were] reserved for the non-Zionists while all the strident and truculent ones [were] for the Zionists." Silver's fellow Zionists for the most part joined with him, and the fifty-fourth convention of the ZOA in Atlantic City provided the setting for addresses that denounced Ben-Gurion. Silver delivered a lengthy and vigorous attack, interrupted more than a dozen times by applause, once again defending the role of American Zionists and rejecting definitions of Zionism that excluded leaders such as he.[11]

The twenty-third World Zionist Congress held in Jerusalem in August 1951 featured a renewal of the bitter political fight between Ben-Gurion and Silver as the former sought successfully to diminish (Silver said undermine) the authority of diaspora Zionists and their organizations (especially the Zionist Organization of America) and together with his Mapai followers he soundly defeated the Silver forces. The ZOA, of course, linked itself with the General Zionists, Ben-Gurion's major political adversaries, who had won twenty seats in the recent Israeli elections (Mapai won forty-five seats), and the ZOA demanded a partnership with Israel that included participation in the distribution of money and a substantial share in shaping Israeli policies. Ben-Gurion furiously fought this brazen demand and generally succeeded in beating back the diaspora challenge. Silver however left the Congress enraged at Ben-Gurion.[12]

Ironically, Ben-Gurion may also have been responsible for blocking the most serious opportunity Silver had to move permanently to Israel. When Selig Brodetsky resigned from the presidency of the Hebrew University in 1952, David Senator, executive vice-president of the board of governors, informed George Wise, the chairman of the board of governors, on 4 September 1952 that Abba Hillel Silver was the board's first choice to replace Brodetsky. He had "the biggest personality" and was "most influential in American Jewry," the key constituency for successful fundraising. In addition he had the "highest scholastic background, and would surely be

acceptable to the faculty." The board of governors asked Emanuel
Neumann to explore the position with Silver and he quickly wrote
to Silver (on 17 September 1952) with the preliminary offer. Silver
responded that he was interested but asked to know how Ben-
Gurion had reacted to his candidacy, rightly sensing that the president of Israel's only university would have to get along well with the
head of the government, especially in light of the university's
serious financial difficulties and its need to select a site for a new
campus. Ben-Gurion's response, according to Senator and Wise,
noted that the government must remain neutral in such a matter,
but if he could express an opinion he would not be "over-enthusi-
astic." Several members of the board continued their efforts to
convince Silver to take the job, and as late as March 1953, after
Albert Einstein, Nelson Glueck (president of the Hebrew Union
College—Jewish Institute of Religion), and Abe Sachar (president
of Brandeis University) had all rejected inquiries about their possible candidacies, the Israeli daily *Ha-Aretz* reported that Silver was
about to accept the position. He did not, nor did he ever express
any interest in the position after learning of Ben-Gurion's lukewarm
response, and both the state and the university lost an opportunity
to lure Silver away from The Temple.[13]

Silver's years of service to Israel's cause, his constant lobbying of
Eisenhower, Dulles, and other government officials during the
1950s, the alliance of General Zionists (Silver's party) and Mapai
(Ben-Gurion's party), and the clear awareness that Silver posed no
threat of any kind to Ben-Gurion led the prime minister finally to
embrace Silver, and the rabbi genuinely returned the gesture. The
site of their public rapprochement was Kefar Silver, the agricultural
training school where dedication ceremonies took place on 29
March 1956 and the prime minister attended. He used the occasion
to deliver an emotional address that praised Silver as the greatest
American Zionist since Henrietta Szold (1860–1945) and declared
that none had surpassed his courage in the struggle to establish the
state of Israel.[14]

From this point until his death, Silver would telephone, write, and meet with Ben-Gurion frequently, and he was honored by the Labor government in April-May of 1958. At their last meeting in July 1963 a few months before Silver died and while he was attending the sixty-sixth annual ZOA convention—the first ever in Israel—the rabbi noted that "all friction and misunderstanding . . . seemed to have been washed away." Thousands cheered at the Tel Aviv Sheraton on 14 July as Ben-Gurion hailed Silver as "the greatest and most courageous Zionist fighter in American Jewry," and he was toasted by leader after leader, especially those who had relentlessly battled him fifteen years earlier. He later presided over convention sessions in the same hall in which, at the twenty-third World Zionist Congress twelve years earlier, opponents such as Goldie Myerson (Golda Meir) had delivered bitter attacks against him and he had walked out after announcing that he would never attend another (he never did). Ben-Gurion later claimed several years after Silver's death that Silver had told him during their last meeting that he would soon come to Israel to settle permanently. There is no evidence to confirm this besides Ben-Gurion's recollection; Silver died too soon after the convention for such plans, even had they been contemplated, to be set in motion.[15]

With Silver's exit from the politics of Zionism, he once again had the opportunity and time to return to what was, perhaps, his first love, scholarly reading and writing. In 1950 and 1951 he began to read seriously once again in rabbinic literature, medieval Jewish philosophy, Greek thought, early Christian and Moslem writings, and contemporary Jewish and non-Jewish scholarship on the primary sources he was devouring. The books he had compulsively purchased over several decades but frequently had not had time to read now began to be opened, studied, marked, and digested. He already possessed an extensive grasp of biblical and rabbinic literature—passages flowed off his pen as he crafted lectures and sermons over thirty-five years. But now he supplemented this knowledge with careful reading in some texts he had not studied since his undergraduate years and in others that he explored for the first time.

In addition to the Hebrew scriptures, New Testament, Josephus,

Koran, Mishnah, Midrash, Zohar, and Jewish liturgy, Silver read
and marked works by several Jewish philosophers (Philo, Saadia,
Maimonides, Halevi, Crescas, and Albo), classical writers (Cicero,
Herodotus, Plato, Aristotle, Suetonius, Plutarch, Marcus Aurelius,
Vergil, and Sophocles), early Christian writers (Augustine,
Irenaeus, Ignatius, Clement, Tertullian, Ambrose, Justin, and
Aquinas), and contemporary scholars (Lieberman, Klausner,
Scholem, Goitein, Zeitlin, Rosenthal, Buttenweiser, Spesier, Roth,
Fischel, Schechter, Marmorstein, Finklestein, Abrahams, Lauter-
bach and Wolfson, Whitehead, Pritchard, Albright, Frankfort,
Goodenough, Driver, Engnell, Frazer, Toynbee, Moore, Murray,
Niebuhr, and Barth). He did not neglect scholarly journals in
German and Hebrew and even found the opportunity to read parts
of the *Mahabharata* and *Bhagavad-Gita*. Silver subsequently used
every one of these authors in writing his most widely read work,
Where Judaism Differed (New York: Macmillan, 1956).

As his ideas took form in 1951 and especially 1952, he delivered
addresses at The Temple that without much revision became the
basis for several chapters of the book. As a master of the pulpit and
platform, Silver developed very early into a master in the field of
human communication. He understood almost instinctively what
his hearers already knew and what they did not know, what was
clear and what was vague, and how to say what needed to be said in
an impressive and memorable way. The book is clear and effective
and reveals the exceptional orator's skill of making the difficult
thought relatively simple and the vague idea crystal clear.

The volume presents massive and original scholarship, and for
the most part Silver does not present his own opinions and call
them "normative Judaism" but lets the classical sources and authors
speak for themselves. While recognizing that Jews and Christians
do share some things in common and hence one can speak of the
Judeo-Christian tradition, Silver's emphasis is on the differences
between Judaism and Christianity (and all other religions as well).
He does not deprecate the worth of other faiths while demonstrat-

ing the uniqueness of Judaism. He is rarely defensive, and his eloquent arguments are filled not only with mastery of the rabbinic and philosophical tradition but also with pride and confidence in the intrinsic worth of Judaism.[16]

Silver's own liberal outlook does slip through the pages of a generally fair presentation of the richness of the Judaic past. His optimism, hope, and faith in humanity, despite the recent Nazi extermination of millions of his people, is of a piece with Reform Jewish thought of the first postwar decade, and his lack of attention to the centrality of the commandments, to *halacha*, the belief in a personal messiah, resurrection, and immortality, led careful readers to notice once or twice that his own deeply felt convictions are equated with "normative Judaism." The unity of structure and character that he sees in Judaism, especially its "moral" and "spiritual" genius, is sometimes no more than an attempt to ground his own Judaism in the Judaism of the past. He does, however, especially in chapter 6, recognize the many apparent contradictions in Jewish religious thought and reveals their psychological harmony in Jewish life.[17]

This introduction to Judaism appealed to scholars, clergy, and laypeople alike. The book quickly became a staple of "Introduction to Judaism" courses at university Hillel Foundations and synagogues around the country and was possibly as widely read by non-Jews as it was by rabbis and laity. This was somewhat surprising in a decade of ecumenism and goodwill, for Silver does not subordinate the differences between Judaism and Christianity to interfaith understanding, explicitly arguing that such understanding grows out of respect for the differences between religious traditions.[18]

The manuscript itself had a rather troubled start before it was accepted by Macmillan and went through printing after printing. Silver received a close and critical reading from Professor Solomon Zeitlin during 1954 and, as the final chapter or two was being written, early in 1955. Zeitlin encouraged him in letters and in person to send it to Harper & Brothers and Silver did so in March

1955. He brought the manuscript to New York and met at some length with the senior editor, explaining to him that the book had been written over a period of three to four years and not consecutively, so that some "repetitions undoubtedly crept in," and that it would surely be "a controversial book" because the differences between Judaism and other religions were pointed out "forthrightly," albeit with "deference and respect." The senior editor rejected it, explaining that it was "too long" as well as "too verbose" (words such as theogony, theomachy, chiliastic, and soteriological had long been part of Silver's lecture vocabulary) and it would therefore require "a considerable number of changes."[19]

Silver decided to try another publisher and sent it to M. Lincoln Schuster at Simon & Schuster. Mr. Schuster himself read it and told Silver that he was "deeply stirred by the erudition and Talmudic wisdom of your truly inspiring study of Judaism" and would seek the approval of his senior editor, Justin Kaplan. Kaplan called it "a wise and inspiring book, a *magnum opus*, deserving of the widest possible audience" and correctly observed that "the distinctive wisdom of Judaism" stood at the heart of the manuscript. Kaplan, however, demanded that Silver eliminate the extensive "historical and scholarly documentation" as well as the "highly technical and detailed material," and more critical still, resented what he termed the "invidious comparisons of Christianity with Judaism", which might offend and repel people of other faiths."[20]

Silver rejected Kaplan's critique and his suggestions for revision, insisting that the scholarly apparatus remain intact and that he had delineated all the differences with respect. At this point, however, he asked a distinguished Jewish intellectual and novelist, Ludwig Lewisohn, on the faculty of Brandeis University, to edit the manuscript, and Lewisohn responded with a careful, sometimes line-by-line, list of suggestions that Silver almost entirely accepted. He also asked his good friend from AZEC days, Harold Manson, to edit the manuscript. Manson, giving up his own writing project, sent Silver chapter after chapter during the summer of 1955 and Silver substantially reworked the manuscript in response to his suggestions as well. Most interestingly, perhaps, in terms of these two critiques, Silver needed to clarify whether he was writing about the past (where Judaism differed) or the present (where Judaism differs). Both agreed that Silver meant both the past and the present and helped him to clarify this in the text by paying closer attention to verb tenses.[21]

By the fall the revised manuscript was ready to be sent off, this time to Macmillan, and it was immediately accepted for publication without revisions. By January 1956 Silver had a contract and the book was ready for an autograph party at Halle's Cleveland store on 19 September 1956. With twenty-five hundred member families at The Temple, seventeen hundred women in the sisterhood, and eight hundred men in the brotherhood as well as an order from the Jewish Publication Society for three thousand copies for a 1957 edition, Macmillan was taking only a small gamble. The book went into a second printing before the end of the year and Macmillan reprinted it in 1957, 1961, and 1972.[22]

In 1961 Silver published his final book, *Moses and the Original Torah,* a scholarly study of what (if any) portion of the Pentateuch is actually Mosaic and how subsequent biblical authors, such as the prophets, interpreted this Mosaic material. To frame his argument Silver draws upon biblical scholarship from journals and books, comparative Semitics and comparative religion, rabbinic traditions, and, especially, a careful analysis of biblical Hebrew and the biblical material itself. His conclusions, though rather radical in parts, draw upon studies of widely respected scholars, and his abundant notes offer quite original and important interpretations. His argument as a whole remains compelling.

Silver correctly argues that the ancient Israelites, who had many stories, most cherished the story of how their ancestors had once escaped from Egyptian bondage by crying out to their God for freedom. Their God responded through Moses, who brought about their deliverance and who led them to Mount Sinai, where through his mediation the law of their God was offered to them. Silver argues persuasively that some early legal materials were indeed Mosaic, or part of what he calls "the original Torah which Moses taught." These were the apodictic laws, the general, unconditional laws or divine imperatives at the very core of the biblical faith. Some of these, such as the Ten Commandments and other parts of the law codes buried within Exodus, Leviticus, and Deuteronomy have been preserved, but much of this material, predating the case laws and customary laws, has been lost. Silver here is on firm ground: biblical scholars generally believe that some early legal materials, based perhaps on some form of the Ten Commandments, were given to and accepted by the people.

Furthermore, he argues that this original Torah was "given by [God] to His people," and here the "aristocratic" and learned Reform rabbi, trained in an institution that attributed the cardinal spiritual and ethical teachings of the Bible to the literary prophets, parts company with his Reform rabbinic colleagues and the biblical scholars he applauds elsewhere. Silver literally believed that to which so many colleagues paid lip service, that the core of the Torah was "spoken by [God] Himself and by Him to all the people directly."[23]

God thus revealed actual words to Moses and the Hebrews and they were accepted by the people at Mount Sinai. Silver is not just saying that, following ancient Near Eastern models, these legal formulations were understood as commands of the deity during the time of Moses, but that, as the Orthodox rabbis of his youth and as his own father had argued, God revealed Torah to Moses and His people.

Silver correctly emphasizes the centrality of this Moses-Sinai material in the Northern Kingdom of ancient Israel and correctly observes that "the Northern tradition, set deeply in the events of the Exodus, is dominated . . . by the personality of Moses." Moses is certainly the critical figure from Israel's past in the narratives that were shaped a few centuries after Moses (ca. ninth century B.C.) in the north. These tribes (rather than Judah or the Southern Kingdom, which he points out rightly have their own Davidic traditions) find their identity and even their potential unity in this early Mosaic material. Silver argues with merit, and Moses becomes the model for the later prophetic figures who will also stand between the deity and the people. Thus a prophet such as Amos will recall the sacred story of the exodus and covenant (Amos 2:9–11) and use it to legitimize God's words of condemnation, which Amos brings to the people of his day.

The northern state fell to Assyria in 722 B.C., but this material did not of course disappear. The Moses-Sinai/Exodus-Covenant tradition was preserved, ordered, written down, and taken to Judah in the south where it was incorporated into the traditions of the Judah tribes and continued to inform the lives of what remained of the people of Israel for "a time far off, and for many days hence." This original Torah, which Silver powerfully "reclaims" as Mosaic (had not Orthodox Judaism always insisted upon it?) has surely "never los[t] its magnetic appeal."[24]

The "magnetic appeal" that Silver attributed to the "original" words of the Torah was frequently used by those who honored Silver to describe his own words. Although *Moses* was his last published book, he continued to use the public platform at The Temple as well as in halls and stadiums until his death. He died suddenly, stricken with a heart attack while sitting down with his wife, sons, daughters-in-law, and grandchildren for Thanksgiving dinner on 28 November 1963. Rushed to the hospital in the family car from his home (19810 Shaker Boulevard), he died in the hospital at 3:40 P.M. surrounded by the family with whom he lived in great harmony. Not surprisingly, he had completed his Sunday sermon the previous day—a memorial address for John F. Kennedy who had died one week earlier. His followers never heard that sermon, but four thousand of them filled every room of The Temple and the streets outside a few days later to pay their final respects to Rabbi Silver. David Ben-Gurion's brief eulogy said it best: "When he spoke, people listened."[25]

The type of rabbinate Silver constructed for himself is rare today: stentorian oratory before two thousand worshippers each week, deep involvement in the tense political life of the community, a strong distaste for the pastoral work of the rabbi, constant lectures in other communities, intensive national and even international organizational leadership demanding long absences from the congregation, sustained reading and productive scholarship, formal attire everywhere, and a congregation that left nearly every major decision to Silver's rarely ambivalent preferences.

There is scarcely anyone alive who claims to have known Silver well, while those deceased few friends and enemies (Nahum Goldmann, Emanuel Neumann, Harold Manson, and Ezra Shapiro) who claimed at one time or another to know him well hardly knew more than a part of him. A private person who shunned intimacy, he may never have found a vehicle for his feelings beyond the poetry of his youth, a few adolescent letters to his parents, and a diary kept in France during one month of World War I. Nevertheless, though nobody (save perhaps his wife, who died in 1984) knew how he felt about the critical events and decisions of his own time, that is precisely what the biographer and readers seek to know.

Of course, we can never really know Silver, even if he had shared his personal fears, hopes, joys, and disappointments with friends, or had put them on paper; we cannot even know ourselves. But when we add it all up—Zionist, rabbi, teacher, orator, politician, father, scholar—I fear that we hardly know Silver at all. He remains always in control, rarely allowing us a glimpse of what might have lurked behind the cold, confident, severe personas of the pulpit and organization or the warm, spontaneous, jocular presence in the office or the restaurant. He remained as he was as a teenager when Solomon Freehof first met him: "He had . . . a premature reserve. There seems to have been no triviality about him. He had a hearty sense of humor . . . but very little playfulness. We were rather boyish and he was already in temperament a man."[26] Few, if any, men or women outside his family could be called really close to Abba Hillel Silver. Despite his tremendous capacity for humor, perhaps he appeared to most people to take himself too seriously. He put himself on a pedestal; he was stiff, severe, dignified; and many perceived him as always performing an act.

Outside of his own family, the two people who most admired Silver also seemed to "know" him best. Both Armond Cohen and Shulamith Schwarz Nardi sang Silver's praises to me, but each carefully delineated his faults as well. Cohen, a conservative rabbi in Cleveland for over half-a-century, knew Silver for three decades, while Mrs. Nardi worked with him in the 1940s. Each understood that he presented one face to the congregation, the politicians, and the Zionists, and another to his staff (in New York, Washington, or Cleveland) and to his card-playing buddies. When he spoke, he was certain, and if he was not certain, he did not speak. When he ate, he laughed, and laughed heartily, and when he laughed he put others at ease. He made scripture and Talmud part of the texture of his magnificent eloquence, and he told Yiddish jokes at Cleveland and New York delis with timing that would rival the best stand-up comedians of his generation.

Silver's legacy, of course, is not his sense of humor, for most of those who heard him whether at The Temple, in lecture halls around the country, or at rallies, protests, and forums arranged for political purposes knew little of the boyishness thinly concealed beneath the serious exterior. His significance, as I have discussed it throughout this book, was in his organizational work on behalf of Zionism at the AZEC, his lobbying skills at the United Nations, on Capitol Hill, and with cabinet members in the administrations of Roosevelt, Truman, and Eisenhower, as well as his eloquent and consistent challenges to President Roosevelt. In addition, he made important and lasting contributions to the political life of Cleveland and Ohio; John Gunther, for example, called Silver

Cleveland's "most distinguished citizen." And last but certainly not least in the hearts of two generations of members of The Temple, he ministered to an enormous congregation.

His legacy to Reform Judaism is also considerable. When he came into the rabbinate and for many years afterward in many major congregations, rabbis and congregants had negated the particularistic elements in Jewish peoplehood and had affirmed Israel's universal mission to disseminate a special ethic—the prophetic ideals of social justice. Influenced by the optimism and social Darwinism of the nineteenth and early twentieth centuries, they meant by this that Judaism was to be a religion of universal significance, not a particular national community. Just as mankind was evolving from a particularistic to a universalist community of faith, so too was Reform Judaism a step (a very advanced one, too) along the way.

The disillusionment caused by World War I coupled with the rise of Nazism destroyed this optimism and sense of progress. In its place Silver developed a childhood Zionist commitment (probably more oriented toward Ahad Ha'am's emphasis on a Hebrew cultural revival than to an actual "state") into a thorough reevaluation of the universal mission of Judaism and the resulting dramatic and powerful, intense and even passionate, assertion of Jewish national particularism. This took the form of Ahad Ha'am's cultural emphasis (an insistence on the importance of the Hebrew language and Hebrew culture) as well as Herzl's political program (the euphemistic "National Home," which early on yielded to "Jewish State"). This commitment made him no longer able to subordinate Jewish national particularism to anything.

Silver felt the disillusionments of civilization very deeply, and he combined this with deep reading about the Jewish historical experience. These combined to convince him to shift his Zionist concerns from the next highest rung on the ladder, just below social justice, to the top rung. Certain beyond doubt, in contrast to most of his reform colleagues, that Jewish nationalism was the normative historical experience and that only within a sovereign state of their own could the majority of the world's Jews find succor, he feverishly wrote and spoke on behalf of Zionism. For only in Palestine, he asserted, with their own state could the Jews hope to be fully free (the Herzl influence), while only in Zion could a Jewish community hope to evolve a vibrant, contemporary Hebrew culture (following Ahad Ha'am) and radiate that cultural center to world Jewry.

I have not ignored the fact that a small, and perhaps even significant, minority of Reform Jews were outspoken Zionists before Abba Hillel Silver came to national political attention in the 1940s, and even during the previous two decades when he made Zionism an important but not the most important item on his lecturing agenda. Stephen S. Wise, James Heller, Louis Newman, and others spoke frequently from lecterns and worked actively in Zionist organizations on behalf of Zion. Their involvement for the most part was on behalf of the political struggle for the establishment of the Jewish state; they were Reform rabbis who were Zionists.

Silver was primarily a Zionist for whom Jewish statehood and Hebrew culture were increasingly the highest values of his career, and for whom the constant use of Hebrew demonstrated the importance he attached to cultural Zionism throughout his life. He was above all else a Zionist, albeit of the American kind for whom personal *aliyah* (return) or even the *aliyah* of other American Jews was of little importance. And it was this commitment to Zionism that he managed to convey to the American people as a whole, personally and institutionally, through the decade or so before Israel proclaimed itself a state. If Rabbi Milton Steinberg was right when he said in 1942 that "American public opinion is crucial—it is necessary; its sympathy must be won," then Silver certainly was the key American leader in creating that sympathy.[27]

The controversies with fellow Zionists, especially Israeli leaders, took place superficially over managing the fundraising dollars raised in the United States, but, more deeply, they involved these leaders' perception of whether the domination of Zionist affairs ought to rest with those men (and a woman) who had in fact made *aliyah,* or with those Zionists, committed though they might be, who renounced any personal "return" to Zion. It was, simply stated, the Israel-centered Zionism of Ben-Gurion and his colleagues versus the diaspora-centered Zionism of Silver and his friends.

We have seen, of course, that the ideological conflict was strengthened by Silver's autocratic, or at least authoritarian, personality and leadership style, which drove a significant number of his colleagues to repress (some better than others) a strong dislike for his manner, while others tossed abuse and criticism at him when they could not control their anger and jealousy. The emergence of the State of Israel gave these leaders abundant confidence, and they quickly set about to stem the possible domination by American Zionists and to settle a few scores along the way. Silver was powerless in the face of this attack, having alienated, even while accomplishing much, most of those with whom he might have allied had he sufficient interest in continuing the battle.

So, while Ben-Gurion and his colleagues began to court non-Zionist American Jewish leaders, heightening their awareness of Israel's position as a bulwark of democracy in a volatile geographic area and a haven of refuge for Jewish survivors of the European catastrophe, Silver went home to his congregation and family in Cleveland, content in the last fifteen years of his life to offer advice to President Eisenhower, to minister to his congregants, and to immerse himself once again in the scholarship he had put on hold during the previous decade of service to the cause of Zionism.

For his congregants at The Temple as well as for non-Jews to whom he spoke scores of times in churches and schools, civic clubs, auditoriums, and organizational meeting rooms, he continued to offer a strong affirmation of Jewish values, a vigorous defense of Judaism, and a treasury of Jewish sources to audiences probably largely unfamiliar with the Jewish contribution to western civilization. Melvin Urofsky, the biographer of Stephen S. Wise, notes that Wise never claimed anything more for his extraordinary oratory than that it was an instrument, at times quite powerful, in his constant battles against social and personal injustice. Silver would agree, but he could claim much more.[28]

Not only did his voice serve as a vehicle to convey his ideas about Jewish and general themes, but its content was to be contemplated as a text. To this end, Silver continued to print scores of his talks and to distribute them widely. So he continued to use his oratory to engender concrete action, to stimulate reflection and thought, and to serve as a permanent guide to contemporary issues as well as *historica Judaica*. But he was, in short, more than an orator. A great speaker of the old school of oratory, he had immense intelligence and read voraciously. It wasn't just his voice or even his vocabulary. He had something significant to say.

His enemies, and they were many, knew this well. He provided them with an adversary who raised their often petty squabbles to a higher level, for he usually set the rules of the battles and maintained his dignity while rolling up his sleeves. He was a man to fear, as Nahum Goldmann pointed out (while claiming never to have feared him), but this fear stimulated many to serve Jewry well even as they were trying to topple the "Jewish lord."

Note on Sources

In addition to contemporary newspaper accounts, this book was based almost exclusively on primary historical materials such as private memoranda, organizational minutes (especially from executive committees), and private correspondence. (The question of whether a really satisfactory life can be written is essentially the question of whether letters have been preserved.) The archival collections I used most extensively included the Abba Hillel Silver Papers (The Temple, Cleveland), Harold Manson Papers (The Temple), Minutes, Board of Directors (The Temple), Eliezer Kaplan Papers (Central Zionist Archives, Jerusalem), Israel Goldstein Papers (CZA), Nahum Goldmann Papers (CZA), Jewish Agency for Palestine, American Section, New York Files (CZA), Jewish Agency for Palestine, American Section, New York Files (CZA), Moshe Shertok (later Sharett) Papers (CZA), David Ben-Gurion Papers (S'de Boker), Minutes, Board of Governors (Hebrew University Archives), Chaim Weizmann Papers (Weizmann Institute, Rehovoth), American Zionist Emergency Council Papers (Zionist Organization of America Archives, New York), Annual Reports, Proceedings and Minutes of the ZOA Annual Conventions (ZOA Archives), Stephen S. Wise Papers (American Jewish Historical Society, Waltham, Mass.), Dwight D. Eisenhower Library (Abilene, Kan.), Student Records (University of Cincinnati Archives), United Jewish Appeal Archives (New York) and the Foreign Office Records (Public Record Office, London).

List of Oral Interviews

I have also utilized interviews with the following individuals and have indicated in references the date of the interview, the location of the tape (T = The Temple; HU = The Hebrew University; MU = Marshall University), and the name of the interviewer, if not the author.

David Ben-Gurion	12 Nov 1969 (HU; Noah Orion)
Florence Michaelson Bernstein	19 Dec 1984 (T)
Irene Broh	19 Nov 1974 (MU; Elizabeth Ann Smarr)
Elizabeth Rice Carson	13 Feb 1985 (T)
Armond Cohen	12 Nov 1984 (T)
Eliahu Epstein (later Elath)	5 Jun 1975 (HU; Mel Urofsky)
Eliahu Epstein	15 Jul 1986 (T)
Leon Feuer	14 Jun 1983 (T)
Benjamin Friedman	5 Mar 1985 (T)
Alice Goldman	30 Dec 1986 (T)
Nahum Goldmann	12 Apr 1975 (HU; Mel Urofsky)
Israel Goldstein	12 Sep 1973 (HU; Menachem Kaufmann)
Israel Goldstein	29 May 1977 (HU; Menachem Kaufmann)
Rose Halperin	? Oct 1971 (HU; David Shapira)
Melbourne Harris	27 Mar 1986 (T)
Richard Hirsch	23 Jul 1986 (T)
Isaiah L. Kenen	27 Mar 1985 (T)
Moshe Kol	4 Jan 1975 (HU; Mel Urofsky)
William Kramer	25 Aug 1983 (T)
Miriam Leikind	9 Dec 1986 (T)
Irving Liebow	29 Jan 1985 (T)

Arthur Lourie	9 Jun 1975 (HU; Mel Urofsky)
Harold Manson	4 Nov 1971 (HU; David Shapira)
Golda Meir	10 Jun 1975 (HU; Mel Urofsky)
Henry Montor	14 Oct 1975 (HU; Jeff Hodes)
Shulamith Schwarz Nardi	23 Jul 1986 (T)
Benzion Netanyahu	26 Jul 1986 (T)
Emanuel Neumann	21 Jul 1967 (HU; Yehudah Bauer)
Emanuel Neumann	7 Jan 1975 (HU; Mel Urofsky)
Ezra Shapiro	10 Jun 1975 (HU; Mel Urofsky)
Joseph Silbert	11 Nov 1984 (T)
Daniel Jeremy Silver	14 Aug 1986 (T)
Daniel Jeremy Silver	27 Aug 1986 (T)
Raphael Silver	11 Feb 1987 (T)
Jack Skirball	31 Aug 1983 (T)
Earl Stone	18 May 1986 (T)
Jacques Torczyner	31 Jan 1975 (HU; Menachem Kaufmann)

Notes

Preface

1. James Russell Lowell, *Literary Essays*, vol. 1 (Boston, 1864), p. 353.

2. Sigmund Freud, *Leonardo da Vinci*, trans. A. A. Brill (New York, 1947), p. 109.

3. Leon Edel, "The Biographer and Psycho-Analysis," *New World Writing*, 18 (Winter 1961): 50–64, and idem, "Biography and the Science of Man," in *New Directions in Biography*, ed. Anthony M. Friedson (Honolulu, 1981), pp. 8–10 (where Edel enunciates four useful principles for the writing of biography).

Chapter One

1. "Inspection Card, Abe Silver, 1902," in The Abba Hillel Silver Archives, The Temple, Cleveland, Ohio; Bessie R. Liebow, *Keepsake: An Autobiography* (New York, 1951), pp. 15–26.

2. Liebow, *Keepsake*, pp. 15–26; Eliezer Rivlin, *Silver Goblet to Rabbi Moses Silver*, Hebrew (Jerusalem, 5701 [1941]), pp. 7–9. Several long and unusually fluent Hebrew letters from teen-age Abe Silver are preserved in his personal correspondence; see especially AHS to Daniel Perksy, Tevet 5672 [1912].

3. Liebow, *Keepsake*, p. 24; Rivlin, *Silver Goblet*, pp. 9–14.

4. Liebow, *Keepsake*, pp. 25–26.

5. Liebow, *Keepsake*, p. 26. On P.S. 62, see *Junior College Journal*, 18 November 1925, where AHS discusses Marc Hoffman, his favorite teacher, and see also AHS to Isaac Siegel, 18 June 1924, PC 1923–24.

6. Silver, "Autobiography," typescript, p. 1.

7. Edward D. Coleman, *Keepsake* (New York, 1929), p. 5.

8. Jesse Schwartz, "The Dr. Herzl Zion Club," *Jewish Tribune*, 7 November 1924, p. 8; Solomon Cohen to AHS, 19 May 1924, PC 1923–24.

9. Coleman, *Keepsake,* pp. 6–7.

10. For a roster of club members, see Coleman, *Keepsake,* pp. 18–72.

11. Emanuel Neumann, "Abba Hillel Silver," in *A Galaxy of American Rishonim* (New York, 1967), p. 5; Neumann, *In the Arena* (New York, 1976), p. 21; oral interview with Neumann, 7 January 1975; *New Palestine,* 7 January and 28 February 1936.

12. Coleman, *Keepsake,* pp. 6–8, *New York Evening Mail,* May 1909; *The Theatre* (April 1903): 3.

13. Baruch [Benjamin] Friedman, "Dr. Herzl Zion Club," *Central Conference of American Rabbis Journal,* 12, 3 (October 1964): 25–26 (Hebrew); Neumann, *In the Arena,* p. 23; Leon L. Wolfe, *Abba Hillel Silver: Spokesman for Zion* (New York, 1974), pp. 8–9.

14. On the Educational Alliance, see Moses Rischin, *The Promised City: New York's Jews, 1870–1914* (New York, 1962, 1970), pp. 101–03. See also "The Reminiscences of George Sokolsky" (Oral History Research Office, Columbia University, 1956), pp. 3–4.

15. Sokolsky, "Reminiscences," pp. 2, 8–9.

16. Silver, "Autobiography," pp. 3–4.

17. Max Raisin, *Great Jews I Have Known* (New York, 1952), pp. 121–22.

18. Isidore Singer, "Hirsch Masliansky—the Tribune of the Russian-American Jews," *Menorah Journal,* 49, 1–2 (Autumn–Winter 1962): 138–39.

19. Hayim R. Rabinowitz, *Portraits of Jewish Preachers,* Hebrew (Jerusalem, 1967), pp. 393–94; Silver is quoted on the dust jacket of Zevi Hirsch Masliansky, *Sermons,* trans. Edward Herbert and ed. Abraham J. Feldman (New York, 1926); Lipsky, *A Gallery of Zionist Portraits* (New York, 1956), p. 193.

20. The College of the City of New York, transcript, Abraham H. Silver, 1488 Fifth Avenue, 1909–10.

21. Editorial, *The Hebrew Herald,* published by the Dr. Herzl Zion Club on its fifth anniversary, n.d., Mss/Ty 11–6; Susan N. Kohut, Director of Student Records, University of Cincinnati, to Raphael, 8 May 1984. Silver not only accelerated through the entire Hebrew Union College preparatory program and the first year of the five-year rabbinic program, but he completed the four-year university program with a major in Greek in three years. He graduated, however, with his own class.

22. Jacob Tarshish, "History of the Class of '15," *Hebrew Union College Monthly*, 2, 1 (June 1915): 47.

23. Max Silverman to AHS, 18 January 1922, PC 1921–22; Neumann, "Silver," p. 6.

24. Friedman, "Dr. Herzl Zion Club," p. 27; Wolfe, *Abba Hillel Silver*, p. 11.

25. Silver, "Autobiography," p. 6; Joseph Guttmann, "Agudat Ivreeyah," *HaDoar*, 19, 29 (9 June 1938); *Jewish Daily Forward*, 20 February 1912 (Yiddish).

26. Solomon B. Freehof, "Recollections of Abba Hillel Silver," in *Therefore Choose Life: Selected Sermons, Addresses and Writings of Abba Hillel Silver*, ed. Herbert Weiner, Vol. 1 (Cleveland, 1967), p. xiv. *American Israelite*, 18 and 25 April 1912; *Cincinnati Times Star*, 9 April 1912; *University Weekly News*, 10 and 24 April 1912; William R. Blumenthal to AHS, 23 April 5672 [= 1912], PC 1912–13.

28. *University Weekly News*, 14 and 21 May 1913; *Cincinnati Times Star*, 18 May 1913.

29. *The Cincinnatian* 1912, 1913, and 1914. Receipts from the religious literature department of Chas. Scribner's & Sons reveal that AHS spent much of his limited income on books.

30. A collection of AHS's manuscript poetry is in Mss/Ty 10–1, 10–2, 10–3, 10–4, 11–1, 11–2, 11–3, 11–4, 11–5, 12–1, 13–1, 15–1. Among AHS's poems I would call attention to those in the *Maccabean*, 19 (August 1910), *College Mercury*, 28 March 1911, *University Weekly News*, 8 November 1911, *American Israelite*, 16 November 1911, and *Young Judaean* (December 1913).

31. Samuel S. Cohon to AHS, 14 October 1914, PC 1914–17; Henry Berkowitz to AHS, 29 August 1915, PC 1914–17; Henry Englander to AHS, 22 May 1914, PC 1914–17; AHS, "Dreams and Visions," *Hebrew Union College Monthly*, 2, 3 (December 1915); Silver, *Therefore Choose Life*, pp. 13–16. "The Am HaAretz" appeared in three installments in the *Hebrew Union College Monthly*, 1, 3 (December 1914); 1, 4 (January 1915); and 1, 5 (February 1915).

32. Charlotte Goldberger to AHS, 18 November 1914, PC 1914–17; AHS to F. L. Wormser, 8 April 1915, Correspondence 11–1–33; Ely Liebow to AHS, 10 November 1914, PC 1914–17; George Zipin to AHS, 12 August 1914, PC 1914–17; Julius Rosenberg to AHS, 9 May 1914, PC

1914–17. Abraham Shinedling erroneously lists Silver as serving Huntington's Ohev Sholom in 1912–13; see Abraham Shinedling, *West Virginia Jewry: Origins and History, 1850–1958*, Vol. 2 (Philadelphia, 1963), p. 907.

33. *Chelsea Evening Record*, 4 October 1913; *Huntington Advertiser*, 21 and 26 September 1914; *Huntington Herald-Dispatch*, 30 September 1914.

34. Freehof, "Recollections," pp. xi–xii.

35. Neumann, "Abba Hillel Silver," p. 6.

36. Ibid.

Chapter Two

1. As late as his ordination (June 1915) Silver had no job, having applied unsuccessfully to Congregation Anshe Chesed (in Scranton) and to Temple Israel (in Terre Haute). His despair at that time is reflected in an undated letter to the departing Wheeling rabbi, Morris Lazaron, Correspondence 11–1–32, and in AHS to F. L. Wormser, 8 April 1915, and Jacob Kaplan to AHS, 7 May 1915, Correspondence 11–1–33.

2. This affection was by no means limited to teenage girls, though several of them wrote to him in Cleveland for some years. Letters from Virginia Horkheimer were quite formal ("My dear Mr. Silver" and "Always, Virginia") while those from Paulin Kirtz and Rose Front were usually seductive ("Mon cher Rabbine"). See especially Personal Correspondence 1917–18, 1918–19, and 1922–23.

3. Shinedling, *West Virginia Jewry*, 3:1442 (for the 1849 date); M. Sonneborn to AHS, 22 and 23 June 1915, Correspondence 11–1–32; Miscellaneous letters, PC 1917–18; Silver, "Autobiography," B:1. Louis Horkheimer, Virginia's father, owned Horkheimer Brothers Wool of Wheeling, with an office and a warehouse in Boston and in Columbus, Ohio, respectively; PC 1922–23. Rabbi Hyman Iola officiated at Abba and Ginny's wedding in Wheeling, and they took their honeymoon at White Sulphur Springs, West Virginia; PC 1922–23.

4. Anne Wallace Efland, "The Woman Suffrage Movement in West Virginia, 1867–1920," M.A. thesis, West Virginia University, 1983, pp. 50, 51 and 141; Irene D. Broh, Oral interview with Elizabeth Ann Smarr, 19 November 1974, Huntington, West Virginia, Oral history tape 119, at

Marshall University, Huntington, West Virginia; J. Broh to AHS, 3 and 7 June 1915, Correspondence 11–1–32; Mrs. E. W. Venable to AHS, 20 September and 20 November 1916, PC 1915–16.

5. *Wheeling Daily News,* 25 September 1915; Virginia Horkheimer to AHS, n.d., PC 1917–18; *Wheeling Register,* 15 May 1917.

6. *Wheeling Register,* 22 November 1915.

7. *Wheeling Intelligence,* 6 March 1917; *Charleston Leader,* 7 March 1917; *Wheeling News,* 7 March 1917; *Wheeling Register,* 7 and 10 March 1917; *New York Times,* 8 March 1917; Correspondence 8–1–30 ("The La Follette Incident").

8. Abe Feinberg to AHS, 21 June 1917, PC 1917–18; Abraham L. Feinberg, *Storm the Gates of Jericho* (New York, 1964), p. 191; Feinberg to Raphael, 23 April 1984. Other rabbinical students whose warm letters of affection attest to young Silver's influence on their careers include Leon and Maurice Feuer, PC 1922–23.

9. Harry Cutler to AHS, 21 March 1916; Kaufmann Kohler to AHS, 3 March 1916, PC 1914–17.

10. AHS to Samuel Mayerberg, 4 October 1916, PC 1914–17; Mayerberg to AHS, 2 October 1916, Correspondence 8–4–40 and A. A. Benesch to AHS, 1 March 1917, PC 1917–18. Wolsey wrote AHS, before the latter had left Wheeling, that "Gries and I did not get on well together," that he genuinely welcomed Silver's arrival, and that he looked forward to working with him; Louis Wolsey to AHS, 14 May 1917, Correspondence 11–1–31. See also Freehof to AHS, 17 May 1917 and Lee Levinger to AHS, 7 May 1917; Correspondence 8–4–39.

11. *The Temple,* 3, 31, (6 May 1917).

12. *The American Jewish Chronicle* (Fall 1916), p. 798; Samuel Mayerberg to AHS, 2 October 1916.

13. *The Temple,* Annual Reports [Eighteenth Annual [sic] of The Temple, etc.]; Minutes of the Meetings of the Executive Board of The Temple, June 1899–March 1904 and April 1904–September 1913. Rabbi Melbourne Harris, who served with Silver at The Temple for ten years, claims that Gries not only opposed the presence of a Torah in the synagogue but the ark as well; Oral interview with Melbourne Harris. For Rabbi Isaac Mayer Wise's opposition to Gries, see *American Israelite,* 30 December 1897, cited in Lloyd P. Gartner, *History of the Jews of Cleveland* (Cleveland, 1978), p. 353.

14. Benjamin Lowenstein to AHS, 30 April 1917, PC 1916–17; *The Temple.* 3, 31, (6 May 1917). The official synagogue history disagrees with AHS's assessment of the impact of his reform, noting that there was "considerable opposition." See *The Temple: A History,* p. 28.

15. *Jewish Record and Observer,* 17 August 1917 and *Jewish Independent,* 17 August 1917.

16. AHS, Diary, 19 August 1918.

17. *Cleveland Plain Dealer,* 22 September 1918; *The City,* 18 September 1918; *American Israelite,* 10 October 1918.

18. *Oklahoma City Times,* 13 November 1918; *Tulsa News,* 15 November 1918; *Carthage Evening Press,* 19 November 1918; *Muskogee Phoenix,* 16 November 1918; *Jewish World* (Yiddish), 17 April 1919; AHS, "Europe Revisited: Impressions of 1920, and My Earlier Impressions of 1918 and 1919," 10 October 1920 (Sermon 40).

19. *Jewish Record and Observer,* 14 September 1917, and *Cleveland Plain Dealer,* 27 August 1917.

20. *Youngstown Vindicator,* 14 January 1919; *Rochester Bumblebee,* 13 February 1919; *Chicago Tribune,* 7 March 1919; *Toledo Israelite,* 17 April 1929.

21. *St. Louis Star,* 20 October 1920; Oral interview with Jack Skirball; *Ft. Worth–Dallas Jewish Monitor,* 30 January 1920; *New Orleans Times-Picayune,* 1 April 1920.

22. Melvin I. Urofsky, *American Zionism from Herzl to the Holocaust* (New York, 1975), pp. 270–79; George L. Berlin, "The Brandeis-Weizmann Dispute," *American Jewish Historical Quarterly,* 60, 1 (September, 1970): 37–68. AHS's letters to Horace Kallen in 1918–19 reveal him to be already deeply interested in the political and ideological quarrels among European and American Zionists.

23. *London Jewish Chronicle,* 9 July 1920; *B'nai B'rith News* (September 1920); *American Hebrew,* (30 July 1920): 271.

24. *London Jewish Chronicle,* 16 July 1920, pp. 6, 19 and 24.

25. *The Jewish Monitor,* 30 January 1920; *Ft. Wayne News,* 4 February 1920; AHS to Moses J. Gries, 26 April 1917, PC 1917–18; AHS to Stephen S. Wise, 11 May 1917, in Stephen S. Wise Papers, Box 119. Among the Zionist talks of 1919–20 are "The Future of Palestine" (5 January 1919), "Palestine as I Saw it" (12 October 1919), "Joseph Trumpeldor" (1920) and addresses in New York City (19 April 1920—Carnegie

Hall, and 1 June 1920—Extraordinary Zionist Conference), London (12 July 1920—English Zionist Federation).

26. Yonathan Shapiro, *Leadership of the American Zionist Organization, 1897–1920* (Urbana, Ill., 1971), pp. 145–50.

27. Memorandum of a conversation with Justice Brandeis in Washington, on Tuesday morning, 12 October 1920, in Louis D. Brandeis Papers, University of Louisville, Reel 85–184, Film 475–78; AHS to Louis D. Brandeis, 21 October 1920, Brandeis to AHS, 23 October 1920, and miscellaneous letters, all in PC 1920–21.

28. Proceedings of the Twenty-Third Regular Annual Convention of the ZOA, 25–28 November 1920 (Buffalo, N.Y.), pp. 149–78, ZOA Archives; Esther Panitz, "Louis Dembitz Brandeis and the Cleveland Conference," *American Jewish Historical Quarterly*, 65, 2 (September 1975): 140–62; Shapiro, *Leadership*, pp. 150–58 and 162–67. Some of the pre-conference bargaining is described in Weizmann, *Trial and Error: The Autobiography of Chaim Weizmann* (Westport, Conn., 1949, 1972), pp. 267–69 (Judge Julian Mack confronted Weizmann before he could even disembark from his ship) and Philippa Strum, *Louis D. Brandeis* (Cambridge, 1984), p. 284.

29. Stenographic Minutes of the Cleveland Convention, 5 June–8 June 1921 (Cleveland, Ohio), Book 1, Third Session, 6 June, pp. 8–44, ZOA Archives; Shapiro, *Leadership*, pp. 135–44 and 161–62; Esther L. Panitz, "'Washington versus Pinsk': The Brandeis-Weizmann Dispute," *Herzl Year Book*, 8 (New York, 1978): 77–94; Berlin, "The Brandeis-Weizmann Dispute"; *Cleveland Plain Dealer*, 6 June 1921.

30. Jacob de Haas, *Louis D. Brandeis: A Biographical Sketch* (New York, 1929), pp. 144–45; Report of the Proceedings of the Twenty-Fourth Annual Convention (New York, 1921), pp. 120–21; *Cleveland Plain Dealer*, 7 and 8 June 1921.

31. Stenographic Minutes, pp. 35–37.

32. Ibid., pp. 40–43, 47 and 49–56.

33. Proceedings of the Twenty-Third Regular Annual Convention of the ZOA, 1920 (Buffalo).

34. *Minneapolis Morning Tribune*, 24 August 1922; *Portland Telegram*, 28 August 1922; *B'nai B'rith Messenger*, 1 September 1922; *San Francisco Call & Post*, 1 September 1922; *San Francisco Chronicle*, 1 September 1922.

35. *Pittsburgh Jewish Criterion*, 18 May 1921; *Dos Yiddische Folk*, 6

January 1922; *Detroit Jewish Chronicle*, 9 December 1921 and 7 April 1922; *Scranton Argus* (February 1922); *Reading Pennsylvania Times*, 15 February 1923.

36. The details of this lecture tour come from Silver's correspondence, arranged by city, in "Speaking Engagements," Correspondence 2:1, 2:2, and 3:2; *Boston Globe*, 7 April 1924.

37. *Erie Times* (June 1922).

38. Leonard J. Mervis, *The Social Justice Movement of the American Reform Rabbis, 1890–1940*, Ph. D. dissertation, University of Pittsburgh, 1951; AHS, *Therefore Choose Life*, pp. 117–18.

39. *Cleveland News*, 29 October 1920 and 3 January 1921; *Cleveland Press*, 22 October 1922; *Cleveland Plain Dealer*, 23 October 1922; Will Hays to AHS, 10 August 1922, and Dale Brown to AHS, 22 May 1922, Correspondence 5–3–89; *Akron Daily-Beacon*, 3 August 1924.

40. Silver, "Labor and the War," 17 February 1918 (Sermon 88).

41. Raymond Boryczka and Lorin Lee Cary, *No Strength Without Union: An Illustrated History of Ohio Workers, 1803–1980* (Columbus, 1982), p. 161.

42. Boryczka and Cary, *No Strength*, pp. 164–67; David Brody, *Steelworkers in America: The Nonunion Era* (Cambridge, 1960), pp. viii and 242; Brody, *Labor in Crisis: The Steel Strike of 1919* (Philadelphia, 1965), p. 152.

43. Silver, "The Right and Wrong of Strikes," 19 October 1919 (Sermon 14).

44. Benjamin Lowenstein to Silver, 2 August 1919 and AHS to Lowenstein, n.d., PC 1919–20.

45. Silver, "Labor Relations in Cleveland," 28 March 1920 (Sermon 33); *Cleveland Plain Dealer*, 29 March 1920; George L. Fairbanks to AHS, 23 February 1931, PC 1919–20.

46. Silver, "The Coming Industrial Struggle—The Open vs. the Closed Shop," 19 December 1920 (Sermon 49).

47. *Cleveland Plain Dealer*, 3, 6, 7, 17, 18, 20, 24–28, 30 and 31 May, and 1–2, 4, 8, 10 and 11 June 1921. Associated Plumbing Contractors of Cleveland, Ohio to AHS, 27 May and 2 June 1921; Conference Committee of the Journeymen Plumbers' Union to AHS, 3 June 1921; Landis's Wage Schedule, Joint Conciliation Board to AHS, 3 June 1921; six pages

of handwritten notes from one of the hearings—all in Correspondence 5–3–90.

48. Silver, "Coal: An Interpretation of the Coal Strike," 21 May 1922 (Sermon 96); *Cleveland Plain Dealer,* 22 May 1922; Research Department, Commission on the Church and Social Service, Federal Council of the Churches of Christ in America, *The Coal Controversy* (n.p., 1922).

49. *Cleveland Plain Dealer,* 25 and 26 April 1923; *New York Times,* 26 April 1923; *Cleveland Press,* 25 April 1923; *Cleveland Times,* 26 April 1923; *Jewish World* (Yiddish), 29 April 1923; AHS to Newton D. Baker, 1 December 1922; Baker to AHS, 1 March; AHS to Baker, 8 March; Chairman, Committee on Labor Relations to *Cleveland Citizen,* 20 March; Baker to AHS, 28 March; AHS to Baker, 5 April; Baker to AHS, 11 April; Frank Johnson to AHS, n.d.; Charles James to AHS, 3 May; *Cleveland Topics,* 5 May, p. 1; AHS to Cleveland Chamber of Commerce, 2 June; Baker to Chamber of Commerce, 1 and 10 July; AHS to Chamber of Commerce, 12 and 26 July; AHS to Newton D. Baker, 26 July 1923— all in Correspondence 5–3–90. This voluminous and remarkable exchange of letters between two eloquent, strong-willed, and nationally known men, who were totally at odds but enormously respectful of each other, deserves its own study. See also Orrin J. Sayers to AHS, 27 April 1923, a dentist who assured Silver that he knew "other members who feel as you do that have not dared to make it public"; PC 1922–23.

50. "The Committee of Forty-Eight. The Aims of the Committee," Correspondence 6–1–17; Committee of Forty-Eight to AHS, n.d., Correspondence 6–1–84; *New York Times,* 29 October 1924; *American Jewish World,* 31 October 1924; AHS to Stephen S. Wise, 16 October 1920, Correspondence 6–1–93. Although Silver did vigorously defend Senator Warren G. Harding (Rep.-Ohio) against those who claimed he was anti-Semitic, he was not enthusiastic about Harding's candidacy for president; Correspondence 6–1–93.

51. Sam L. Guggenheim to AHS, 10 October 1925 and S. B. Abrams to AHS, 5 January 1926, PC 1925–26; Selma Strauss to AHS, 5 October 1922, PC 1922–23.

52. *Cleveland Plain Dealer,* 16 June 1924 and 24 May 1925.

53. AHS to Leon M. Wolfe, 12 June 1920, Correspondence 8–4–42; *Steubenville Herald-Star,* 2 September 1924; *Cleveland Press,* 20 September

1924; *Cleveland Plain Dealer*, 20 September 1924; *Cleveland News*, 20 September 1924; Irma Kraft to AHS, 1 December 1924, PC 1924–25.

54. Richard R. Standwood, "Temple Tifereth Israel, Cleveland," *The Architectural Forum*, 43 (November 1925): 257–60.

55. Benjamin Lowenstein to AHS, 8 February 1923 and Lowenstein to AHS, 2 May 1925, PC 1922–23 and 1925; The Temple, Minutes, May 1918–June 1928, pp. 123 and 194. AHS's salary quickly skyrocketed, but he seems to have come to Cleveland well-paid. Brooklyn's *Shaarei Zedek* hired his brother Maxwell for $3,000 in 1919, while Silver's successor in Wheeling received $2,100 in 1918. AHS's total income (salary plus honoraria) for 1918 was almost $6,000; PC 1917–18 and 1918–19 (including individual income tax return for calendar year 1918).

56. [Overland Park, Kansas] *Jewish Chronicle*, 5 December 1924; The Temple, Minutes, May 1918–June 1928, pp. 148, 153–54 and 156–57.

57. Solomon Cohen to AHS, 15 February 1923; AHS to Julian Morgenstern, 20 February 1923, PC 1922–23.

58. AHS to Maxwell Silver, 11 March 1925; Pearl Silver Matlaw to AHS, 17 October, 3 and 19 November, and 4 December 1925; AHS to Friends of Neustadt Jewry, 1 December 1925—all in PC 1925–26.

59. *Steubenville Herald-Star*, 18 January 1922; *Reading Pennsylvania Times*, 15 February 1923; *Pittsburgh Jewish Criterion*, 29 February 1924; Oral interview with Rose Halperin.

60. *Ohio State Journal*, 24 April 1919; *Wheeling Telegraph*, 9 February 1921. AHS's personal appointment books, extant from 1922, reveal that he tried to leave his early mornings free for reading, that he filled his midday hours with appointments, and that he tried to write in the afternoon.

61. *Scranton Argus* (February 1922).

62. *Steubenville Herald-Star*, 18 January 1922; *Allentown Morning Call*, 24 May 1923.

63. *Boston Globe*, 7 April 1924; *Pittsburgh Jewish Criterion*, 29 February 1924.

64. Silver, "Autobiography," D:3. Nearly every rabbi who ever served at The Temple with AHS noted his memorization of his sermon and the curious fact that he never ate before his addresses (but ate generously afterward!). AHS himself noted that "I rarely eat before a lecture"; PC 1922–23.

65. *Steubenville Herald-Star*, 18 January 1922.

66. H. H. Mandelzweig to AHS, 13 December 1929 and AHS to A. A. Benesch, 20 September 1929 (both in PC 1929–30).

67. PC, miscellaneous.

Chapter Three

1. *New York Times*, 18 January 1926; *Wisconsin Jewish Chronicle*, 19 February 1926; David Winchester to AHS, 15 March 1927, PC 1926–27.

2. Oral interview with Leon Feuer and AHS to Feuer, 27 May 1927, PC 1926–27.

3. Oral interview with Feuer.

4. "Applications and Recommendations for Assistant Rabbi, Successor to Feuer, 1934–35," Correspondence 8–4–56.

5. Oral interview with Feuer.

6. Feuer to AHS, 4 August [1927], PC 1926–27.

7. "Notes: Assistant Rabbis," PC 1934–35. AHS to Melbourne Harris, 23 January 1935. Correspondence 8–4–56.

8. Raphael, *Profiles in American Judaism: Reform, Conservative, Orthodox and Reconstructionist Judaism in Historical Perspective* (San Francisco, 1984), pp. 107–09.

9. *Cleveland Press*, 27 May 1929; *Jewish Tribune*, 7 June 1929; "The New Temple Policy," in The Temple, *Yearbook* 1929–30, pp. 1–2; The Temple, *Minutes, June 1928–June 1933*, pp. 91–96, 107 and 146. See also the *Boston Jewish Advocate*, 11 July 1929.

10. "What is Behind the DAR Blacklists"? *Literary Digest*, 97 (14 April 1928): 5–6; "Blacklist Party," *The Nation*, 126 (23 May 1928): 580–81; "Dishonoring the DAR," *The Nation*, 129 (25 September 1929): 323–25; Margaret Gibbs, *The DAR* (New York, 1969), pp. 118–34. A few years later Elizabeth Dilling, in *The Red Network: A "Who's Who" and Handbook of Radicalism for Patriots* (Chicago, 1934), called both Newton D. Baker and Silver "communists" and contributors to "one or more phases of the Red movement in the United States." See especially pp. 121, 129, 258–59 and 321.

11. *Cleveland Plain Dealer*, 13 and 19 October 1927, 21 April 1928; *Cleveland News*, 19 October 1927.

12. *Cleveland Press,* 4 and 10 July 1929; *Cleveland Plain Dealer,* 10 July 1929 and 19 October 1931.

13. Silver, "*Messianic Speculation in Israel,* Reaction, 1927–28," Correspondence 8–1–96.

14. *London Jewish Chronicle,* 30 December 1927; *Menorah Journal,* 14, 4 (April, 1928): 412; *Ha-olam* (London), 2 March 1928, 180 (Hebrew); *Hadoar* (New York), 2 March 1928, 281–83 (Hebrew).

15. AHS to Henry Berkowitz, 4 June 1928, PC 1928–29, and "Speaking Engagements, Los Angeles, 1922–52," Correspondence 3–1.

16. AHS to Sam Gross, 22 May 1929, Speaking Engagements, Denver, Correspondence 2–4.

17. On philanthropy, see PC 1927–28, 1928–29, 1929–30; on loans, see AHS to Jack Matlaw, 25 March 1927, PC 1926–27, AHS to Matlaw, 8 January 1929, PC 1929–30, Solomon Bloom to AHS, 15 October 1928, PC 1928–29, AHS to Bloom, 1 October 1928, PC 1928–29; oral interview with Armond Cohen; oral interview with Earl Stone (for AHS's generosity during the 1950s); Joseph S. Shubow to Israel Goldstein, 15 July 1943, Israel Goldstein Papers A364/1504.

18. AHS to Sam Hartman, 2 December 1927, PC 1927–28; AHS to Samuel Ungerleider, 12 September, 14 October and 21 November 1928, 14 January and 7 June 1929, PC 1928–29; AHS to Schultz Bros. & Co., 1 February 1929, PC 1928–29; AHS to Maxwell Silver, 5 December 1927, PC 1927–28; AHS to Samuel Ungerleider, 4 November 1929, PC 1929–30; AHS to Robert Gries, 21 February 1930, PC 1929–30; The Temple, Minutes, June 1928–June 1933, p. 422.

19. AHS to Nathan Krass, 30 April 1929, PC 1928–29, and numerous letters in PC 1926–27 and 1928–29.

20. *Cleveland Plain Dealer,* 3 March 1930, and *Providence Journal,* 20 March 1930.

21. *Columbus Dispatch,* 17 and 18 February 1931; *Cleveland News,* 24 and 25 March 1931; 72nd Congress, Senate Bill No. 25 (1931).

22. *Cleveland News,* 21 August and 13 November 1931; *Cleveland Plain Dealer,* 15 November 1931; *Cleveland Press,* 16 November 1931; *Atlanta Journal,* 24 February 1932; *Atlanta Constitution,* 24 February 1922.

23. *Cleveland Press,* 4 April 1932; *Cleveland Plain Dealer,* 9 October 1932; AHS, "A Rabbi Reviews Politics," 8 October 1932 (City Club lecture), Mss/Ty 32–7.

24. James F. Lincoln, *Criticism of Suggested Ohio Unemployment Insurance Bill* (Columbus, [1932]), p. 11; Ohio Chamber of Commerce, *Critical Analyses of the Report of the Ohio Commission on Unemployment Insurance* (Columbus, [1932]), pp. 3–5 and 24; *Cleveland Plain Dealer,* 12 January 1933.

25. *Cleveland Plain Dealer,* 11, 12 and 30 January 1933, 27 March 1934, 16 April 1937; *Cleveland Press,* 30 May and 13 June 1933, 21 February 1935, Dennis I. Harrison, The Consumers' League of Ohio: Women and Reform, 1909–1937, Ph.D. dissertation, Case Western Reserve, 1975.

26. *New York Herald,* 23 March 1933; *Cleveland Press,* 15 May 1933; *Philadelphia Inquirer,* 5 June 1933 and 9 April 1935; *Cleveland Plain Dealer,* 11 September 1933; *New York Times,* 4 December 1933, 15 February and 23 November 1934, 11 April 1935 and 5 May 1938; *Jewish Daily Bulletin,* 7 December 1933; Raphael, *Jews and Judaism in the United States: A Documentary History* (New York, 1983), pp. 319–29. See also Silver's response to Palestinian Jewish trade with the Nazis in Edwin Black, *The Transfer Agreement: The Untold Story of the Secret Agreement between the Third Reich and Jewish Resistance* (New York, 1984), pp. 320–21.

27. *Cleveland News,* 2 April 1925 and 7 May 1927; *Cleveland Plain Dealer,* 10 June 1930.

28. The Temple, Minutes, May 1918–June 1928, p. 418 (1927–28); *Cleveland News,* 27 October 1930; *Cleveland Plain Dealer,* 24 April 1932; *Jewish Daily Bulletin,* 19 May 1931; oral interviews with Leon Feuer, Melbourne Harris and Richard Hirsch. Despite the Hebrew instruction, The Temple did not offer a formal bar mitzvah ceremony during the 1920s or 1930s. This followed a pattern established by a majority of the more than one hundred Reform congregations I surveyed.

29. Leo M. Ascherman to ASH, 11 February 1935, PC 1934–35.

30. Stern to AHS, 17 January 1928, PC 1927–28.

31. "Columbus Zionist District, 1933–34," Correspondence 5–4–14 and "Columbus Zionist District, 1934–35," Correspondence 5–4–15; AHS to Morris Rothenberg, 12 January 1935, PC 1934–35; AHS to Rothenberg, 16 January 1935, Correspondence 5–4–15.

32. *Cleveland Plain Dealer,* 20 January 1935; *Cleveland Jewish World,* 25 and 26 January 1935; *American Jewish World,* 1 February 1935; AHS, Palestine Day address, 19 January 1935, Correspondence 5–4–16.

33. *Jewish Daily Bulletin,* 18 November 1934 and 16 December 1934.

See also Max Kadushin's angry letter to the editor (*Jewish Daily Bulletin*, 2 December 1934) in which he distorts AHS's argument and defends bureaus of Jewish education. For Silver to attack such bureaus and Hebrew schools would have been strange indeed; he helped found the Bureau of Jewish Education in Cleveland in 1924 and served as its first president for nearly eight years.

34. *American Jewish World*, 1 February 1935; Morris Rothenberg to AHS, 11 January 1935, Correspondence 5–4–16; Rothenberg to AHS, 14 January 1935; AHS to Rothenberg, 16 January 1935, Correspondence, 5–4–15.

35. *American Jewish World*, 1 February 1935, Correspondence 5–4–16; *Cleveland Plain Dealer*, 13 February 1935; oral interview with Armond Cohen.

36. "Minutes of the Meeting of the Administrative Committee of the Zionist Organization of America, Held Sunday, March 3, 1934," ZOA Archives.

37. Ibid.

38. *Cleveland News*, 27 February and 4 March 1935; *Cleveland Plain Dealer*, 28 February, 5 and 6 March 1935; *Cleveland Press*, 4 March 1935; *Jewish Daily Bulletin*, 7 March 1935; *Hartford Jewish Ledger*, 29 March 1935; *New Palestine*, 1 March 1935.

39. Memorandum, 7 and 17 March 1935, Correspondence 5–4–16; *Jewish Daily Bulletin*, 22 March 1935; F. M. Falkman to AHS, 27 June 1936, Correspondence 5–4–17; AHS to Morris Margulies, 26 May 1936, Correspondence 5–4–17; Falkman to AHS, 11 June 1936, Correspondence 5–4–17.

40. *Cleveland Press*, 1 March 1932; *Cleveland Plain Dealer*, 26 February 1937; Miscellaneous letters and telegrams, Correspondence 5–4–17.

41. W. H. O. McGhee to AHS, 20 November 1918 and AHS to W. H. O. McGhee, 1 December 1918; J. E. Cutter to AHS, 30 April 1928—all in Correspondence 11–1–28; Miscellaneous memos and notes in Correspondence 11–1–30.

42. Miscellaneous memos and notes in Correspondence 11–1–29; Solomon Goldman to Julian Mack, 11 March 1927, quoted in Jacob J. Weinstein, *Solomon Goldman: A Rabbi's Rabbi* (New York, 1973), p. 232.

43. Weinstein, *Goldman*, p. 17.

44. Robert E. Vinson to AHS and to Solomon Goldman, 9 April 1929,

in Correspondence 6–1–84; Oral interview with Armond Cohen; AHS to Julius Siegel, 11 May 1930, PC 1929–30.

45. *New Palestine*, 24 April 1925 and 28 September/5 October 1928; *New York World*, 30 June 1926; *Philadelphia Inquirer*, 4 June 1926; *Pittsburgh Press*, 2 July 1928; *Jewish Tribune*, 13 July 1928.

46. *New York Times*, 30 July 1929, 9 December 1930, 19 April 1931, 25 and 26 August 1935, 8 August 1937; *Jewish Daily Bulletin*, 20 August 1929; *St. Louis Times*, 17 April 1931.

47. *Chicago Sentinel*, 11 October 1934; *New York Times*, 5 and 6 March 1936.

48. *Modern View*, 1 July 1937; *American Hebrew*, 2 July 1937; *New York Times*, 8 August 1937; *Jewish Chronicle*, 13 August 1937; *Canadian Zionist* (September, 1937); *Cleveland Post*, 23 September 1937.

49. *Jewish Daily Bulletin*, 29 July 1931; *Boston Evening American*, 16 August 1938; Oral interviews with I. L. Kenen, Joseph Silbert and Melbourne Harris.

50. The quotations are taken from easily identifiable letters in PC 1923–24, 1927–28, 1928–29, 1930–31, 1942–43 and 1948–49. See also the pleas from Saul Appelbaum (1930), Baruch Braunstein (1949), Adolph J. Feinberg (1944), Maurice Feuer (1933), Joseph Fink (1932), Samuel Halperin (1931: "Lord knows, I deserve a decent pulpit"), Melbourne Harris (1931) Isaac Landman (1931), Irving Levey (1928) and Irving Reichert (1929). Even when Silver "cut" sessions at the annual rabbinical convention to swim, he did so alone. See AHS to Morris Lazaron, 29 June 1931, PC 1930–31 and AHS to Joseph Silbert, 6 July 1946, PC 1945–46.

Chapter Four

1. On the Congress, see *New Judaea* (September 1939).

2. Harold Manson, "Abba Hillel Silver—An Appreciation," in *In The Time of Harvest: Essays in Honor of Abba Hillel Silver on the Occasion of his 70th Birthday*. Edited by Daniel Jeremy Silver (New York, 1963), p. 11; Neumann, *In the Arena*, p. 147.

3. *Congrezion: Bulletin of the 21st Zionist Congress*, no. 4 (21 August 1939): 1–10 and no. 5 (22 August 1939): 1–6, ZOA Archives; *New York Times*, August 1939; Mss/Ty 39–31 ("World Zionist Congress"). Silver

wrote the latter speech in longhand on five sheets of stationary from the Hotel Cornavin in Geneva.

4. *Congrezion,* no. 5 (22 August 1939); *The Day,* 9 September 1939; *New York Times,* 20 August 1939; AHS, Vita, p. N:3; David Ben-Gurion, *Memoirs,* comp. Thomas R. Bransten (Cleveland, 1970), p. 195.

5. ZOA, *Annual Report for the 46th Annual Convention* (Atlantic City, 1944), p. 59. The American Emergency Committee for Zionist Affairs became the American Zionist Emergency Council in September of 1943.

6. Memorandum, submitted to the ECZA by David Petegorsky, 30 March 1942, typescript, Manson Files, The Temple, I-40; Neumann, *In the Arena,* p. 187; AECZA, Minutes of Office Committee Meeting, 1 June 1943.

7. Chaim Weizmann to AHS, 30 April, 15 May, 1 and 14 June 1942, and AHS to Weizmann, 5 June 1942, Manson Files, I-50; Weizmann to Lewis Namier, 27 June 1942, in *The Letters and Papers of Chaim Weizmann,* ed. Michael J. Cohen (New Brunswick, N.J., 1979), 20: 316, Weizmann to AHS, 28 September 1944, in *Letters and Papers of Chaim Weizmann,* 21: 214, and Weizmann to Stephen S. Wise, 26 December 1944, in *The Letters and Papers,* 21: 261–62; AHS to Weizmann, 12 January 1943, Correspondence 11–1–23; Weizmann to AHS, 28 January and 21 June 1943, Chaim Weizmann Archives; Weizmann to Numa Torczyner, 14 December 1943, in *The Letters and Papers,* 21: 111; Wise to Weizmann, 10 February 1943, Weizmann Archives. Wise pays tribute to AHS's tough negotiating skills in Wise to Goldmann, 4 August 1943, Stephen S. Wise Papers (Box 109, Folder 12), but depressed by what AHS demanded, he comforted himself with the hope that "there are still people inside and outside the Zionist movement who . . . imagine that my name means something in American life."

8. AECZA, Minutes, 26 August 1943, Executive Minutes, 26 August 1943; AHS to Melbourne Harris, 12 August 1943, PC 1943–44; AHS to Stephen S. Wise, 30 July 1943, PC 1943–44; Israel Goldstein, conversation with Dr. Silver, 30 July 1943, Israel Goldstein Papers, A364/1656B; Memorandum of Accord [between the three leaders], 9 August 1943, Correspondence 11–3–19 (the agreement is also in Israel Goldstein Papers, A364/1656B.) One day after the agreement was signed, it was accepted, "with something less than graciousness," by the office

committee; Meyer Weisgal to "Chief" Chaim Weizmann, 11 August 1943, Weizmann Archives.

9. AZEC, Executive Minutes, 26 August 1943; Memorandum of Accord, Correspondence 11–3–19.

10. AHS to Charles Rosenbloom, 30 July 1943, Correspondence 11–3–19.

11. See various press releases in Correspondence 11–3–19, and *Jewish Telegraphic Agency,* 27 July 1943.

12. See the letters and telegrams from Israel Goldstein, Stephen S. Wise, and Emanuel Neumann to AHS and from AHS to Neumann, 30 July 1943, Correspondence 11–3–19, and Elihu D. Stone to Goldstein, 23 July 1943 and Goldstein to Jerome J. Greenberg, 12 August 1943, Israel Goldstein Papers, A364/1504.

13. AHS to Emanuel Neumann, 6 August 1943; Neumann to AHS, "Sunday," Correspondence 11–3–19; [Recommendations for ZOA Executive], 26 August 1943, Israel Goldstein Papers, A364/1504; Goldstein to AHS, 2 August 1943, Goldstein Papers, A364/1656B; Stephen S. Wise to AHS, 3 August 1943, Goldstein Papers, ibid.; Meyer Weisgal to "Chief" [Weizmann], 11 August 1943, Weizmann Archives; oral interview with Neumann. Some interesting details of the Silver-Goldstein compromise are in Jacob Richman's article in the *Philadelphia Jewish Inquirer,* 20 August 1943, in the *Hartford Jewish Ledger,* 13 August 1943, and in a speech Gershon Agronsky delivered in Cleveland on 20 February 1949 (see *Israel Speaks,* 18 March 1949). Weizmann immediately wired congratulations and, a few months later, wrote of the "great gifts of devotion, courage, and eloquence" AHS would bring to the position. Weizmann to Numa Torczyner, 14 December 1943, in *The Letters and Papers,* 21: 111.

14. Emanuel Neumann to AHS, 5, 9 and 17 August 1943; AHS to Joseph Silbert, 6 August 1943; Silbert to AHS, 6 August 1943, Correspondence 11–3–19; Israel Goldstein to Louis E. Levinthal, 16 August 1943, A364/1504; Goldstein to AHS, 2 August 1943, Goldstein Papers, A364/1656B.

15. *Canadian Zionist* (September, 1937); *London Jewish Chronicle,* 6 August 1937, p. 21 and 13 August 1937, p. 26.

16. For the Biltmore resolutions, see Extraordinary Zionist Conference, Stenographic Protocol (New York, 1942).

17. *New Palestine,* 31 January 1941 and 23 January 1942; AHS to Simon Marks, 13 May 1942, Manson Files, I-20; Silver, "In War and Peace—A Jewish Palestine," Columbia Broadcasting System, 18 January 1942.

18. Extraordinary Zionist Conference, Stenographic Protocol, pp. 464–65 (the entire speech is on pp. 456–78).

19. AHS to Viscount Halifax, 27 April 1942, Manson Files, I–20; *The Scotsman,* 16 March 1942; *Southport Guardian,* 18 March 1942; *Manchester Guardian,* 20 March 1942; *Yorkshire Post,* 23 March 1942; *Birmingham Post and Mail,* 24 March 1942; *Birmingham Evening Dispatch,* 24 March 1942; *Zionist Review,* 20 and 27 March 1942; Weizmann to AHS, 30 April 1942, Manson Files, I-50; Report of Dr. Weizmann to the Office Committee of the Emergency Committee, 17 April 1942, Strictly Confidential, Z5/1415, Central Zionist Archives.

20. *New Palestine,* 10 September 1943, p. 19.

21. The American Jewish Conference, Proceedings of the First Session, 29 August to 2 September 1943, ed. Alexander Kohanski; Louis Lipsky, "The Drama of the Conference," *Brooklyn Jewish Center Review,* November, 1943, p. 47; I. L. Kenen, *Israel's Defense Line: Her Friends and Foes in Washington* (Buffalo, 1981), p. 12. For the opening speech of one of the non-Zionists urging unity but no discussion of statehood, see Joseph Proskauer, *A Segment of My Times* (New York, 1950), pp. 200–05. According to several accounts of the conference, the morning after Stephen S. Wise's speech, at a closed meeting of leaders, AHS gave Wise "an awesome tongue-lashing" for his docility. See, for example, Kenen, *Israel's Defense Line,* p. 13 and Neumann, *In the Arena,* p. 192.

22. *New York Times,* 31 August 1943; Lipsky, "Drama," p. 47.

23. *Jewish News,* 3 September 1943; *The Day,* 31 August 1943; Proceedings of the First Session.

24. Nahum Goldmann to Moshe Shertok, 19 March 1946, Z6/69, Goldmann Papers, 1944–46; Neumann, *In the Arena,* pp. 190–92; Goldmann to Shertok, 16 September 1943, S5/773, Goldmann Papers, 1941–45, Organizational Department of the American Zionist Executive; Lipsky, "Drama," p. 48; *New Palestine,* 10 September 1943, p. 17; *The Day,* 4 September 1943, p. 1, and 5 September 1943, p. 1. Arthur Lourie wrote to Palestine during the conference about the unappealing speeches of Wise and Goldstein and the "outstanding power" of AHS's address; Lourie to

Leo Lauterbach, 2 September 1943, S5/773, Organizational Department of the American Zionist Executive, Goldmann Papers. 1941–45. Jacques Torczyner recalled thirty years later how AHS's speech had "electrified the atmosphere" (Oral interview with Torczyner).

25. American Jewish Conference, Proceedings of the First Session.

26. Arthur Lourie to Leo Lauterbach, 2 September 1943, S5/773, Goldmann Papers, 1941–45; *New Palestine*, 10 September 1943, p. 19. A useful discussion of the conference is in the *National Jewish Monthly*, October 1943.

27. [Reorganization Plan], 17 August 1943, Manson I-27.

28. Manson, "Abba Hillel Silver," pp. 12–13; Oral interviews with Shulamith Schwarz Nardi, Harold Manson, I. L. Kenen, Eliahu Epstein (1986) and Emanuel Neumann (1975).

29. AZEC, Executive Minutes, 15 November and 13 December 1943; Goldmann to MS, 22 November 1943, S25/1504, Goldmann Papers, 1940–46; AZEC, Minutes, 5 October 1943 and 1 October 1946. One historian claims that more than four hundred emergency committees existed; Doreen Bierbrier, "The American Zionist Emergency Council: An Analysis of a Pressure Group," *American Jewish Historical Quarterly*, 60 (September 1970): 90. On the local committees, see AZEC, *An Outline of Activities for Local Zionist Emergency Committees* (New York, 1943), ZOA Archives. On Montor's leaving, see Neumann, *In the Arena*, pp. 193–94.

30. AZEC, Executive Minutes and Minutes, August 1943–June 1944; History of American Zionist Emergency Committee, 20 September 1944.

31. "Taking Stock of 1943—A Retrospect and Prospect," 2 January 1944 (Sermon 633); Goldmann to Isaac Gruenbaum, 5 April 1943, Z6/2762, Goldmann Correspondence, 1938–46; Goldmann to Moshe Shertok, 3 June 1943, S35/1504, Goldmann Papers, 1940–46.

32. AHS to Arthur Lourie, 22 April 1944, Manson Files, II-43; Leon Feuer, "Abba Hillel Silver: A Personal Memoir," *American Jewish Archives*, 19, 2 (November 1967): 120.

33. Feuer, "Abba Hillel Silver," p. 111. A detailed summary of AHS's lobbying during October 1943 is in Z5/391, CZA.

34. Silver, Confidential Notes, 1943–44.

35. Ibid. On his lobbying, see the many letters from those he "lobbied" in Manson Files, II-63.

36. Oral interview with Shulamith Schwarz Nardi. For a detailed dis-

cussion of how the Emergency Council organized Christian support, see Bierbrier, "American Zionist Emergency Council," pp. 92–95; Carl Hermann Voss, "The American Christian Palestine Committee," in *Essays in American Jewish History to Commemorate the Tenth Anniversary of the Founding of the American Jewish Archives*, ed. Jacob Rader Marcus (Cincinnati, 1958), pp. 242–62; and Joseph Schechtman, *The United States and the Jewish State Movement: The Crucial Decade, 1939–1949* (New York, 1966), pp. 64–67.

37. Feuer, "The Forgotten Year," *American Zionist* (November–December 1967): 18; Samuel Halperin, *The Political World of American Zionism* (Detroit, 1961), p. 185.

38. AZEC, Confidential Bulletin, I:1 (n.d.), p. 2, ZOA Archives; Bierbrier, "American Zionist Emergency Council," p. 103; The American Zionist Emergency Committee Report of Activities, 1940–46, in Goldstein Papers, A364/1656D.

Chapter Five

1. Emanuel Celler to AHS, 12 October 1943; Elihu Stone to Henry Montor, 17 December 1943; Leon Feuer to Stone, 23 December 1943; AHS to Stone, 21 December 1943; Stone to AHS, 24 December 1943 (all in Manson Files, I-92); AHS to Chaim Weizmann, 10 January 1943, Correspondence, 11–1–23; AZEC, Executive Minutes, 3 January 1944.

2. *Congressional Record*, 90, 18 (1 February 1944); Robert A. Taft to AHS, 23 February 1944, Manson Files, II-72; *Foreign Relations of the United States, Diplomatic Papers, 1944*, vol. 5, *The Near East, South Asia, and Africa, The Far East* (Washington, 1965), p. 563; Neumann to AHS, 28 January 1944, Manson Files, II-54; Feuer to AHS, 24 March 1944, Manson Files, II-63; *New Palestine*, 34, 12 (3 March 1944): 281–82 and 284–86.

3. *Jewish Telegraphic Agency Daily News Bulletin*, 10 February 1944; Silver, *Vision and Victory*, pp. 23–37; *New Palestine*, 34, 11 (18 February 1944): 258.

4. Leon Feuer to AHS, 24 March 1944, Manson Files, II-63; Melvin Urofsky, *We Are One: American Jewry and Israel* (New York, 1978), p. 57;

AHS to Senator Wallace H. White, Jr., 17 January 1944, Manson Files, II-63; *The Memoirs of Cordell Hull*, (London, 1948), 2: 1534–35. In private letters and at AZEC meetings during March of 1944, Silver correctly identified all of these reasons as responsible for the sudden State and War Departments' opposition, and he sensed that the real threat was political, not military, and that it originated in the State, and not the War, Department. AHS to Joel Gross, 7 March 1944, PC 1943–44; Confidential Notes, 7 February 1944, Manson Files, II-78. David Niles, too, told Silver and Feuer that the War Department "had gone to the front for the State Department"; interview with David Niles, 23 February 1944, Manson Files, II-72. The oil argument was favored by *Time, The Nation, New Statesman, Saturday Evening Post*, and columnist Drew Pearson, among others; the military explanation was favored by the War Department, Secretary of Navy Knox, and *New Judaean*.

5. *New York Times*, 5 and 22 March 1944; Leo Sack to AHS, 23 February 1944, Manson Files, II-75; Elihu Stone, "The Zionist Outlook in Washington," *New Palestine*, 34, 13 (17 March 1944); Confidential Memorandum for Dr. Silver from Mr. Leo Sack, 9 February 1944, Manson Files, II-75; *Foreign Relations of the United States*, 1944, 5: 563–64, 567, 574–76, and 591.

6. *New York Times*, 10 March 1944; AHS, Confidential Notes, 9 March 1944; *Foreign Relations of the United States*, 1944, 5: 586–88; *The Memoirs of Cordell Hull*, 2: 1535–36. The Ibn Saud–Roosevelt correspondence was not made public until 19 October 1945—after Roosevelt's death.

7. AZEC, Executive Minutes, 28 February, 13, 20 and 27 March 1944; Evan M. Wilson, *Decision on Palestine: How the United States Came to Recognize Israel* (Stanford, 1979), p. 40; AHS, *Vision and Victory*, pp. 39–46; I. L. Kenen to AHS, 4 February 1944, Manson Files, II-63. One State Department official recalled that the administration was indeed "buried under an avalanche of paper from American Jews" (Wilson, p. 31). On the executive session of the House Foreign Affairs Committee, see AHS's summary of his phone conversation with Representative Wright, 17 March 1944, Manson Files, II-63. Meyer Weisgal told Weizmann that Felix Frankfurter, David Niles, and other Jews in the administration ("all the boys in the *cheder*") were "very unhappy about . . . Silver's performance";

they felt he ought to have quit his activity after FDR told him he would "eventually" support a Jewish state. Weisgal to "Chief" [Weizmann], 4 April 1944, Weizmann Archives.

8. This conclusion comes from a study of the AZEC Executive Minutes and the AZEC, Confidential Bulletin, issued every few weeks during November 1943–June 1944, ZOA Archives.

9. Memorandum, Emergency Conference to Save the Jewish People of Europe (New York, 1943), pp. 13–14.

10. AHS, Confidential Notes, 12 October 1943.

11. AHS, Confidential Notes, 18 October 1943; Goldmann to Moshe Shertok, 19 May 1944, S25/1504, Goldmann Papers, 1940–46.

12. Various letters in PC, 1943–44 and 194–45.

13. AHS, Confidential Notes, 12 June 1944; Robert A. Taft to AHS, 13 June 1944 and AHS to Taft, 15 June 1944, Manson Files, II-84.

14. Peter Bergson to Weizmann, 2 April 1945, Manson Files, II-48; *The Answer: A Non-Sectarian Approach to the Problems of the Hebrew People in Europe and Palestine*, 2, 7 (15 June 1944): 6. This issue of *The Answer* also has useful biographical sketches of Bergsonites.

15. *Palestine*, 1, 7 (June 1944). Peter Bergson also faced attacks from his former allies: the New Zionist Organization of America broke off from the Bergsonites in June of 1944 and "repudiated any association, organizational, ideological, or political, with the 'so-called' Hebrew Committee for National Liberation" (*Zionews*, 5, 2 (July 1944): 12).

16. Judd Teller, *Strangers and Natives: The Evolution of the American Jew from 1921 to the Present* (New York, 1968), p. 202.

17. Feuer, "The Birth of the Jewish Lobby: A Reminiscence," *American Jewish Archives*, 28, 2 (November 1976): 114; Feuer, "Forgotten Years," 19; *Contemporary Jewish Record*, 8, 4 (August 1944): 403. See also the strong denunciations in AZEC press releases in Manson Files, II-39, the AZEC mailings in Manson Files, I-68, and Stephen S. Wise's aggressive attacks on Bergson in Monty Penkower, "In Dramatic Dissent: The Bergson Boys," *American Jewish History*, 70 (March 1981): 293–95.

18. See the letters and miscellanea in Manson Files II-20 and the *Chicago Sun*, 19 February 1944.

19. Manson Files, II-39, II-48, and II-88; Solomon Bloom to Silver, 8 June 1944, Manson Files, II-75.

20. Jesse Z. Lurie, "Confusion Worse Confounded: An Exposé of the

Bergson Group," *Congress Weekly,* 14, 8 (21 February 1947): 8–11; Meir Grossman, "Self-Appointed Liberators," *Congress Weekly,* 11, 20 (26 May 1944): 5–7; *Washington Post,* 3, 4 and 5 October 1944.

21. Goldmann, *The Autobiography,* p. 228; Samuel Katz, *Days of Fire* (Garden City, N.Y.), p. 209; Bierbrier, "The American Zionist Emergency Council," 101; AZEC, Minutes, 30 May 1945; Peter H. Bergson to AHS, 9 October 1945, Personal Correspondence, June–December 1945. Golda Meir near the end of her life recalled AHS's sympathy with the revisionists; oral interview with Golda Meier.

22. AZEC, Minutes, 3 April and 1 May 1944; AZEC, Executive Minutes, 3 April 1944.

23. AHS, "A Rabbi Reviews Politics," 8 October 1932, Mss/Ty 32–7; *New York Times,* 20 August 1933; *Cleveland Plain Dealer,* 5 March 1934; AHS, "The Roosevelt Administration: Its Achievements and Its Failures," 3 May 1936 (Sermon 455); AHS, "Fictitious Issues in the Campaign," 18 October 1936 (Sermon 459); Oral interview with Harold Manson.

24. AHS, "A Third Term for President Roosevelt?" 31 March 1940 (Sermon 554); *New York Herald Tribune,* 9 August 1940; *Washington Post,* 10 August 1940; *Cleveland Plain Dealer,* 1 April 1940 and 16 February 1942; AHS to Weizmann, 3 March 1944, Central Zionist Archives; oral interview with Emanuel Neumann, 21 July 1967 (where he explained how AHS "played the political game"); oral interview with Eliahu Epstein (1975) and Israel Goldstein, 12 September 1973 (where the latter explains AHS's politics as a result of Stephen S. Wise being "taken in by Roosevelt who was tremendously clever and would put his arm around Wise's shoulder and say 'You don't have to worry; everything will be fine'."); another interview with Goldstein, 29 May 1977, (where he explains that Silver "wasn't really a Republican" but "quite a liberal" who had "a fine strategy" of "playing off the two major parties, one against the other"); and oral interview with Jacques Torczyner (where he explains AHS's political strategy at length and how "in those days it was heresy to speak against Roosevelt and against the Democratic Party"). The quotation about "rotation in office" is from AHS, "Thoughts on the Coming Election," 27 October 1940 (Sermon 559), wherein he argues that Wilkie and Roosevelt are so similar that it would make little difference which man wins the election.

25. Robert A. Taft to AHS, 4 April 1944; AHS to Taft, 2 June 1944

(both in Manson files, II-84); Goldmann to AHS, 5 May 1944; AHS to Goldmann, 5 May 1944 (both in Manson files, II-69).

26. Harrison E. Spangler to AHS, 20 June 1944, Manson Files, II-63; AHS, Confidential Notes, 4 June 1943–20 September 1944.

27. AHS to Nathaniel L. Goldstein, 15 June 1944; Goldmann to AHS, 15 June 1944 (both in Manson Files, II-69); Taft to AHS, 25 June 1944; AHS to Taft, 26 June 1944 (both in Correspondence 8-4-24).

28. AHS, Memo to Shulman, n.d.; AHS, Memo to Neumann, n.d.; AHS, Memo on Conversation with Wise, n.d. (all in Correspondence 8-4-24).

29. AHS to Neumann, 27 June 1944; AHS to Neumann, 28 June 1944 (both in Manson Files, II-69).

30. Taft to AHS, 30 June 1944 and AHS to Taft, 1 July 1944 (both in PC July–December 1944).

31. "Final Draft of Palestine Resolution Included in the Republican Platform," Manson Files, II-16.

32. AHS to Wise, 28 June and 1 July 1944, Wise Papers (Box 119, Folder 20); AZEC, Executive Minutes, 10 July 1944; AHS to Neumann, 17 July 1944, Manson Files, II-54.

33. Goldstein to AHS, 11 July 1944, PC July–December 1944; AHS to Goldmann, 11 July 1944, PC; AHS, Confidential Notes, 10 July 1944.

34. AHS, Confidential Notes, 14 and 17 July 1944; Leo Sack to AHS, 5 July 1944, Correspondence 4-2-51; Wise to Doris I. Byrne, 16 July 1944, Wise Papers (Box 67, Folder 9); Wise to AHS, 29 June 1944 (Box 119, Folder 20); Wise to Louise Waterman Wise, n.d. and Wise to Samuel I. Rosenman, 18 July 1944 (Box 67, Folder 9). Morris Lazaron (1888–1979) served in Wheeling for one year, 1914–15, and married Virginia Horkheimer's older sister, Paulin. Prior to her untimely death in 1933, the two rabbinic couples had cordial relations but infrequent visits together. With the in-law connection dissolved and Lazaron moving from vigorous Zionism to founding the anti-Zionist American Council for Judaism, he and Silver had little contact. In his "autobiographical-biography," *As I See Him* (Gerrards Cross, England, 1978), Lazaron wrote about himself in the third person!

35. Leo Sack to AHS, 22 July 1944, Correspondence 4-2-51; Stephen S. Wise to Louise Waterman Wise, n.d. and Wise to FDR, 19 July 1944 (both in Wise Papers, Box 67, Folder 9); Wise to AHS, 21 July 1944,

Correspondence 4–2–68. See Correspondence 11–1–45 for the claim that "I have never stumped." AHS had informed Wise that the AZEC lobbyists in Washington expected the State Department (through Senator Connally) to oppose a plank in the Democratic Party platform and that he would not have an easy job in Chicago; AHS to Wise, 1 July 1944, Goldstein Papers, A364/1656B.

36. AHS to Wise, 20 July 1944, Correspondence 4–2–68; AHS to Wise, 21 July 1944, Wise Papers (Box 119, Folder 20); AZEC, Minutes, 24 July 1944; *Foreign Relations of the United States*, 1944, 5: 615–16 (Roosevelt's endorsement, 15 October, and Dewey's endorsement, 12 October 1944).

Chapter Six

1. AZEC, Minutes, 20 December 1944.

2. James T. Patterson, *Mr. Republican: A Biography of Robert A. Taft* (Boston, 1972), p. 281; AZEC, Executive Minutes, 12 October 1944; *Foreign Relations of the United States*, 1944, 5:618; AHS, Confidential Notes, 5 September 1944; AHS to Taft, 26 September 1944; Taft to AHS, 12 October and 28 December 1944 (all in Correspondence 4–2–64).

3. AZEC, Minutes, 30 October and 9 November 1944; *The Diaries of Edward R. Stettinius, Jr., 1943–1946*, ed. Thomas M. Campbell and George C. Herring (New York, 1975), p. 164.

4. For Wise's account, see Wise to Julius Livingston, 18 December 1944, in *Stephen S. Wise: Servant of the People*, ed. Carl Hermann Voss (Philadelphia, 1969), p. 267.

5. *The Diaries*, pp. 169–70 and 174; AZEC, Minutes, 21 November 1944; Oral interview with Neumann, 21 July 1967.

6. Memoranda of Conference of Dr. Silver and Mr. Leo Sack with Senator Connally in the Office of the Senate Committee on Foreign Relations, 27 November [1944], Manson Files, II-30; AZEC, Executive Minutes, 14 November 1945; AZEC, Minutes, 7 and 9 December 1944; Solomon Bloom to Israel Goldstein, 13 December 1944, Goldstein Papers, A364/1656B; Melvin Urofsky, "Rifts in the Movement: Zionist Fissures, 1942–1945," in *Essays in American Zionism, 1917–1948*, ed. Melvin I. Urofsky (New York, 1978), p. 211, n. 32.

7. *New York Times*, 30 November 1944; *Jewish Telegraphic Agency Daily News Bulletin*, 30 November 1944; AHS, Confidential Notes, 28 November 1944; 78th Congress, 2d Session, H–R, Report No. 1997, 30 November 1944, pp. 1–4; AZEC, Executive Minutes, 26 November 1945.

8. *Foreign Relations of the United States*, 1944, 5:640–42.

9. Wise to Stettinius, Jr., 1 and 3 December 1944, Wise Papers (Box 66, Folder 3); Franklin Delano Roosevelt to Wise, 21 December 1944 (Box 68, Folder 44); Notes on AHS meeting with Robert Wagner and Edward J. Stettinius, Jr., 4 December 1944, Correspondence 4–2–51; AHS, Confidential Notes, 4 December 1944; AHS to Neumann, 15 December 1944, Correspondence 4–2–26; Stettinius, Jr. to AHS, 15 December 1944, Correspondence 4–2–61; Feuer to Goldstein, 5 January 1945 and Goldstein to Lawrence W. Crohn, 12 February 1945, Goldstein Papers, A364/1546; Wise to Stettinius, Jr., 4 December 1944 (the full telegram), Goldstein Papers, A364/1656A.

10. *The Day*, 14 December 1944; *Washington Post*, 15 December 1944; AZEC, Minutes, 7 December 1944; *Foreign Relations of the United States*, 1944, 5:643–44, 644–46, and 655; AZEC, Executive Minutes, 11 December 1944; Wise to Stettinius, Jr., 12 December 1944; Stettinius, Jr., to Wise, 15 December 1944; Wise to AHS, 15 December 1944 (all in Wise Papers, Box 66, Folder 3).

11. Goldstein to Leon Feuer, 14 December 1945, Goldstein Papers, A364/1546; *Foreign Relations of the United States*, 1944, 5:645–56; Neumann to AHS, 15 December 1944, Correspondence 4–2–26; AZEC, Minutes, 7 and 9 December 1944.

12. For the origins of the Jewish Agency's political department in Washington, see Chaim Weizmann to Moshe Shertok, 31 March 1943; Minutes, Office Committee Meeting, AECZA, 1 June 1943; Plan for a Branch of the Political Department of the Jewish Agency Executive in the United States, 11 June 1943; Weizmann to Silver, 21 June 1943—all in Weizmann Archives.

13. Oral interview with Goldmann; Solomon Bloom to AHS, 23 September and 30 October 1943; Goldmann's Conversation with Sol Bloom, 22 September 1943 (both in Manson Files, I-93); Minute of Conversation with Judge Samuel Rosenman, 3 November 1943; AHS to Goldmann, 5 November 1943; Goldmann to AHS, 9 November 1943 (all in Manson Files, I-70);

14. AHS to Goldmann, 10 November 1943, Manson Files, I-70.

15. Goldmann to AHS, 30 December 1943, Z6/2306, Goldmann Papers, 1943–47; AHS to Wise, 18 August 1944, PC 1944–1945; AHS, Confidential Notes, 8 and 10 February 1944; Weisgal, *So Far: An Autobiography* (London, 1971), p. 186.

16. Miriam Cohen to Goldmann, 1 March 1944 and Goldmann to AHS, 11 January 1943, S25/1504 (both in Goldmann Papers, 1940–46); Goldmann to Weizmann, 7 June 1944, Z6/2759, Goldmann Correspondence, 1944–48.

17. Goldmann to AHS, 14 September 1943, 85/773, Organization Department of the American Zionist Executive, Goldman Papers, 1941–45; AHS to Weizmann, 5 April 1944, Manson Files, II-43; Neumann to AHS, 13 April 1944, Manson Files, II-54; AHS to Weizmann, 3 March 1944, Z5/391, Central Zionist Archives; Weizmann to AHS, 1 May 1944, Z6/2306, Goldmann Papers, 1943–47; AHS to Weizmann, 3 March 1944, in *Letters and Papers of Chaim Weizmann*, 21:168.

18. Goldmann to AHS, 18 May 1944; Goldmann to Weizmann and Wise, 10 August 1944 (all in Z6/2759, Goldmann Correspondence, 1944–48); AHS to Neumann, 16 August 1944, ZOA Archives; AZEC, Executive Minutes, 14 August 1944; Goldmann to AHS, 10 August 1944, PC 1943–44; AHS to Goldmann, 28 August 1944 and Goldmann to AHS, 1 September 1944, both in Goldmann Papers, A364/553. Goldmann wrote a letter to Weizmann, similar to his 18 May correspondence with AHS, about Silver's clumsy handling of the resolutions; *The Letters and Papers*, 21:130. See also Weizmann to Weisgal, 1 October 1944, where Weizmann expressed doubt that his letters to AHS re: Silver vs. Goldmann will do any good; *The Letters and Papers*, 21: 219.

19. AZEC, Executive Minutes, 14 August and 25 September 1944; AHS to Neumann, 16 August 1944, ZOA Archives; Meeting of the Program Committee, 22 August 1944, Goldstein Papers, A364/1656B; AHS to Neumann, 12 September 1944, Correspondence 4-2–26; Goldmann to AHS, 12 September 1944 and Leo Sack to AHS, 15 September 1944 (both in Correspondence, 4-3–43). The Emergency Council, on 28 August, rejected Silver's resignation, but three days later he reaffirmed it and continued to do so until an understanding with Goldmann was effected; AZEC, Executive Minutes, 28 and 31 August 1944. Goldmann agreed to inform AHS in advance of his scheduled meetings with govern-

ment officials and reaffirmed this agreement periodically in 1945. Silver nonetheless continued to tell Zionist colleagues of Goldmann's complete disregard of this agreement; Goldstein to A. K. Epstein, 7 September 1944, Goldstein Papers, A364/1546; Zionist Executive to AHS, 10 September 1945, Goldmann to AHS, 18 September 1945, Silver to committee of eight, Memorandum, 26 October 1945 (all in Goldstein Papers, A364/553). Weizmann formed a Zionist executive branch in the United States in 1942; it included Weizmann, Goldmann, Wise and Silver.

20. Goldmann to Weizmann, 7 June 1944, Z6/2759, Goldmann Correspondence, 1944–48; Goldmann to Weizmann, 1 July 1944, Weizmann Archives. With respect to his "vacation," Goldmann complained to Ben-Gurion one summer that AHS refused to "be available at twenty-four-hours notice" and insisted on a family vacation. See Goldmann to Ben-Gurion, 20 June 1946, Z6/2759, Goldmann Correspondence, 1944–48.

21. Wise to AHS, 3 and 6 February 1944, Manson Files, II-95.

22. AZEC, Minutes, 7 and 9 December 1944; AZEC, Executive Minutes, 12 October 1944; AHS to Neumann, 27 October 1944, Correspondence 4–2–25; Press Release, 1 January 1945, Correspondence 4–2–27; Wise, Sermon on Reelection of Roosevelt (Boston), 5 November 1944, Wise Papers (Box 68, Folder 9); Solomon Bloom to Goldstein, 13 December 1944, Goldstein Papers, A364/1656B.

23. Address, B'nai Zion Dinner, 31 March 1946, Mss/Ty 46-4; AHS, "Some Thoughts on the Campaign and the Coming Election," 5 November 1944 (Sermon no. 644); Leo Sack to Rep. Adolph J. Sabath, 27 August 1947, Manson IV-53.

24. Wise to Roosevelt, 18 January 1944, Manson Files, II-95; Roosevelt to Wise, 14 March 1944, Wise Papers (Box 68, Folder 9); Wise to Roosevelt, 19 December 1944, Corrrespondence 11–1–50; AHS to Neumann, 9 January 1945, PC January–June 1945; "Statement by Dr. Abba Hillel Silver," Jewish Press Service, 5 January 1945, p. 6. Many AZEC members noted how lifeless the organization seemed before Silver took over; in addition, Weizmann noted in early 1943 how it was "a bulky, unwieldy body utterly inadequate to deal with the complexities of the situation." See Weizmann to Mrs. E.T.D. [Mrs. Edgar Dugdale, or "Baffy"], 6 January 1943, Weizmann Archives, as well as Weizmann to AHS, 19 February 1943 and Weizmann to Shertok, 31 March 1943, in Weizmann Archives.

25. AHS to Neumann, 20 December 1944, Manson Files, II-72; oral interview with Harold Manson; *New York Times,* 28 December 1944; *Boston Jewish Advocate,* 28 December 1944; Goldmann to Eliezer Kaplan, 12 January 1945, Z6/69, Goldmann Papers, 1944–46, General; Report on Controversy in Emergency Council, n.d., Goldstein Papers, A364/1656C. Shlomo Grodzensky, writing in *Der Yiddishe Kemfer* (6 April 1945), was an exception to the general trend in the Yiddish press. He called Silver the "ousted Messiah" and claimed that he was "too much intoxicated with the sonorous words he uttered and with the wide swing of his majestic gestures."

26. AZEC, Minutes, 28 December 1944; AZEC, Executive Minutes, 2 January and 3 April 1945; ZOA, Executive Minutes, 1 April 1945 and Summary of Discussion of Internal Controversy at Meeting of ZOA Executive Committee, 1 April 1945 (both in IG Papers, A364/1513C); IG to A. K. Epstein, 5 February 1945, Goldstein papers, A364/1546; AHS to Leo Sack, 14 and 30 January 1945, Correspondence 4-2-51; Urofsky, "Rifts," p. 208; Harry S. May to Saul Spiro, n.d., Goldstein Papers, A364/1656C; Charles J. Rosenbloom to William H. Sylk, 5 February 1945, Goldstein Papers, A364/1656D. Wise kept the "Chief" abreast of his resignation strategy during December; see Wise Papers (Box 68, Folder 9), especially Wise to Chief, 12 December 1944. A lengthy discussion of the AZPC is in the oral interview with Harold Manson, 4 November 1971.

27. Philip Slomovitz to Leon Fram, 8 April 1945, Correspondence, 4-2-43. The "purge" to which Slomovitz refers was the ZOA's systematic removal of AHS supporters during the autumn of 1944 from positions of leadership, and AHS responded by calling the ZOA leaders "power-hungry politicians"; AHS to Bernard H. Arnold, 5 February 1945, Israel Goldstein Papers, A364/1656C.

28. "A Time to Speak" [1945], Goldstein Papers, A364/1656D; *Opinion,* 15, 3 (January 1945): 3; Robert Szold to Carl Alpert, 23 March 1945, Goldstein Papers, A364/1656D; Neumann to AHS, 30 April 1945, Correspondence 4-2-26; *New York Times,* 8 and 30 April, and 17 July 1945; Elias Goodstein to Louis E. Levinthal, 17 March 1945, Goldstein Papers, A364/1656B; Levinthal to Louis Lipsky, 14 June, Lipsky to Levinthal, 18 June, and Levinthal to Lipsky, 20 June 1945 (all in Goldstein Papers, A364/1584); *New Palestine,* 35, 20 (27 July 1945).

29. Voss, *Stephen S. Wise,* pp. 79–80.

30. Wise to Editor, *American Jewish Chronicle* (n.d.), Correspondence 11–1–47; Voss, *Stephen S. Wise*, pp. 97, 99, and 220; *Ft. Worth News*, 4 February 1920; Wise to AHS, 28 April 1920, Correspondence 11–1–49; Wise to AHS, 28 May 1924, PC 1923–24; Wise, "Zionist Division and Strife: Could they Have Been Avoided?", Sermon, 5 January 1945, Wise Papers (Box 19, Folder 2).

31. Urofsky, "Rifts," p. 203, n. 18; Wise, "Zionist Division"; Zvi Ganin, "Activism versus Moderation: The Conflict between Abba Hillel Silver and Stephen Wise during the 1940s," *Studies in Zionism*, 5, 1 (Spring 1984): 73 and 83.

32. Goldmann, *Autobiography*, p. 230; Wise, "Zionist Division."

33. Goldmann to Weizmann, 19 April 1945, Z6/2759, Goldmann Correspondence, 1944–48; AHS to Neumann, 16 August 1944, zoa Archives; Wise to Goldmann, 8 January 1947, in Voss, *Stephen S. Wise*, p. 275; Goldmann to Ben-Gurion, 4 October 1945, Z6/2762. Goldmann Correspondence, 1938–46; Wise to Goldmann, 11 September 1946, Weizmann Archives. Wise frequently wrote AHS about his ill health; typical is this passage from a letter of 2 March 1944 mailed from Miami Beach: "I have been far from well and suffering great pain because of the organic disease which I suffer" (Manson Files, II-95).

Chapter Seven

1. Robert J. Donovan, *Conflict and Crisis: The Presidency of Harry S. Truman, 1945–1948* (New York, 1977), p. 314; *Foreign Relations of the United States, 1945,* 8: 734–36 (31 August 1945 memo by Merriam); Francis Williams, *A Prime Minister Remembers: The War and Post-War Memoirs of The Rt. Hon. Earl Attlee* (London, 1961), pp. 187–89; *Manchester Guardian*, 24 September 1945 (editorial); *The New Statesman and Nation*, 29 September 1945, p. 208; Truman, *Memoirs*, vol. 2, *Years of Trial and Hope* (New York, 1956), pp. 132, 137–38; Hadley Cantril, *Public Opinion, 1935–1946* (Princeton, 1951), p. 385 (On 22 November 1945, 80 percent of the respondents stated that a Jewish state in Palestine is a good thing and every possible effort should be made to secure it).

2. The text of Harrison's report is in the U.S. Department of State, *Bulletin*, 13 (30 September 1945): 456–63, and reprinted in *New York*

Times, 30 September 1945 as well as J. C. Hurewitz, *Diplomacy in the Near and Middle East: Documentary Record, 1914–1956* (New York, 1956), 2: 249–57. On the Jewish Agency petition (in mid-June), see Jewish Agency Executive, *Political Report 1946,* p. 23 (CZA) or *New Judaean,* 21, 11–12 (August–September 1945): 190. On the visit to G. G. Hall, see Weizmann to Shertok, 20 August 1945, in *The Letters and Papers of Chaim Weizmann,* ed. Joseph Heller (Jerusalem, 1979), 22: 35, and Christopher Sykes, *Crossroads to Israel* (Cleveland, 1965), p. 332.

3. Robert F. Wagner to AHS, 2 July 1945, Correspondence 4-2-49; Williams, *Prime Minister,* pp. 183–84; "Harry S. Truman Press Conference," 16 August 1945, Manson Files, III-69; Truman, *Memoirs,* 2:136; AHS, *Vision and Victory,* p. 91. See also the praise of Truman in *New Judaean,* 21, 11–12 (August–September 1945): 189.

4. Menachem Begin, *The Revolt: Story of the Irgun* (Tel Aviv, 1964), p. 316. Weizmann complained about AHS's militancy toward England in May while his friends attacked Silver's "warlike message . . . against Britain and America" in March; Weizmann to Ernst D. Bergmann, 17 May 1945, in *The Letters and Papers,* 22: 8 and Wise to Weisgal, 6 March 1945, Z6/2306, Goldmann Papers, 1943–47.

5. AHS to Goldmann, 6 November 1945, Z6/2306, Goldmann Papers, 1943–47.

6. *Foreign Relations of the United States,* 1945, 8: 740–41; "Record of Chaim Weizmann Phone Call," 15 September 1945, Manson Files, III-71; Williams, *Prime Minister,* pp. 189–90 (for Attlee's 16 September 1945 telegram); *New York Times,* 1 October, 14 November, and 11 December 1945 (on Bevin's humanitarianism).

7. *The Day,* 24 September 1945; AZEC, Executive Minutes, 24 September and 2 October 1945, ZOA Archives.

8. AHS to Feuer, 27 September 1945, PC 1944–45; Goldmann to AHS, 18 September 1945, Goldstein Papers, A364/553.

9. Goldmann to Shertok, 16 October 1945, Z6/2759, Goldmann Correspondence, 1944–48.

10. Michael J. Cohen, "The Genesis of the Anglo-American Committee on Palestine, November 1945: A Case Study in the Assertion of American Hegemony," *The Historical Journal,* 22, 1 (1979): 185–207; *Foreign Relations of the United States,* 1945, 8: 771–819 and 821–40 (cables between Byrnes and Bevin); Wise and Silver to Truman, 30 October 1945,

attached to AZEC, Executive Minutes, 29 October 1945 and in Manson Files, III–62; Truman, *Memoirs*, 2: 142; Williams, *Prime Minister*, p. 193.

11. *Foreign Relations of the United States*, 1945, 8: 756 and 767; *New York Times*, 19 October, 14, 15, and 19 November 1945; *Parliamentary Debates*, 415 H.C. Deb, 5s., 13 November 1945, 1927–35 (especially 1934); Donovan, *Conflict and Crisis*, p. 314; AZEC, Executive Minutes, 14 November 1945. The date of 13 November was carefully selected so as not to announce Truman's support of another inquiry committee until after the New York mayoralty elections in which the Democrat faced a Jewish Republican.

12. AHS to Herbert Bayard Swope, 21 November 1945, Manson Files, III-62; *Boston Jewish Advocate*, 22 November 1945; *Hartford Jewish Ledger*, 23 November 1945; AHS to Goldstein, 3 January 1946, Manson Files, III-62; Bartley Crum, *Behind the Silken Curtain: A Personal Account of Anglo-American Diplomacy in Palestine and the Middle East* (New York, 1947), pp. 24–28; AZEC, Executive Minutes, 14, 26 and 30 November, 7 December 1945; Small Zionist Actions Committee, 11 December 1945, S5/363 (CZA); Joseph Heller, "The Anglo-American Committee of Inquiry on Palestine (1945–46): The Zionist Reaction Reconsidered," in *Zionism and Arabism in Palestine and Israel*, ed. Elie Kedourie and Sylvia G. Haim (London, 1982), pp. 137–70.

13. Richard Crossman, *Palestine Mission: A Personal Mission* (London, n.d.), p. 66; William Phillips, *Ventures in Diplomacy* (Boston, 1952), p. 426; James G. McDonald, *My Mission in Israel, 1948–1951* (New York, 1951), pp. 24–26; Neumann to AHS, 17 March 1946, Manson Files, III-82; Arthur Lourie to AHS, 25 January, 3, 5, and 7 February, 3, 13, 15, and 21 March, 6, 11, and 16 April 1946, Manson Files, III-83; *Foreign Relations of the United States*, 1946, 7: 585–87; *New Judaea*, 22, 8 (May 1946): 140–49.

14. *Foreign Relations of the United States*, 1946, 7: 588–89; Truman, *Memoirs*, 2: 146. For the evidence that AHS drafted Truman's statement, see the original longhand draft (on St. Regis Hotel letterhead) and much else in Correspondence 4–3–5 and AHS, Confidential Notes, 28 April 1946. On Attlee's and Bevin's pleas for consultation, see *Foreign Relations of the United States*, 1946, 7: 584–85 and 587–88. On Attlee's resentment, see Francis Williams, *Twilight of Empire: The Memoirs of Prime Minister Clement Attlee* (New York, 1960), especially chap. 12. See also Attlee's

speech in the House of Commons in *Parliamentary Debates,* 422 H.C. Deb, 5s., 1 May 1946, pp. 197–99, a speech that led one member of the committee of inquiry, Fred Buxton, to call Attlee "an incredibly stupid man" (Isaac Zoar, *Rescue and Liberation: America's Part in the Birth of Israel* [New York, 1954], p. 183). See also Francis Williams, *Ernest Bevin: Portrait of a Great Englishman* (London, 1952), p. 260, where Williams describes Bevin's reaction to Truman's response as "one of the blackest rages" of his career.

15. Crum, *Silken Curtain,* p. 281; Heller, "Anglo-American Committee," p. 160; *Foreign Relations of the United States,* 1946, 7:587–88; Michael J. Cohen, *Palestine and the Great Powers, 1945–1948* (Princeton, 1982), p. 206; Goldmann to Wise, 18 April 1946, Wise Papers (Box 109, Folder 12); AHS, Confidential Notes, 28 and 29 April 1946. There is some evidence from his private letters that had Truman been left alone by the Zionists ("I received about 35,000 pieces of mail and propaganda from the Jews in this country. . . . I put it all in a pile and struck a match to it.") Truman would have enthusiastically endorsed the entire report; Truman to Claude Pepper, 20 October 1947, quoted in Cohen, *Palestine,* p. 110. Goldmann had worked intensively both to prevent Silver from launching public protests against the committee's recommendations and to influence the committee during its deliberations in Switzerland. He wrote AHS in March that "I decided to go to Palestine in order to be around when the Commission [the name the British used] is there, and from there I will go to Switzerland to be there when the Commission will work in Switzerland"; Goldmann to AHS, 4 March 1946, Z6/2306, Goldmann Papers, 1943–47. Goldmann probably greatly influenced the decision of Crum and McDonald to see AHS in New York before meeting with the president.

16. AZEC, Executive Minutes, 3, 13 and 29 May, 7 June 1946; AZEC, Minutes, 9 May 1946; Truman, *Memoirs,* 2: 149; *New York Journal American,* 13 June 1946; *New York Herald Tribune,* 13 June 1946; Dean Acheson, *Present at the Creation: My Years in the State Department* (London, 1969), p. 173; Memorandum from AHS to AZEC Delegates (n.d.), Manson Files, III-17; AHS and Wise to Acheson, 18 and 31 May 1946, attached to the Executive Minutes of 29 May 1946.

17. AHS, *Vision and Victory,* p. 93; Neumann to AHS, 14 June 1946, Correspondence 4-4-24; John Snetsinger, *Truman, the Jewish Vote, and*

the Creation of Israel (Stanford, 1974), p. 38; Neumann, *In The Arena*, p. 207; Benjamin Akzin to AHS, 17 July 1946, Manson Files, III-41; AZEC, Executive Minutes, 15 July 1946; *New York Times*, 10 and 11 July 1946; *Boston Herald*, 11 July 1946. See also Wise's discussion of his loan approval position in a conversation with Weizmann in *The Personal Letters of Stephen Wise*, ed. Justine Wise Polier and James Waterman Wise (Boston, 1956), p. 273, and Goldmann's record of Wise's explanation of his intervention when they both met with Hall, in Nahum Goldmann, "Secret Report on Interview with Mr. Hall in London," 15 August 1946, Z6/2762, Goldmann Correspondence, 1938–46.

18. Williams, *Ernest Bevin*, p. 260; McDonald, *My Mission*, pp. 24–26; *Foreign Relations of the United States, 1946*, 7: 603–27; Acheson, *Present at the Creation*, pp. 172–73; *Public Papers of the President of the United States: Harry S. Truman 1946* (Washington, 1962), pp. 218–19.

19. *Foreign Relations of the United States, 1946*, 7: 636–43; Williams, *Prime Minister*, pp. 193–97; AZEC, Executive Minutes, 7 and 11 June, 3 July 1946; Joseph Alsop's column in the *New York Herald Tribune*, 18 August 1946; Acheson, *Present at the Creation*, p. 169.

20. *Foreign Relations of the United States, 1946*, 7: 644–70 (the complete text of Morrison-Grady is on pp. 652–67 and Byrnes's perplexity is described in his 22 July letter to Ambassador Harriman, on pp. 648–49). Grady's acceptance of the plan, strongly opposed by all Zionists, disappointed them. Grady, a college friend of Rabbi Louis Newman and an inveterate Zionist, was the object of steady (albeit gentle) pressure from AHS and his AZEC associates. Grady, representing Secretary of State Byrnes faithfully, carefully adhered to the State Department position. See especially AZEC, 1945–46, "Benjamin Akzin," Correspondence 4-3-2.

21. *Foreign Relations of the United States, 1946*, 7: 623–24, 627, 648–49, 671–74; AZEC materials and Akzin to AHS, 17 July 1946, Manson III-41; *Jewish Telegraphic Agency Daily News Bulletin*, 1 August 1946; *New York Times*, 27 July and 1 August 1946; McDonald, *My Mission*, p. 11; AZEC, Executive Minutes, 25 and 26 July 1946.

22. AZEC, Executive Minutes, 30 July and 1 August 1946; *Foreign Relations of the United States, 1946*, 7: 673–82; Williams, *Prime Minister*, p. 199; *New York Herald Tribune*, 1 August 1946. Parliament debated the plan on 31 July and 1 August 1946.

23. The text of the statement by Acheson on 8 August 1946 is in Manson Files, III-1; Acheson's memorandum is an agreement with the summary of the meeting with Truman provided to the AZEC by Frank Buxton, a member of the Anglo-American committee, in Arthur Lourie to AHS, 12 August 1946, Manson Files, III-92. See also *Foreign Relations of the United States*, 1946, 7: 679–82. The Bergsonites, too, condemned Morrison-Grady and rallied several senators and representatives to opposition.

24. *New York Times*, 11 October 1946; AZEC, 1946–47, "L," Correspondence 4–4–17; *Foreign Relations of the United States*, 1946, 7: 701–04.

25. *Foreign Relations of the United States*, 1946, 7: 704–05.

26. AZEC, Executive Minutes, 14 October 1946; *New York Post*, 16 and 17 October 1946; *The Day*, 10, 16, and 24 October 1946; *The Morning Journal*, 7 October 1946 (Yiddish).

27. *Modern View*, 1 July 1937; *New York Times*, 8 August 1937; *Canadian Zionist*, September 1937; *Cleveland Press* and *Cleveland News*, 23 September 1937. At an AZEC executive meeting in 1946 Wise reminisced for a minute about how he and AHS stood beside Ussishkin and opposed partition in 1937; Executive Minutes, 10 September 1937.

28. David Ben-Gurion to AHS, 9 April 1946, PC 1946–47; Meeting Between the Right Hon. Ernest Bevin and Mr. David Ben-Gurion, Foreign Office, 12 February 1947, 9:45 A.M., 13 p., in Jewish Agency, Ben-Gurion, 1947–48, Correspondence 7–1–9; AHS, Abstract of Address Delivered on 22 September 1937, Mss/Ty 37–16.

29. AZEC, Minutes, 9 May 1946; Goldmann, *The Autobiography*, pp. 231–32; AZEC, Executive Minutes, 7 August 1946; Goldmann to Wise, 5 August 1946, Wise Papers (Box 109, Folder 12).

30. Goldmann to Ben-Gurion, 5 August 1946, Wise Papers (Box 109, Folder 12); AHS, Confidential Notes, 6 and 7 August 1946; Goldmann, *The Autobiography*, p. 233; *Foreign Relations of the United States*, 1946, 7: 679–82.

31. *New York Times*, 12 August 1946; AHS, Confidential Notes, 10 August 1946; *National Jewish Post and Opinion*, 13 September 1946; Goldmann to Weizmann, 10 August 1946, Z6/2759, Goldmann Correspondence 1944–48; *New York Times*, 14 August 1946; Goldmann, *The Autobiography*, pp. 233–35.

32. AHS to Fishman Gold Shapiro, 9 August 1946, Manson Files, III-64; *New York Times*, 22 August 1946; Goldmann, The Autobiography, p. 236; Goldmann to Bartley C. Crum, 10 September 1946, Z6/2759, Goldmann Correspondence 1944–48.

33. Goldmann to Acheson, 30 August 1946, Z6/2759, Goldmann Correspondence, 1944–48; Crum to Goldmann, 27 August 1946, Manson Files, III-64; AHS to Ben-Gurion, [14] August 1946, Manson Files, III-88; AHS, Confidential Notes, 10 August 1946; AHS to Louis Segal, 9 September 1946 and Wise to Goldmann, 11 September 1946, Weizmann Papers.

34. Ben-Gurion to AHS, 15 August 1946, in Dr. Abba Hillel Silver, Z6/2306, Goldmann Papers 1943–47; Eliahu Epstein to Ben-Gurion, 2 September 1946, Z6/69, General, Goldman Papers 1946–49; AHS to Ben-Gurion, 5, n.d., 14 and 19 August 1946, Manson Files, III-88; AHS to Crum, 6 December 1946, Manson Files, III-96.

35. *New York Post*, 28 October 1946; *New York Times*, 26 and 29 October 1946; *Jewish Telegraphic Agency Daily News Bulletin*, 1 November 1946.

36. AHS to Benjamin Akzin, 7 November 1946, Manson Files, III-41.

37. Memorandum, Interview with Mr. Ernest Bevin in the Presence of Lord Inverchapel at the Waldorf-Astoria, 14 November 1946, in AHS, Confidential Notes; Memorandum of Conversation by Acting Secretary of State with Lord Inverchapel, 22 November 1946, in *Foreign Relations of the United States*, 1946, 7: 723–26; Memorandum of Inverchapel, 16 November 1946, in FO 371/52565, Public Record Office, London; Record of Conversation between the Secretary of State and Doctor Silver on Palestine, at the Waldorf-Astoria Hotel, 14 November 1946, Foreign Office 537/1787, Public Record Office, London; [Summary of second meeting], 21 November 1946, Foreign Office 371/52565/E 11549, Foreign Office, London.

38. *Congrezion*, 2, Fourth Session, 11 December 1946 and 9, Seventeenth Session, 19 December 1946; AHS, Confidential Notes, 14 November 1946; *New York Times*, 8 December 1946.

39. *The Day*, 13 December 1946; *New York Times*, 17 December 1946; Wise to Goldmann, 8 January 1947 and Goldmann to Wise, 31 December 1946, Wise Papers (Box 109, Folder 12); Wise to Goldmann, 22 July 1947,

Wise Papers (Box 68, Folder 9); *Cleveland Press*, 3 January 1947; oral interview with Eliahu Epstein (1986); Weizmann to Albert K. Epstein, 11 April 1946, in *The Letters and Papers of Chaim Weizmann*, 22: 115 and Weizmann to Joseph I. Linton, 5 April 1946, in *The Letters and Papers*, 22: 115. Jacques Torczyner, in a 1975 interview, claimed that AHS sent him to Paris in advance of the Congress to prepare a Silver–Ben-Gurion alliance against Weizmann, a "pathetic figure," according to Torczyner (oral interview with Torczyner); and ZOA, Torczyner, 1946–47, Correspondence 11–4–81). Weizmann and Ben-Gurion had been at odds throughout the 1940s and Weizmann's letters are filled with disgust with him. In early 1943 in summing up Emergency Committee meetings he had been attending, he blamed the group's "demoralization" on Ben-Gurion who came to meetings "always ranting, always shouting, always in a state of hysteria." Weizmann to E.T.D. [= Mrs. Edgar Dugdale, or "Baffy"], 6 January 1943, Weizmann Papers.

40. Goldmann, *The Autobiography*, pp. 239–40; Wise to Goldman, 8 January 1947, Wise Papers (Box 109, Folder 12); *Congrezion*, 1–13, 10–24 December 1946; *South African Jewish Times*, 21 February 1947. AHS had been elected to the World Zionist Executive for the first time in August of 1945.

41. *The Day*, 5 January 1947; *New York Times*, 4 January 1947; *The New Statesman and Nation*, 4 January 1947; *Detroit Jewish Chronicle*, 10 January 1947; *Jewish Spectator*, February, 1947; *Jewish Morning Journal*, 9 January 1947.

42. These conclusions, from AHS's meeting with Bevin in November, are not in conflict with the scholarly literature on Attlee, Bevin, and British foreign policy.

43. *Foreign Relations of the United States, 1947, 5, The Near East and Africa* (Washington, 1971), pp. 1001–3, 1008–11, 1014–15, 1017–18, 1021–23, 1024–28, 1031–32, 1033–35, 1035–37, 1038–39 and especially 1040–42. A detailed summary of the 11 February meeting, by Neumann, is in Manson Files, IV-44. See also David Horowitz, *State in the Making* (New York, 1953), pp. 141–42 and *Parliamentary Debates*, 433 H.C., Deb 5s, 25 February 1947, 2007.

44. *Foreign Relations of the United States, 1947*, 5: 1048; *New York Post*, 17 February 1947; AZEC, Executive Minutes, 24 February 1947; Moshe

Shertok, Press Conference, 26 February 1947, Correspondence 7–1–53.

45. *New York Times,* 27 February 1947; *Foreign Relations of the United States,* 1947, 5: 1056–57; Truman, *Memoirs,* 2:153–54; *Parliamentary Debates,* 433 H.C., Deb 5s, 25 February 1947, 1908.

46. AHS, Confidential Notes, 1, 4, 5, and 14 February 1947; AZEC, Executive Minutes, 29 January 1947.

47. Jewish Agency Executive, Minutes, 14 and 18 March 1947, 44/2, Central Zionist Archives; *New York Herald Tribune,* 10, 11 and 12 March 1947; *New York Times,* 6, 14, 15, 23, and 25 March 1947; AZEC, Memorandum, 25 March 1947.

48. *New York Times,* 3, 23, 28, and 29 April 1947; AZEC, Press-Radio Luncheon, 5 May 1947, Correspondence 4–4–37; Shertok to Acheson, 24 April 1947, Correspondence 7–1–53; *Foreign Relations of the United States,* 1947, 5:1067–68.

49. AZEC, Executive Minues, 7 April 1947 and Minutes, 19 May 1947; *New York Times,* 8 May 1947.

50. *Foreign Relations of the United States,* 1947, 5: 1080–81. AHS discusses the spring lobbying in his speech to the opening session of the World Zionist Actions Committee, 26 August 1947 (Zurich), Mss/Ty 47–6.

51. *New York Sun,* 8 May 1947. The full text of AHS's address is in the *New York Times,* 9 May 1947.

52. *Foreign Relations of the United States,* 1947, 5: 1085–86. On AHS's impact, see Jorge Garcia-Granados, *The Birth of Israel: The Drama as I Saw It* (New York, 1948), pp., 249–50; and Sykes, *Crossroads,* pp. 244–45. The UNSCOP consisted of Australia, Canada, Czechoslovakia, Guatemala, India, Iran, Netherlands, Peru, Sweden, Uruguay, and Yugoslavia.

53. AZEC, Executive Minutes, 4 June 1947; Minutes of UNSCOP's Private Meetings on 7 August 1947, Correspondence 7–1–66; Horowitz, *State,* p. 208; AHS, Suggestions Regarding Witnesses Before Committee on Inquiry of the U.N., Correspondence 7-1-60, and numerous memos on strategy for working with the UNSCOP, Correspondence, ibid. On the UNSCOP in Jerusalem, see William J. Porter's reports in *Foreign Relations of the United States,* 1947, 5: 1094–96, 1102, 1107–12 (UNSCOP in Palestine—The First Week), 1113–16, The Second Week, 1117–20, The Third Week, 1124–28, The Fourth Week, 1128–31, The Fifth Week.

54. For the UNSCOP report, see *Foreign Relations of the United States, 1947*, 5: 1143. Also, AZEC, Executive Minutes, 4 June and 17 July 1947; *Jewish Telegraphic Agency Daily News Bulletin*, 1 October 1947.

55. Hurewitz, *Struggle*, pp. 295–98. Australia endorsed neither the majority nor minority report; *The recommendations of the UNSCOP (1947)*. The full text of the UNSCOP report is also in *New York Times*, 9 September 1947.

56. AZEC, Executive Minutes, 17 September 1947; *New York Times*, 10 September and 3 October 1947; *New York Herald Tribune*, 3 October 1947; *Jewish Standard*, 12 September 1947; *Foreign Relations of the United States, 1947*, 5: 1281–82.

57. AZEC, Executive Minutes, 17 September 1947.

58. *New York Times*, 3 October 1947; *Foreign Relations of the United States, 1947*, 5: 1153–58, 1165; Jacob Robinson, Jewish Agency in Palestine, 20 October 1947, Memo 32 (a detailed analysis of strategy re the 17 Resolutions submitted to the Ad Hoc Committee) and idem. to Executive of the Jewish Agency, 26 September 1947 (analysis of the General Assembly debate on the Palestine Question), both in Correspondence 7–1–50.

59. *New York Times*, 25 and 27 September 1947; *Foreign Relations of the United States, 1947*, 5: 1147–51, 1164, 1166–70 and 1180; Special U.N. Bulletin, 13 October 1947, Correspondence 7–1–61. The full text of Johnson's announcement is in the *Cleveland Press*, 11 October 1947. On the Soviet motives, see Arnold Krammer, "Soviet Motives in the Partition of Palestine, 1947–8," *Journal of Palestine Studies*, 2, 2 (Winter 1973): 102–19.

60. AZEC, Executive Minutes, 17 September and 13 October 1947; Truman, *Memoirs*, 2: 156–58; AHS telephone calls to Moshe Shertok (24 October) and Senator McGrath (7 November) 1947, Correspondence 7–1–53; Jewish Agency Executive, American Section, Minutes, 22 and 30 October 1947, Z5/2374 and Z5/2375, CZA; Meeting of the Non-Zionist Organizations and the Jewish Agency, Minutes, 26 October 1947, Z5/2375, CZA. See also the letters, memos, and reports of Leo Sack in Manson IV-49, Correspondence 4–4–37, AZEC, Executive Minutes, 13 October 1947 and AHS's letters to Senators White, Thomas, George, and Green, in Manson Files, IV-49.

61. AZEC, Executive Minutes, 13 October 1947; Barnet Litvinoff, *Weizmann: Last of the Patriarchs* (New York, 1976), p. 252.

62. *Foreign Relations of the United States, 1947*, 5: 1290–91; *United Nations Resolutions on Palestine and The Arab-Israeli Conflict, 1947–1974*, ed. George J. Tomeh (Beirut, 1975), Appendix D and p. 4–14 (these pages contain the entire text of Resolution No. 181); AHS, *Diary 5708* (1947–48); V. K. Wellington to AHS and Gonzalo R. Jaramillo to AHS, 28 November 1947, Manson Files, IV-53; *Cleveland News*, 15 October 1947; Wellington to Robert F. Wagner and Jaramillo to Wagner, 28 November 1947, Manson Files, IV-49; Goldmann, *The Autobiography*, pp. 244–45; Horowitz, *State*, p. 301. See also Sumner Welles, *We Need Not Fail* (Boston, 1948), p. 63; Herbert Feis, *The Birth of Israel: The Tousled Diplomatic Bed* (New York, 1969), pp. 44–45; Solomon Bloom, *The Autobiography of Sol Bloom* (New York, 1948), pp. 296–97; Eddie Jacobson, "Diary," *Washington Post*, 6 May 1973; Kenneth R. Bain, *The March to Zion: United States Policy and the Founding of Israel* (College Station, Tex, 1979), pp. 178–82; Vera Weizmann, *The Impossible Takes Longer* (New York, 1967), p. 220; *The Forrestal Diaries*, ed. Walter Millis (New York, 1951), pp. 346–47; *Chaim Weizmann: A Biography by Several Hands*, ed. Meyer W. Weisgal and Joel Carmichael (New York, 1963), p. 302. Sumner Welles's conclusion, cited below, is typical: "By direct order of the White House, every form of pressure, direct or indirect, was brought to bear by American officials upon those countries outside the Moslem world that were known to be uncertain.") Representative Emanuel Celler and several other congressmen telegraphed Truman on 27 November urging the U.S. delegation to intervene with wavering delegations. One should not ignore the Arab lobbying either; see, for example, Garcia-Granados, *Birth*, pp. 263–64. For Silver's summary of Truman's role, see AZEC, Executive Minutes, 11 December 1947.

63. Address of Dr. Abba Hillel Silver, Chairman of the American Section of the Jewish Agency for Palestine and of the AZEC, 29 December 1947, in Mss/Ty 47–13. Not all Zionists enthusiastically embraced the United Nations decision; Isaac Zoar, for example, a Revisionist, argued that "a state under such handicaps [size] is not a state," and felt disappointment in AHS's willingness to accept the vote, despite the fact that the boundaries "entail a very heavy sacrifice on the part of the Jewish people" [AHS's words]. See Zoar, *Rescue*, pp. 249–50.

64. Address of Dr. Emanuel Neumann, president of the ZOA, 29 December 1947, in Mss/Ty 47–13.

Chapter Eight

1. AHS to Neumann, 2 December 1947, Personal Correspondence, July–December 1947; Robert H. Ferrell, *George C. Marshall* (New York, 1966), p. 190; *Foreign Relations of the United States, 1947,* 5: 1249, 1289, 1298, 1301–02, and 1313–14; Weizmann, *Impossible,* p. 223; Frank E. Manuel, *The Realities of America-Palestine Relations* (Washington, D.C., 1949), p. 343.

2. *Foreign Relations of the United States, 1948,* vol. 5, pt. 2, *The Near East, South Asia, and Africa* (Washington, 1976), pp. 545–54, 563–66, 587–89, 600–03, 619–25, 651–54, 742–44; Michael J. Cohen, "Truman and Palestine, 1945–1948: Revisionism, Politics and Diplomacy," *Modern Judaism,* 2, 1 (February 1982): 1–22; Joseph B. Schechtman, *The United States and the Jewish State Movement: The Crucial Decade, 1939–1949* (New York, 1966), pp. 250–97; Ganin, *Truman,* pp. 163–89; Truman, *Memoirs,* 2: 160–69; Snetsinger, *Truman,* pp. 73–78 and 81–114; Horowitz, *State in the Making,* pp. 312–49; Manuel, *Realities,* p. 341; Eban, "Tragedy," pp. 309–10; Millis, *Forrestal Diaries,* pp. 347 and 360; *Foreign Relations of the United States, 1947,* 5: 1283 and 1313; Eddie Jacobson to Josef Cohn, 30 March 1952, in "Two Presidents and a Haberdasher—1948," *American Jewish Archives,* 20, 1 (April 1968): 3–15.

3. AZEC, Executive Minutes, 6 January, 8 and 30 March, and 6 April 1948; Donovan, *Conflict and Crisis,* p. 319.

4. "Zionist Rally in Paris," 8 January 1948, Mss/Ty 48–14; Diary, 5708, 1947–48; *New York Times,* 28 and 29 January 1948; Jewish Agency Executive, Minutes, 4 January–19 August 1948, 45/2, CZA; Notes of a Conversation between His Excellency, Sir Alan Cunningham, and Dr. Abba Hillel Silver, on 27 January 1948, S25/22, CZA; Zionit to AHS, 12 January 1949, in Messages of Condolence; JAE, Minutes, 25 February 1948, Z5/2377, Central Zionist Archives.

5. *Foreign Relations of the United States, 1948,* 5: 608–09; Diary, 5708, 1947–48; *New York Times,* 23 February and 13 March 1948; Silver, *Vision*

and Victory, pp. 161–74; "Statement of Abba Hillel Silver . . . Before the United Nations Security Council," Mss/Ty 48–14. The best example of Silver's sensitivity to the Latin American political arena is his instructions to Moshe Sharett before the latter addressed the Security Council; Jewish Agency Executive, American Section, Minutes, 26 February 1948, Z5/2378, Central Zionist Archives. See also the same organization's minutes of 8, 12, 17, 23, 25, and 26 February as well as 1, 4, 9, 11, 12, 15, 20, 22, and 23 March 1948, in Z5/40–41, Central Zionist Archives.

6. AHS to Daniel Jeremy Silver, 7 March 1948, Personal Correspondence, January–June 1948. Silver preferred personal meetings to the telephone since he was convinced that his hotel phone and the Jewish Agency Executive phone lines were tapped by the United States and British governments during 1947 and 1948.

7. *Foreign Relations of the United States,* 1948, 5: 728–29 and 748–50; Schechtman, *United States,* p. 275; *New York Times,* 20 March (headline) and 1 April 1948; *South African Jewish Times,* 30 April 1948; AHS, "Reaction to Report on Palestine Presented by the United States," in *Vision and Victory,* pp. 175–80. On the 18 March joint session of Congress, see *New York Times,* 19 March 1948. For Austin's speech, see Security Council, *Official Records,* 3rd Year, Nos. 36–51, 3–31 March 1948, pp. 157 and 167–69, and *The Jewish Agency for Palestine Before the Security Council of the United Nations* [1948], pp. 21–34 (Statement), 35–38 (Reaction, 19 March), and pp. 39–41 (Reply, 19 March).

8. *Foreign Relations of the United States,* 1948, 5: 742–44 and Clark M. Clifford, "Factors Influencing President Truman's Decision to Support Partition and Recognize the State of Israel," in *The Palestine Question in American History,* ed. Clark M. Clifford et al. (New York, 1978), p. 36; Oscar Gass to Eliahu Epstein, 7 April 1948, in Israel State Archives, *Political and Diplomatic Documents, December 1947–May 1948* (Jerusalem, 1979), p. 571; Jewish Agency Executive, American Section, Minutes, 20 March 1948, Z5/2384, Central Zionist Archives. On Truman and Weizmann, see Sharef, *Three Days,* pp. 233–34, 239–40, and 242–44; Weizmann, *Impossible,* pp. 228–31; *The Letters and Papers of Chaim Weizmann,* (August 1947–June 1952), ed. Aaron Klieman (New Brunswick, 1980), 23: 109, n. 3; Ganin, *Truman,* pp. 167 and 179; Maurice Bisgyer, *Challenge and Encounter: Behind the Scenes in the Struggle for Jewish Survival* (New York, 1967), pp. 188–94. Every State Department

official with whom AHS met during the weeks after Austin's speech conveyed the sense that the government intended to press fully for the trusteeship plan.

9. *The Day,* 5 and 23 April 1948; *The Forward,* 23 April 1948; *New York Times,* 6 and 20 March, 1 and 5 April 1948; Mss/Ty 48: 3, 48: 8, 48: 11 and 48: 12.

10. Jewish Agency Executive, American Section, Minutes, 3 May 1948, Z5/43, Central Zionist Archives; AZEC, Executive Minutes, 6 and 27 April 1948; Schechtman, *United States,* pp. 294–95; *New York Times,* 5 April 1948; Ian J. Bickerton, "President Truman's Recognition of Israel," *American Jewish Historical Quarterly* 58 (December 1968): 173–240.

11. *Foreign Relations of the United States,* 1948, 5: 930 and 972–76; Jewish Agency Executive, American Section, Minutes, 3 May 1948; Neumann, *In the Arena,* pp. 259–60; Sharef, *Three Days,* pp. 87–89; *Cleveland Plain Dealer,* 15 May 1948; Clifford, "Factors," pp. 38–45. For Dean Rusk's comments about AHS, see *Foreign Relations of the United States,* 1948, 5: 878.

12. Committee for Progressive Zionism, Correspondence 12–1–4; AHS to Allen Klivans, 14 December 1948, Correspondence 10–4–48.

13. Jewish Agency Executive, Minutes, 22 August–3 September 1948, S5/323 and S5/324, CZA; Committee for Progressive Zionism, Correspondence 12–1–4; Keynote address, Manhattan Zionist Region, second anniversary of UN Palestine Resolution, New York, 29 November 1949, Mss/Ty 49–9.

14. Israel Goldstein to AHS, 22 September 1948, Goldstein Papers, A364/1657. Silver arrived in New York City on 7 September 1948.

15. *New Palestine News Reporter,* 22 July 1947 (courtesy of Esther Togman); Henry Montor to Goldstein, 10 September 1948, Correspondence 10–4–48; oral interview with Henry Montor.

16. Montor to Goldstein, 10 September 1948.

17. Goldstein to AHS, 22 September 1948. Goldstein, not the Jewish Agency treasurer, kept Silver informed of Montor's plans.

18. Goldstein to Montor, 27 September 1948 and Montor to United Palestine Appeal, 24 January 1949 (both in Correspondence 10–4–48); AHS to Berl Locker, 28 October 1948, Correspondence 10–4–48.

19. Jewish Agency Executive, American Section, Minutes, 17 January 1949, Goldmann Correspondence, Z6/2760; AHS to Goldstein, 30 July

1948, Goldstein Papers, A364/1657; AHS to Daniel Jeremy Silver, 3 February 1949, PC 1948–49.

20. AHS to Daniel Jeremy Silver, 21 January 1949, PC 1948–49 and AHS to Goldstein, 12 December 1948, Goldstein Papers, A364/1657.

21. Henry Montor and Isidor Coons, Report to Members of the National Campaign Council, 12 and 18 March, 14, 21, and 28 April, 2 October 1947, Montor to Records Dept., 7 March 1947 (all in United Jewish Appeal Archives, New York City); Joseph Greenleaf to AHS, 4 June 1949, PC 1948–49; Montor to Raphael, 17 January and 19 February 1981.

22. Montor to Raphael, 19 February 1981; *New Palestine,* 15 February 1949; *American Hebrew,* 18 February 1949; Judith Epstein, Hadassah Press Release to Presidents and Political Chairmen, 18 February 1949, ZOA; AHS, Statement to Jewish Agency Executive, American Section, 3 January 1949; Ben-Gurion to Montor, 12 December 1948, Eliezer Kaplan Papers. Jacques Torczyner explained Ben-Gurion's position as part of a strategy to reduce the importance of the Zionist movement in the United States. See oral interview with Torczyner. But Ben-Gurion, in a (largely incoherent) 1969 interview, claimed that Montor was the "American Zionist most devoted to Israel [as opposed to men such as AHS who were devoted] only to Zionism." Oral interview with Ben-Gurion.

23. Jewish Agency Executive, American Section, Minutes, 29 November, 6 and 27 December 1948; *New York Herald Tribune,* 21 January 1949; *Zionist Review,* 28 January 1949. One of the best summaries of AHS's hatred for Montor is in AHS's lengthy list of reasons for this feeling; AHS, Notes for WZO, 7 February 1949, Mss/Ty 49–2.

24. AHS to Goldstein, 30 July 1948 (Silver mentioned a gathering in Richmond (6 March 1947) at which Morgenthau addressed forty men, mostly non-Zionists), Henry Morgenthau, Jr. to Goldstein, 16 September 1948, Goldstein to Silver, 4 November 1958 [sic], all in Goldstein Papers, A364/1657; AHS to Members of the Jewish Agency Executive, American Section, 19 January 1949, Correspondence 10–4–48. A series of attacks on Silver, disguised as news articles, appeared in the *Forward* (in Yiddish) early in 1949. They were usually signed by "Ehrenreich," but all of them were written by the Labor Zionist, Baruch Zuckerman (1887–1970). See especially the issues of 19 February, 8 and 9 March 1949.

25. AHS to Neumann, 20 January 1949, Correspondence 12–1–22; Berl Locker to Members of the Jewish Agency Executive, American

Section, 20 January 1949, Correspondence 10–4–48; *The Day*, 23 and 26 January 1949; Press Release, Jewish Agency Executive, Plenary Session, [9 February 1949], Goldmann Papers, A364/1573.

26. AHS to Henry Morgenthau, Jr., 14 February 1949, Morgenthau to AHS, 14 February 1949, AHS to Goldstein, 14 February 1949 (all in Correspondence 10–4–48); *New York Times*, 17 February 1949; *New York Herald Tribune*, 21 January and 17 February 1949; *American Hebrew*, 18 February 1949; *Detroit Jewish Chronicle*, 4 March 1949; Selig Brodetsky to Weizmann, 20 February 1949, Weizmann Papers.

27. *Israel Speaks*, 18 March 1949.

28. Oral interview with Goldmann; Joseph Greenleaf to AHS; Daniel Frisch to Ben Gordon, [1949], Correspondence 8–2–31; *New York Times*, 18 April 1949; Addresses of Neumann and Torczyner, 52nd Annual ZOA Convention, New York, 28 May 1949, ZOA Archives. Among those Zionists who recorded on tape or in print their dislike of Silver are David Ben-Gurion, Nahum Goldmann, Rose Halperin, Gottlieb Hammer, Ezra Shapiro, and Chaim Weizmann.

29. AHS, Address, 52nd Annual ZOA Convention, 29 May 1949, Mss/ Ty 49–11. On the "Draft Silver" movement, see *Detroit Jewish Chronicle*, 25 May 1949, *New York Times*, 9 and 17 May 1949, Correspondence, 12–1–26; AHS to Solomon B. Freehof, 13 April 1949, PC 1948–49; *New York Herald Tribune*, 16 July 1949; and AHS to Jacob Billikopf, 16 June 1949, PC 1949–49.

30. Alan S. Green to AHS, 17 October 1946, 3 April and 17 June 1947, PC 1946–47.

31. AHS to Irving Kane, 14 September 1948, AHS to Julian Morgenstern, 17 September 1948, Norman Goldburg to Silver, 27 April 1949, and Goldburg to Virginia Silver, 2 June 1949 (all in PC 1948–49).

32. Ariel L. Goldberg to AHS, 31 March 1949 and Goldburg to Earl Stone [ca. Fall 1949]—all in PC 1948–49.

Chapter Nine

1. Solomon B. Freehof and AHS, "Symposium: The American Rabbinate in Our Lifetime," *Central Conference of American Rabbis Year Book*, 73 (1963): 163.

2. Freehof and Silver, "Symposium," 161; Oral interviews with Elizabeth Rice Carson and Earl Stone. Rabbis of AHS's generation, especially those active in local politics, national affairs, or scholarship generally placed pastoral work low on their list of priorities. It was commonplace to joke about rabbis who counseled a lot as "out to 'pastor.'"

3. AHS to Louis J. Alber, 13 April 1923, PC 1922–23; AHS to Frances Greenberger, 22 March 1944, PC January–March 1944; oral interviews with Feuer, Harris, Stone, William Kramer, and Carson.

4. Oral interviews with Feuer, Kramer, Daniel Jeremy Silver, and Stone; Robert J. Marx to Raphael, 19 November 1984.

5. Freehof and Silver, "Symposium," 161.

6. Morton C. Fierman to Raphael, 1 May 1985; Marx to Raphael, 19 November 1984.

7. Feuer, "Abba Hillel Silver," 107; oral interview with Kramer.

8. Oral interviews with Carson and Daniel Jeremy Silver.

9. Oral interview with Kramer; Marx to Raphael, 19 November 1984; AHS to Melbourne Harris, 3 January 1944, PC January–March 1944; oral interview with Harris and Stone.

10. "Symposium," 113–16; PC July–December 1943, January–March 1944 and 1948–49; oral interview with Stone.

11. AHS to Henry Schultz, 2 July 1943; AHS to Harris, 20 July 1943; AHS to Bernard Sperling, 14 September 1943—all in PC 1943–44; Carson to I. Vinograd, 4 May 1953, Correspondence 11–1–15; AHS to William Fields, 20 January 1944, AHS to Charles Eaton, 6 April 1944, and AHS to Joseph Schenker, 7 March 1944, all in PC January–March 1944.

12. Carson to Vinograd, 4 May 1953; oral interviews with Carson and Harris.

13. Oral interviews with Carson, Feuer, Halperin; Marx to Raphael, 19 November 1984.

14. Oral interviews with Kramer, Carson, Skirball, Florence Michaelson Bernstein, Daniel Jeremy Silver, Raphael Silver, and Stone; see also Moses Silver's Hebrew letters to his son, PC, 1915–17.

15. Oral interviews with Feuer, Kramer, Stone, Daniel Jeremy Silver, and Silbert.

16. Oral interviews with Skirball and Silbert. AHS's favorite restaurants included Bilker's in Cincinnati and Siegelstein's Deli (1141 East 105th Street) in Cleveland.

17. [AHS] to Daniel Jeremy Silver, 10 October 1947, PC, July–December 1947; AHS to Jacob Rotman, 12 June 1947, PC, January–June 1947; oral interviews with Daniel Jeremy Silver and Raphael Silver.

Chapter Ten

1. AHS to Abba Eban, 10 January 1951, Correspondence 6–1–52, and dozens of letters to and from Ambassador Eban in Correspondence 6–1–53, 6–1–54, 6–1–55, 6–1–56 and 6–1–57; John Foster Dulles to AHS, 1 October 1951, Correspondence 6–1–46; Thomas E. Dewey to AHS, 10 November 1950, Correspondence 6–1–38; Eisenhower to AHS, 14 November 1952 and 22 June 1955 ("I always appreciate your quick understanding and welcome your counsel."), Correspondence 6–1–60.

2. Dewey to AHS, 7 November 1949, Correspondence 6–1–45; *New York Times*, 28 October and 7 November 1949; Dulles to AHS, 27 April 1956, PC 1955–56.

3. ZOA, A Statement by Dr. Abba Hillel Silver, 27 October 1952, ZOA Archives; *New York Times*, 19 and 20 October 1952; *Cleveland Plain Dealer*, 19 October 1952; *Time*, 27 October 1952; *Ha-Aretz*, 20 and 22 October 1952; *Jewish Mail*, 31 October 1952.

4. Arthur Sommerfield to AHS, 30 October 1952, Correspondence 6–1–60 (this file also contains proof that Silver wrote both his own and Eisenhower's letters); Dewey to AHS, 11 November 1952, PC 1951–52; memo of phone conversation with John Bricker, 31 October 1952, Correspondence 6–1–60; Eisenhower to AHS, 14 November 1952, Correspondence 6–1–60; AHS, "Some Reflections on the Present Political Campaign," 26 October 1952 (Sermon 801) and "Some More Observations on the Coming Elections," 2 November 1952 (Sermon 802).

5. Dulles to AHS, 4 and 15 June 1954, Correspondence 6–1–47; Dulles to AHS, 24 August 1955, Correspondence 11–1–8; Dulles to AHS, 19 September 1955, Correspondence 6–1–49; Abba Eban to AHS, 12 February 1953, PC 1952–53; Dulles to AHS, 18 February 1953, Correspondence 6–1–61; Dulles to AHS, 25 August 1953, Correspondence 6–1–55; AHS to Dulles, 25 October 1953, Correspondence 11–1–7; AHS to Dulles, 2 September 1955, 27 April and 24 July 1956, Correspondence 11–1–8; *The Day*, 29 October 1953; *American Zionist*, 20

November 1953; *Cleveland Plain Dealer,* 29 October 1953; Miscellaneous materials, Correspondence 6–3–84, 6–3–85, 6–3–86, and 6–3–87.

6. Eisenhower Diary, 26 April 1956 and Department of State, White House News Conference, 26 April 1956—both in Dwight David Eisenhower Library, Abilene, Kansas; *Cleveland News,* 26 April 1954; *New York Times,* 27 April 1956; *The Day,* 27 April 1956.

7. *Cleveland Press,* 8 July 1953; *Cleveland Plain Dealer,* 9 July 1953; Dulles to AHS, 2 February 1958, PC 1958–59.

8. Ben-Gurion to AHS, 16 June 1949 and AHS to Ben-Gurion, 30 June 1949, PC 1948–49; Sermons 626 (31 October 1943), 627 (7 November 1943) and 721 (1 May 1949), "The First Anniversary of the Establishment of the State of Israel"; Address of 29 November 1949 to Manhattan Zionist Region, Ty/Mss 49–9; Address at ZOA Convention, New York, 29 May 1949, Mss/Ty 49–11; Founders' Day Address, Hebrew Union College, Cincinnati, Ohio, 25 March 1950.

9. *New York Times,* 7 November 1949; Neumann to AHS, 9 November 1949 and AHS to Neumann, 25 November 1949—both in PC 1948–49; *The Day,* 16 November 1949; *Jewish Telegraphic Agency News,* 30 November 1949; *New York Times,* 30 November 1949.

10. The details of Ben-Gurion's refusal to invite AHS are in *Ha-Aretz,* 15, 16, 17, and 18 March, 26 and 29 April 1951; *Davar,* 20, 23 and 26 April 1951; *Yediot Ahronot,* 23 and 25 April 1951; *Ma'ariv,* 26 April 1951.

11. *American Jewish Year Book,* 53 (1952):181; Avraham Avi-Hai, *Ben-Gurion, State-Builder: Principles and Pragmatism, 1948–1963* (New York, 1974), p. 233; *South African Jewish Times,* 29 June and 20 July 1951; AHS, Address to 54th Annual Convention of the Zionist Organization of America, Atlantic City, New Jersey, 14 June 1951, Mss/Ty 51–6.

12. *Ha-Aretz,* 15, 16, and 17 August 1951; *Ha-Boker,* 17 and 19 August 1951; *Ma'ariv,* 17 August 1951; *Fundamental Issues of Zionism,* ed. S. U. Nahon (Jerusalem, 1952), pp. 80–83 (23rd Zionist Congress).

13. David Senator to George Wise, 4 September and 20 October 1952, Senator to Norman Bentwich, 29 October 1952, Wise to Senator, 8 November 1952, Joseph S. Schwartz to Senator, 20 December 1952—all in Board of Governors, 1952, Hebrew University Archives; Senator to Wise, 2 February 1953, S. Horowitz to Wise, 13 February 1953, Wise to Senator, 16 February 1953, Walter Zander to Joseph Mazer, 10 March

1953—all in Board of Governors, 1953, Hebrew University Archives; Neumann to AHS, 17 September 1952, Correspondence 8–2–33.

14. *Ha-Aretz,* 30 March 1956; *Ha-Boker,* 30 March 1956; *Davar,* 3 April 1956.

15. *Ha-Aretz,* 23 April 1958 and 15 July 1963; *Ha-Boker,* 15, 16, 17, 18, 23, and 30 April 1958; *Ma'ariv,* 12 July 1963; *Yedioth Ahronot,* 12 and 15 July 1963; Ben-Gurion to AHS, 1 November 1961, Correspondence 5–1–26; Ben-Gurion to AHS, 17 February 1963, Correspondence 5–1–27; *American Zionist,* September 1963, p. 19. On his way home from the 1958 visit, Silver's El Al flight lost a wheel on its left landing gear as it departed from London and thousands, expecting a crash, watched as the pilot guided the British Britannia turboprop down safely at Idlewild airport after a tense flight (see the New York and Cleveland newspapers of 2 and 3 May 1958).

16. See especially his sermons of 10, 17, and 24 February as well as 2, 16, and 23 March 1952 (Sermons 787–790, 792, and 793), which became chapters 10–15 of *Where Judaism Differed.*

17. See, for example, the scores of sermons by other scholarly rabbis, such as Levi Olan of Dallas and Solomon B. Freehof of Pittsburgh.

18. The book was used, immediately upon its publication in the fall of 1956, at The Ohio State University Hillel Foundation, Miami's Temple Israel, Pittsburgh's *Rodef Sholom,* Chicago's Sinai, and Long Beach California's Temple Israel, to name but a few institutions.

19. AHS to Solomon Zeitlin, 27 January, 7 February, 24 March 1955; Eliahu Epstein to AHS, 22 March and 4 April 1955; AHS to Epstein, 24 March 1955; Epstein to Zeitlin, 5 April 1955 (all in Correspondence 11–1–35).

20. M. Lincoln Schuster to AHS, 11 May 1955 and Justin D. Kaplan to AHS, 31 May 1955 (both in Correspondence, ibid.).

21. Ludwig Lewisohn to AHS, 21 June and 6 July 1955 (both in Correspondence, ibid.); AHS to Manson, 20 January 1956, PC 1955–56.

22. See correspondence with representatives of Halle's in Correspondence 11–1–34. The retail price of the book was $4.50, and a Hebrew edition was published by Massadah Press (in Tel Aviv) in 1961.

23. AHS, *Moses and the Original Torah* (New York, 1961), pp. 76, 127–28, 133–34 and 136.

24. AHS, *Moses*, pp. 172 and 181. This emphasis upon the ethical laws of the original Torah may perhaps be a polemic against the Orthodox insistence that all the laws of the Torah, not just the ethical teachings, are Mosaic in origin.

25. The Kennedy sermon is reprinted in *Cleveland Press,* 29 November 1963. In 1964 friends of Silver memorialized him by creating the Abba Hillel Silver Professorship in Judaic Studies at Western Reserve University; see *Cleveland Plain Dealer,* 27 September 1964.

26. Freehof, "Recollections," pp. xi and xii.

27. Milton Steinberg, who wrote in the *New Palestine,* 6 November 1942, p. 32, is quoted in Samuel Halperin, *The Political World of American Zionism* (Detroit, 1961), p. 295.

28. Melvin I. Urofsky, *A Voice that Spoke for Justice: The Life and Times of Stephen S. Wise* (Albany, 1982), 79–80.

Index

Acheson, Dean, 146–47, 153; Silver's meeting with, 150

Adams, Samuel J., 5

Adams, Sherman, 197

AECZA. *See* Emergency Committee for Zionist Affairs

Allon, Gedaliah, 64

American Christian Palestine Committee, 160

American Civil Liberties Union (ACLU), 54

American Friends of a Jewish Palestine, 102

American Jewish Committee: opposition of, to Zionism, xxiv

American Jewish community: in 1930s and 1940s, xix–xxi; organization and mobilization of political power of, xvii; powerlessness of, against Nazism, xxi–xxii

American Jewish Conference of 1943, 87; Silver's speech at, 88–90

American Jewish Congress, 87–88

American League for a Free Palestine, 103

American League for the Defense of Jewish Rights, 63

American rabbinate, xiv

American Zionism: criticism of leadership of, xviii; post–World War I, 27–34; Silver's political leadership of, 77–95. *See also* Zionism

American Zionist Emergency Council (AZEC), 81; "Action for Palestine Week" of, 158; American Jewish Conference of, 88–91; and Bergsonites, 106–7; goals of, 91–92; lobbying by, for Jewish statehood, 161–63; mobilization of American Jewish support for statehood, 146–47; rescue campaign of, 93–95, 97–115; revitalized role of, 133; Silver's organizational work for, 213; Silver's resignation from, 118, 130; Silver-Wise Affair in, 130–34; Wise as chairman of, 130–31; Wise as nominal head of, 134

American Zionist Policy Committee, 130

Anglo-American committee (1946), 142–43; hearing of, 140–41; rejection of partition by, 149

Angoff, Charles, 8

Anti-Semitism, U.S., xix, xx, 99

Anti-Zionism, xxiv; at Hebrew Union college, 10; of Reform Judaism, xxv–xxvi

Arabs, 140; attack on Jews near Tel Aviv, 164; commercial and diplomatic pressures of, 163; meeting with UNSCOP, 159–60; support for, 155–56, 161–62, 169

Armed Neutrality Act, 19

Attlee, Clement, 135, 137–38, 142; opposition of, to Jewish statehood, 143; pressure on, 145; response of, to Truman's Yom Kippur statement, 148; support of binational Palestinian state, 155–56

Austin, Warren R., 170–71

273